D0829930

Preaching with Power

Preaching with Power

Dynamic Insights from Twenty Top Communicators

Edited by Michael Duduit

BakerBooks

Grand Rapids, Michigan

© 2006 by Michael Duduit

Published by Baker Books
a division of Baker Publishing Group
P.O. Box 6287, Grand Rapids, MI 49516-6287
www.bakerbooks.com

Printed in the United States of America

All rights reserved. No part of this publication may be reproduced, stored in a retrieval system, or transmitted in any form or by any means—for example, electronic, photocopy, recording—without the prior written permission of the publisher. The only exception is brief quotations in printed reviews.

Library of Congress Cataloging-in-Publication Data
Preaching with power : dynamic insights from twenty top communicators / edited by Michael Duduit.
    p.   cm.
   Includes bibliographical references.
   ISBN 10: 0-8010-6630-1 (pbk.)
   ISBN 978-0-8010-6630-6 (pbk.)
   1. Preaching. I. Duduit, Michael, 1954–
   BV4211.3.P745 2006
   251—dc22   2006000299

Unless otherwise indicated, Scripture is paraphrased.

Scripture marked KJV is taken from the King James Version of the Bible.

Scripture marked NIV is taken from the HOLY BIBLE, NEW INTERNATIONAL VERSION®. NIV®. Copyright © 1973, 1978, 1984 by International Bible Society. Used by permission of Zondervan. All rights reserved.

Scripture marked NKJV is taken from the New King James Version. Copyright © 1982 by Thomas Nelson, Inc. Used by permission. All rights reserved.

Scripture marked NLT is taken from the *Holy Bible*, New Living Translation, copyright © 1996. Used by permission of Tyndale House Publishers, Inc., Wheaton, Illinois 60189. All rights reserved.

To James and Stephen

Contents

Introduction

It is hard to believe today that just a generation ago, many Christian leaders were pronouncing the "death of preaching" in the church. That notion seems so unlikely today not only because of the biblical foundations of preaching but also because the ministry of preaching has been enjoying a remarkable renaissance over the past two decades.

During the past twenty years, *Preaching* magazine has observed, encouraged, and reported on the state of Christian proclamation. Among the most important (and popular) features of the publication (which I serve as editor) are the personal interviews with outstanding preachers and influencers of preaching. In these interviews, readers have an opportunity to gain insights into the philosophy and methodology of some of the most outstanding Christian communicators of our age.

This book contains a selection of twenty of the best interviews published in *Preaching* during the past decade. (*Communicate with Power* contains interviews from the magazine's first decade.) In these interviews, you'll have an opportunity to learn from classic expositors (like John MacArthur and David Jeremiah), dynamic evangelical pastors (like Adrian Rogers and Jerry Vines), influential voices in today's church (like Rick Warren and Jerry Falwell), creative innovators (like Andy Stanley and Ed Young Jr.), key figures in the emergent church movement (like Brian McLaren and Dan Kimball), and many more. The preachers in this collection represent the rich diversity and dynamic power that characterize the best of today's preaching.

My prayer is that the insights shared by these twenty gifted preachers will be an encouragement and a catalyst for better preaching in your ministry and mine.

Michael Duduit
www.preaching.com
www.michaelduduit.com

What Is Expository Preaching?

An Interview with Bryan Chapell

The book *Christ-Centered Preaching* by Bryan Chapell has become one of the key homiletics textbooks in college and seminary classes in America. That has given Chapell a significant influence in the training of future evangelical preachers. An outspoken advocate of expository preaching, Chapell is president of Covenant Theological Seminary in St. Louis, where he also teaches courses in preaching. Chapell is also a member of *Preaching* magazine's board of contributing editors. This interview appeared in the March-April 2001 issue of *Preaching*.

Preaching: Your book *Christ-Centered Preaching* is subtitled *Redeeming the Expository Sermon*. How do you define or understand expository preaching?

Chapell: In the most basic sense I think it is what Augustine said we try to do, which is to say what God says. As I perceive the Bible to be God's inspired Word, my greatest goal is to be able to say, "This is what God says." That involves identifying a segment of Scripture—an expository unit—and then explain what it means; to demonstrate it if necessary—I believe that most of the time it is necessary to demonstrate what it means—and then to apply it to the hearts and lives of the people to whom I am speaking. It is to say to them, "This is what God says to you."

Preaching: How does the expository sermon vary from other kinds of preaching? For example, in what way does an expository sermon reflect what God said as compared to other models of preaching?

Chapell: These are not new categories, but they are helpful categories. A topical sermon gets its theme or topic from the text, but it is developed elsewhere or according to the nature of the topic. A textual sermon gets its topic plus its main ideas—its main points—from the text, but the development of those points is also outside the text itself. An expository sermon gets its main idea, its main points, and its subpoints or its developmental components from the text as well. So it is by methodology binding the preacher to say what the text is saying. The preacher becomes a bond servant of the text, working according to the thought of the original author.

I don't believe that expository preaching is the only "right" kind of preaching, because one can do textual and topical preaching and still be very true to the Bible's message. The expository method has the advantage as an approach to preaching of making sure that we are walking in the paths of the original writer. We can still make interpretive errors, but at least there is a lesser tendency to be preaching one's opinions or the philosophy of the age when one is approaching [the text] in an expository method.

Preaching: What do you see as the greatest benefit or benefits of using an expository model for preaching?

Chapell: The thing that I think is most advantageous in an expository method is not only are we being bound to the message of Scripture, but the preacher then has the authority of God's Word with which to challenge or encourage people. That one says: "this is not me as a preacher talking. This is what God says to you based upon what this text means." So the chief advantage, I think, is the preacher is allowed to operate with the authority of what God says.

There are other advantages: if one is dealing in an expository approach—main points, subpoints coming from the text—I think you create an informed listener. People who listen to expository preaching over time learn to see how Scriptures develop, and therefore their own interpretative skills grow. There is the advantage that the preacher is not bound to his own thoughts and opinions. Particularly if he moves consecutively through a text, he is forced to deal with subjects that might not normally appear to his own mind.

The advantage of that additionally is he can address subjects that, had he thought them up, might appear to have been too pointed, with perhaps sensitive issues in the congregation. If he is simply moving through the text, he might be able to deal with the subject of gossip, where, if he had simply brought that up as the theme for the week and it had no connections to previous weeks, he might seem to be responding to his own hurt—that somebody gossiped about him and so he was just going to get them back in the sermon this week. So expository preaching has the advantage of authority, has the advantage of teaching, has the advantage of pushing us beyond our own opinions and enabling us to touch sensitive subjects without appearing to pick on people.

Preaching: One of the traditional caricatures or attacks on expository preaching is that it tends to be dry—that it doesn't have the dynamic or the energy of other kinds of preaching. How do you respond to that?

Chapell: It is sometimes a valid criticism if by expository preaching we mean the stereotypical preacher "making a few comments upon the text," where he is just simply making a few extraneous comments—having looked at a few commentaries first—kind of as his thoughts appear to him or as the verses or even the phrases appear in sequence. An expository message is not simply commenting upon the text, it is bringing the meaning of the text to bear upon the biblical needs that that text is addressing, and then connecting those biblical needs to the contemporary needs of people today.

What keeps it from being dry, I think, is first of all an attempt to deal with the mutual condition that we share with the audience or writer of the original text. So that we are immediately saying: God was dealing with an issue or a problem or concern in the original setting, and since there is no temptation or sin or difficulty that is not common to us, then I have some identification with that person.

That means I am not simply preaching for information; I am preaching for a transformative purpose. I am preaching for transformation. I tell my students, "We are not ministers of information primarily; we are ministers of transformation." Information is part of what we do, but we are preaching in order to see lives transformed by the Word of God being brought to bear upon specific situations. If that's the case, then I have the goal not only of dealing with information in the text, but I also have the goal of making sure I am interacting with the lives of the people with whom I am dealing. I am exegeting the text, but I am exegeting the congregation as well. That means that I am considering illustrations that are connecting and have the ability to help people to identify with me. I am using applications that say, "This is where this has meaning today, not just what you should do but where you should do it and why you should do it. What is the motive, and how does God enable you to do that?"

This is more than just a cognitive performance, which is that dry, rationalistic preaching which is rightly criticized. It is an attempt to deal with the whole person regarding the scriptural truth and to show how God is dealing with people today specifically by the eternal truth that he has communicated. That requires that we deal with the truths of the text around the theme, demonstrate its relevance, and apply it to people's personal situations. That's what keeps it from being dry.

Preaching: You entitled your book *Christ-Centered Preaching*. How do you, as an expository preacher, make sure that your preaching is, in fact, Christ-centered?

Chapell: When I use the word "Christ-centered" or the phrase "Christ-centered preaching," I am not attempting to say that Jesus has to be shown to be present in every biblical text. Sometimes people hear the words "Christ-centered preaching" and they are preaching a passage where Israel is wandering in the wilderness, and they say, "Now where is Jesus? Is he behind that bush, or is he in that camel track? I don't see him."

What I am trying to express is that God has redeemed us, delivered us through the work of Jesus Christ. But that message of grace—that means of communicating to us his deliverance from our human condition—is his consistent way of presenting God's working throughout Scripture which finds its culmination in Christ. I am happy to use the words *"redemptive* preaching," as well as *"Christ-centered* preaching," to talk about *grace-focused* preaching as well. My bottom line is that we show how every text in its context is demonstrating that God is the answer to the human condition. We take people away from themselves as the instrument of healing.

So when I talk about *Christ-centered* preaching, I advise students to always come with two lenses in their glasses as they look at Scripture. These two lenses are composed of two questions. The first question is, "What does this text reveal about the nature of humankind that requires the deliverance of God? What does it tell me about the character of mankind?" The second question is, "What does this text tell me about the nature of God who provides for the deliverance of humankind? In essence, what does this tell me about the nature of God?" If I am always asking those questions of the text—what does this tell me about persons, and what does this tell me about God—I will always think redemptively, because persons are being shown in their dependence upon God and their fallenness—in their need for something beyond themselves. We won't just say, "David was a good guy; you be a good guy, too." The Bible is telling us more about David in context, whereby David and God's people require more than David's personal goodness. They required a God who would deliver them. David becomes the means of that deliverance, but God is the hero of the text, not David. The bottom line of *Christ-centered* preaching is always showing people that they are not the instruments of their own healing. That's Christ-centered preaching throughout the whole of Scripture.

Preaching: **In the book there is an element you term the "Fallen Condition Focus." Describe what that is and what role it plays within the expository sermon.**

Chapell: The Fallen Condition Focus is attempting to move beyond the question of "What does this text say?" It is also asking the question, "Why was this text written?" So as I am examining a text, looking for the data, the context, the background, and the exegesis, I am also asking the question, "Why was this text written in its original context? Why did the Holy Spirit inspire this? What needed to be addressed in the condition of the people to whom this message is being written or in the life of the person who wrote it?" When I identify that human condition it may be a sin or it may simply be a matter of living in a fallen world of grief—"I don't know what tomorrow means." "I'm fearful of not knowing all that God has in mind for my life." We identify what is the reason that God wrote the text, and then we identify that fallen condition and we say how we are like those persons.

I often go to 2 Timothy 3:16–17: "All Scripture is given by inspiration of God, and is profitable for doctrine, for reproof, for correction, for instruction in righteousness, that the man of God may be complete" [NKJV]. If all Scripture is given to complete us, then there is a necessary implication: that we are incomplete. So what I want to do is to identify in the Scriptures what incompleteness is being addressed. Now that is to move me beyond thinking about myself. It is to say that if the human is incomplete, then the answer has to be found in God. By dealing with fallen conditioned-ness as the reason behind the text, I always have to bring God's solution into the scene as the answer to the problem.

If we really perceive the Scriptures as dealing with our fallenness when propositional truth is being dealt with, then we ought to be able to look at people around us and we ought to be able to see Swiss cheese—they are incomplete. They have got holes in them. And what identifies Christian preaching is what we say is going to fill the holes. Is it just being a better person, trying harder, working real hard and long? Ultimately that is a human answer to fallenness. If we truly identify in preaching the fallen condition that required the writing of the text, then we are forced to deal with the divine solution to the human condition. So our message has again become redemptively Christ-centered rather than anthropocentric, human-centered. Because I have shown from the very beginning the human answer won't work. We deal with a Fallen Condition Focus, why the text was written, so that we will be able to say what is God's solution to that problem.

Preaching: In the environment in which we live today, what do you see as some of the greatest challenges preachers face as they try to communicate God's Word to congregations?

Chapell: I know the politically correct answer to this question is going to be something about helping people continue to have interest in an age that is habituated to picture thinking; how we work in an oral medium. So how do we convert preaching of a linear mode to a visually oriented culture? I don't think that is the hardest question. I think preachers who love communicating recognize that my greatest task is to say, "How do I make an ancient text understandable, yes, but also relevant to the concerns of contemporary believers?"

We often think in very static terms about what preaching is. We say there is explanation, there is illustration, there is application. It is kind of like when you are being taught the color wheel as an artist. There is red paint, there is blue paint, and there is green paint. You paint a little bit, and you discover that these colors work together. They all implode on one another. So I am not so concerned that we say, "Do we do explanation better, or do we do illustration better, or do we do application better?"

What I encourage people to do is to think, even as they are beginning a sermon, to think in an application mode. It is part of that Fallen Condition Focus mentality of saying, "What is the burden of this text? How does this deal with people to whom I am talking?" Not only think in exegetical terms but—to sound like Dr. Seuss for the moment—to encourage preachers from the very beginning, when they say, "How am I going to make this text real to people?" to go in through the "who" door.

Now the "who" door is asking this question: "Who really needs to hear what this text is about?" I want to think of real people that I know, to invite them into my study—imaginatively, if not really—and to talk to them about what this text means. If I get into the habit of talking to people across the kitchen table about what this text means, then I will do the most natural things in the world. I will talk in fairly plain terms about what the text means. I will demonstrate with real life, identifiable images, and illustrations, and then I'll say this is why you personally need to know this. I will be personal and clear and demonstrative simply by thinking in human terms, "Who needs to hear this?" even as I am preparing the message.

I think that moves us beyond a lot of discussions about whether or not the sermon should be this percentage of illustration, or that percentage of application, or that percent of explanation, or how much of graphic image do you use, or whether you use film clips, or whether you use the overhead. We can debate those issues forever. My own sense is that we have a lot of the debates silenced when we say, "Here is my goal as a preacher: I want to think of real people and the impact of this text upon them, and as clearly and as passionately as I can I want to care for them, telling them what God's Word says to them." That moves us out of the oratorical mode. It also moves us out of the entertainment mode to actually think of pastoring people. When we are pastoring them, we tend to come up with the answers to our relevance-to-culture questions.

Preaching: Are there particular resources that you recommend to pastors and students who want to really develop as expository preachers?

Chapell: The books that are out there are quite helpful, and we have a certain richness of written expression at this point. Haddon Robinson (*Biblical Preaching*) is still, I think, the granddaddy of books that are true to God's Word and in establishing an organized method for expositional preaching. Certainly a good foundation. Your book (*Handbook of Contemporary Preaching*), in which you deal with a number of people on noteworthy issues, is quite helpful as a resource when one moves beyond basics to think about selected issues.

I think the thing that is quite helpful to students is seeing people in action. For anybody who wants to be a good preacher: listen to as much preaching as you can. Listen to certain things that are on the Internet now, places that you can access from the Web for listening to good preaching. Those are wonderful resources for us now that we have not had until recently.

Preaching: Do you have any concern about some of the recent trends in preaching?

Chapell: I'm often asked what I think about some of the modern trends in both media and narrative preaching, so let me comment on both of those things. The trends in narrative preaching—my own sense is that evangelicals are coming to a healthier balance of late. When the narrative preaching movement came through, out of the "new homiletic" and out of the liberal circles, we kind of reacted in two ways as evangelicals. One, I think we just slammed it, and we said, "Well, we know all about storytelling. We don't want too much storytelling, and we just don't need that in our culture. That is going to move us away from expository styles." So at one extreme we kind of slammed it and said they had nothing to tell us.

The other extreme is that we imbibed and said, "Oh, this is great!" For pragmatic reasons we steered a lot of our students and a lot of our pastors into narrative styles, with a very naive understanding of the philosophical underpinnings that said that propositional truth was no longer valid and all there was was experience. Therefore we had to have interlocking conscious views of experience in order to have truth communicated. That is just very dangerous and very unbiblical. I think a lot of what we did to kind of stay up with credibility with liberal scholarship was we had a lot of evangelicals too quickly move down the narrative path and without adequate discretion.

My sense is that there is a healthy critique of the narrative homiletic that is now occurring in evangelical circles, while at the same time there is an understanding that not only our culture but the best preaching in all ages has had a helpful and healthful use of narrative components in messages. We can learn a lot not just from the homiletic of narrative but from the hermeneutics of narrative, which are helpful for us in interpreting Scripture well. There is a helpful balance that is now being achieved, of not accepting the philosophical underpinnings but seeking to understand how narrative works for true expository preaching that is often on narrative passages. I think we are coming to a more healthy balance on that.

The other thing that I think is occurring—which I don't think we have come to a healthy balance on yet—is the use of extra media in preaching. My sense is that we will discover about the uses of film clips and extra audio and lights on stage and so forth that is occurring—we will discover a lot of what we did with the overhead projector movement. That is, it is good for attention—it has a certain didactic power—but ultimately the preaching that lasts and is transformative is the truth of God spoken by a man of God whose character is known and trusted by the people of God.

Our preaching is not going to be most powerful because it is most highly produced in terms of either stage or media production. That's effective, but few people have the time to put into competing with nightly television for what is really professional audio, video, media productions. I certainly want to say that I think those can be valid tools. But I don't think any pastor needs to think that he has done a second class sermon because he hasn't gotten the latest media in it. Media can be a helpful tool, but it will never be the primary means by which preaching communicates what the Scriptures are saying.

Preaching in the Public Square

An Interview with Jerry Falwell

Jerry Falwell started a church in his own hometown, then used it as a platform to speak to the nation. In 1956 he founded the Thomas Road Baptist Church in Lynchburg, Virginia (with a beginning congregation of thirty-five people), and within a year was speaking on radio and television on *The Old-Time Gospel Hour*. The church grew rapidly, his TV program went national in 1971—the same year he founded Liberty University—and Falwell became a well-known public figure. In 1979 he founded the Moral Majority, which became a major political force in the 1980s. In recent years he has aligned with the Southern Baptist Convention, and he continues to be one of the most recognized Christian voices in America through his recent appearances on television talk shows and news programs. This interview appeared in the July-August 2003 issue of *Preaching*.

Preaching: In the past you have described yourself as a "salt and light" preacher. What do you mean by that?

Falwell: I believe that God has called me to be both salt of the earth and light of the world. Light of the world—evangelism, soul winning, world evangelization church planter. Salt of the earth—confronting the culture, speaking out against the ills of society that need a prophetic voice. And I have done both for many, many years—about fifty years. Not everyone agrees with that and approves it, and it is something that my mentor Dr. Francis Schaeffer taught me. I was his student for many years and sometimes like to feel that I am extending his ministry.

Preaching: As you think about those two issues—evangelization and cultural confrontation—how do you relate those? Do you see them as separate themes, or do you see them as connected?

Falwell: They both blend in my ministry. There's hardly a sermon I will preach anywhere in which I will not touch on both somewhere during the message. Always evangelism, always soul winning. Almost always there will be some reference in my ministry to the culture.

Preaching: Has that been a characteristic of your ministry since you began preaching, or is it something that developed over the years?

Falwell: Somewhere in the early 1960s, when Bible reading and prayer were removed from public schools by the U.S. Supreme Court, I began speaking out. I had been taught in Bible college that politics and religion don't mix. Nobody gave me a book, chapter, and verse, but I accepted it. I was raised a Democrat by my father, and I became pretty much a Republican by conviction—but I use the qualifier "pretty much" because there are many Republicans whose views on the social issues lead me not to support them. When I find myself in a quandary—where both candidates are pro-choice, pro–gay rights, anti–strong national defense and so on—I go fishing on election day.

Preaching: The use of preaching to seek to achieve political and social change dates back to the earliest days of American history. Clearly it has been one of the dominant themes in your ministry. How has that impacted your preaching to have such a major emphasis on cultural and political confrontation?

Falwell: To be a salt and light preacher does put you in confrontation from time to time. There are places where I would never be invited to preach, simply because of the fear they might have that I might address the abortion issue, the gay issue, faith and family issues, but it is what I feel definitely called to do. So it is irrelevant to me that there is a price to pay.

My Mars Hill ministry is a ministry to the media—things like *Crossfire*. Five, six, seven times a week I will do national TV shows. I do *Hardball* each Friday night debating somebody on some issue. It's my way of getting the gospel out to what I call the greater public. The greater public is not at church on Sunday morning, and it is not listening to religious broadcasting on television or radio. A primetime debate forum for me is a way to get the gospel—the death, burial, resurrection of Christ—message out to people while confronting the other side on the moral and social issues. The positive side to that is that through the years about five million faithful, conservative, mostly Christian families have come alongside and have asked me informally to be their spokesperson. So I am speaking for that politically incorrect minority of a few million people who don't have in the media another spokesperson, with a possible exception of a Sean Hannity or George Will from time to time.

Preaching: **Have you ever felt pressured or drawn to move more fully into that sphere and not continue in the pastoral role?**

Falwell: No, I watched people make that mistake. I watched Carl McIntyre make that mistake a generation ago, and Billy James Hargis and some others. The primary ministry any preacher of the gospel has is just that, preaching the gospel. But for me a significant part of my ministry is confronting the culture. While I have no intention of running for public office or leaving the pastorate of the local church ever, I feel strongly that I must do what I am doing.

Preaching: **As you look at other preaching in churches across the country, do you think that pastors do enough of that kind of cultural confrontation in their own preaching ministries?**

Falwell: I would have to say, I do not. I believe that we all have a different calling in some areas; each of us is unique. At the same time I don't think that anyone is exempt from being salt of the earth, and when you come to the premier social issue of our time, legalized abortion, I don't think that any person who takes the Bible seriously has the luxury of being silent on this issue. I think we shall stand with bloody hands if we do. But, again, I am not hard on other preachers who are less vocal. Everyone must do what he feels God is calling him to do.

And when I go into other pulpits, I try to be as sensitive as possible to the preferences of that pastor of that church except in rare situations where it demands unacceptable compromise. I can't think of an exception where that would be true. I would not go into a Methodist church and preach on baptism by immersion. If I accept the invitation, I should be a gentleman also. And I don't go into Roman Catholic churches and talk about the gay priest in Boston.

I speak in lots of places because of my political involvement. I debate at Harvard, Yale, most of the major schools on a regular basis. I'm always as kind as I can be to the powers that be in those things that deal with the issues, not personalities. For example, at Princeton, Peter Singer believes that parents should have the right to kill their little born babies up to thirty days after birth. Well, I have spoken at Princeton. I haven't been there lately, but if I were to go now I would go with the understanding that I would not be lashing out at the president or the board of trustees for having Peter Singer on the faculty. I would probably make strong reference to what he is saying without using his name.

Preaching: On average, how many times each week do you speak?

Falwell: I speak over twenty times a week.

Preaching: As pastor at Thomas Road Baptist Church, how do you go about planning what you will do in the pulpit?

Falwell: As a pastor I try to be sensitive to the needs of the congregation. I have preached through books of the Bible many times. More recently I preached on the book of Proverbs, the last year through the Revelation, usually a chapter a Sunday. I leave the Bible teaching in-depth to the classes and to conferences. I deal with issues also, and topics—things that are facing the church or the nation I will address for a period of time. I am primarily an exhorter—I encourage the saints. I try very hard to somehow lift the burden that each congregant might have in every audience. I point them to the promises of God and encouragement that is in Christ.

I am primarily a topical preacher dealing with what is happening in the culture. The subjects that you would be hearing on *Oprah, Montel,* and all the talk shows and the political talk/debate shows of MSNBC, Fox News, CNBC, CNN are topics that I take right to the pulpit. Every week usually has a burning issue, or two or three burning issues. Things are happening so fast it's seldom that one issue has a shelf life of more than two or three weeks and we are on to something else. Right now, for example, the climate is war, and probably somewhere between now and certainly by year's end we will be at war with Iraq. [This interview was conducted early in 2003, prior to the war in Iraq.] Well, that means that in my church—and it is happening now and in the university—young people will be called up, several last week. That is on the minds and hearts of our people. And so it is a matter that we need to be driving people to their knees and praying about and helping them know how to pray for the president, the men and women in combat, for those in authority, for the Pentagon, and for the whole nation that God might get glory out of that difficult situation.

A year ago it was 9/11, and along the way a long wave of the kidnapping and killing of little children. It's a 50 percent divorce rate in this country and still climbing. All these things for me, as a pastor with a prophetic voice in ministry, motivate my sermon preparation. I have people who help me gather research, and I depend heavily on my computer at home and on the road. Then I have several people who are searching out, encapsulating into paragraphs, information that I am able to build into my messages and to books so that when I am speaking we are talking about today—not a month ago—and using Scripture to apply that.

There are people who don't like that. There are some people who want to sit under pure, simple, unapplied Bible teaching. Dr. J. Vernon McGee all of his life, and even on radio since his death, is that type of a teacher-preacher. Much needed, excellent, but his preaching is just as effective now on the air as it was back when he was living, because he did not apply what he was teaching to what is happening in current events. There is a need for that, and the people who want that would not be happy under my ministry. And there are others who get too much into the political and too much into the social and too little edifying people in Christ. I try very hard to keep the balance, where a family leaves church Sunday morning, Sunday night, Wednesday night spiritually fed, their needs met, and also alert and aware of the world they are living in.

Preaching: With the kind of hectic schedule that you must keep, how do you go about the process of preparing for Sunday morning? Could you walk me through what a preparation process for you might be?

Falwell: Early morning by 6:00 a.m. I shower, dress, and study. By 8:00 a.m. I am out heading to the hospital, to the office, to my work. Mid-afternoon I am crawling in the back of our own plane, where I will be going somewhere—usually east of the Mississippi, north of Miami, south of Bangor—to preach that night and come back home that night. And I sleep in the plane. I have a satellite phone in there, so no matter where I am in the world, the office, my wife, my family can call and it rings right by my little desk there. And I have a satellite Internet connection there where I can receive and send emails. I am in instant communication with everybody all the time. And my seat at that desk also folds into a bed, and we have a galley on board.

Some people travel with me, so I get my rest, and if I am shortchanged at night I make it up in two hours flying to wherever I am going. When I get there I will have shaved and refreshed and cleaned up and step off the plane and go to work. Then we hop in the plane, and I sleep all the way home. Then I go directly home and right into bed and the next morning same thing. I've been doing that forty-seven years.

For me sermon preparation is happening in my study, in my private devotions, in my traveling on the plane and then when I catch a couple of hours in the office. Like here today, both on the computer and on the pads here, I am putting together for next Sunday the follow-up message for the super conference.

Preaching: **As you preach in your own pulpit here, what do you carry with you? Do you take notes or write out a manuscript?**

Falwell: All the time, when I hear something that is interesting to me I write it down and stick it in my pocket. Then when I get home at night I put it in a document. For example, at the lunch table today Dr. Rawlings gave a definition of contemporary fundamentalism and what it must be; he said that a contemporary fundamentalist must be consistent in doctrine, moderate in attitude, progressive in methodology, and liberal in spirit. So I wrote that down.

Then I take all these notes. Like anybody else I have the most current Bible study software—every commentary, every Bible translation that I use—and I build the information. It may be towards something down the road that I will come back to later, but I am constantly building frameworks for sermons. Then something will happen today that becomes the catalyst for doing it next Sunday.

It is not easy when we have twenty-four thousand members here. We have seven services on Sunday: five in the morning and two on Sunday night. We only seat something over three thousand at a time, so it is in-and-out, in-and-out. We use our inner city church, and we use Liberty with a campus pastor who's a Thomas Road-er, and a lot of Thomas Road people will come here (to the university campus)—the younger ones especially who like a little better tempo music than we permit at the church. I usually preach the 8:30 and 11:00 a.m. and 6:00 p.m. I preach three times a day on Sundays. We are relocating the church here to Liberty Mountain. We are building a twelve-thousand-seat sanctuary.

I am always preparing sermons. I am listening to everybody from John Maxwell to Bailey Smith. My wife reads to me every night till I fall asleep; she is a prolific reader, and I bring home at least a book a day because I do interviews on *Listen America*. I did Henry Kissinger one week, Sam Donaldson the next, Larry King the next, Geraldo Rivera the next. This last week I did David Horowitz. And they all have books, and I will bring those home and I'll peruse the index and chapter headings. Then I will ask her to read chapter 3 and chapter 4. And then I build that. So I am constantly reading newspapers, magazines, having books read to me by my wife and others while traveling. I get sick while reading in motion, so I have others read to me. The minute I hear something good I make a note.

We try to take the newest books. If anybody were to ask me, "What's the last book you read?" it would be probably the best seller from yesterday. There might be two pages in the book that are worthwhile or one thought, one idea. But at sixty-nine I try to stay relevant and try to stay cutting edge. We have six thousand sharp kids here, and you can't razzle-dazzle them. I speak to them every week at least once, sometimes twice—the whole student body. I have to keep them challenged, on the edge of their seats. That demands a lot of study, a lot of preparation. They are not impressed with shouting, jokes, that stuff—they laugh *at* you, not *with* you. We bring speakers in sometimes to try something that worked at the church. But the kids have been there, done that. It can be a tough crowd.

Preaching: On Sunday morning as you step into the pulpit, do you have notes with you?

Falwell: I do, because we put the full sermon on the website as if it were to be read by somebody. If you were listening to it, it would not be greatly similar to what is written, but it's done so that it is readable and says the same thing, like doing a script. And for the PowerPoint I have headlines right throughout the text so that it will go up on the screen while I am speaking. But it is very unlikely that the script will be very close to what I am saying. I will be saying the same thing but in a different way. Sometimes I totally digress from it. But when I have finished the message I will have covered the same materials scripted. And then they know that they can go right to the website and print out the actual original script and read that, too, which usually reinforces.

Preaching: Over the years you've gotten involved with radio and television and of course now the Internet. Has the use of media changed or influenced your preaching in a significant way?

Falwell: Yes, being a media minister helps you to say more with few words because it's usually only the first two or three sentences, the sound bite as they call it, that the public is accustomed to capture. You will have others who will get it all, you will have many who will get a good bit of it, but most only get the sound bites. So it is important that your first paragraph is attention getting. It is important that at various points of the message where you want to drive home a truth, there is something that will recapture their attention. It is important that the way you end is a memorable ending, because two weeks from now they won't be able to remember the topic—they have heard so much since then.

I try very hard to think of what I am doing at the pulpit as though I were on *Face the Nation* or one of the talk shows when you are across from an opponent. You don't get the chance to go into all of your rationale.

You will be shouted down or talked over. You've got to have two or three sentences that go right through. For example, Friday night I was debating on *Hardball*. I had said in a *60 Minutes* interview, when asked about comparing Moses and Jesus and Muhammad, I said that Jesus and Moses were great models for love, peace, truth, faith, and family, and Muhammad was a man of war and violence. And then he asked, "Well, why do you think Muhammad was a bad example?" I said I think Muhammad was a terrorist, and I think that he got his kicks out of killing and assassinating people. That is if the Muslim biographers are to be believed.

And so I am on *Hardball* and this guy says, "You bigot, why would you say such a thing?" He was screaming at me. I said, "Abraham, now settle down, don't have a stroke. Let me ask you something: You have read the biographies, the Muslim biographies. Did Muhammad kill innocent people?" "What's that have to do . . . ?" "It's a yes or no question, did he kill innocent people?" He wouldn't answer me. I said, "Your refusal to answer does answer it. The answer was, he did. And that is what a terrorist does." And I said, "Now most of you out there have not read a biography of Muhammad and never will. Go to falwell.com—I've printed one out for you there to summarize it." So you've got to say it quickly. We've gotten eighty-two thousand hits since Friday night reading the copy.

So that translates into preaching. The shorter the sermon you're going to bring—and I bring thirty minute sermons—the shorter the sermon, the better prepared you've got to be. In today's world with everybody seeking instant gratification, you've got to be able to say it quickly, say it well, prick their minds, drive them to further research, and tell them where to get it, simply. Really, the preachers of the next generation have got to be smarter than the preachers of our generation. They've got to say it better, quicker, with greater support. People no longer can say as we once did, "This is the way it is." Because they want to know *why* is that the way it is. You've got to build that in and then give them the resources to get the rest. Kids are wide open today, but you can't fool them as once churches could.

Preaching: As you look back over your ministry . . .

Falwell: I have been preaching fifty years; I'm in my forty-seventh year at Thomas Road Baptist Church.

Preaching: . . . are there some things about preaching that you wish you would have known forty or fifty years ago that you have learned since then?

Falwell: The answer is always yes to that. I was listening to Dr. Billy Graham the other day; it was a Youth for Christ sermon that he brought back in the '40s—rapid fire, I had to listen real attentively to hear what he was saying. And that was back when there was Billy Sunday, before he had broken chairs over the pulpit. They didn't have good sound systems. The preacher who really was considered a great preacher back in the '40s and '50s was a guy that could speak 180 words a minute without breathing and then swallow the mike and do it again.

In the early days coming out of Bible college it was very easy to preach forty-five-minute to an hour sermons and sort of get off down rabbit trails and then come back and so forth—literally lose and bore your audience and get by with it. You learn bad habits, and so I would have liked to have known fifty years ago what I know now. I think that with everything we are doing it would be ten times better. But I was not allowed that privilege. We have to live it out and learn it.

Preaching: If you could offer a word of counsel to other pastors, what would it be?

Falwell: I think that the average American evangelical church is spending too little time teaching and preaching the Bible to its people. There are 168 hours in a week. The average evangelical church has its average member less than an hour. And then all the voices of the culture are cry ing out the other 167 hours. Instead of revving up to meet the challenge, churches are canceling Sunday night, Wednesday night, and doing far too few in-depth study programs with their people.

Once a month we do an all day Saturday Bible study special event. For example this year, early this year, we brought Tim LaHaye, our own Ed Hindson, Gary Frazier who works with Tim. Brought them in for a 9:00 a.m. to 3:00 p.m., six hour series on prophecy. Then they stayed on to Sunday and did three hours in the morning and two at night. We had eleven hours of teaching and the same four thousand people in overflow sat through the whole eleven hours and took notes and were tested on them. A month later we brought in Ken Ham, from Answers in Genesis, and did exactly the same thing in two days—people standing around the walls and teaching them. And then we do one on the doctrines of the Bible. We see to it through our Sunday school and church that our teachers and especially our new converts get to these. Besides Sunday morning, Sunday night, and Wednesday night, we have what we call the Equipping Institute with twenty-four different classes. Everybody is in a different class learning different things, men and women. In one year you've been through the average Bible college.

The result is that our young people, our young couples, our older Christians can take a Bible quiz anytime you want to give them one and pretty well do as well as the preachers. And the rush of the day is not a problem. People are hungry for it. It's just that the preachers are not willing to work that hard. They have to be there. They can't just have these things and go off somewhere flitting around. They have to be there moderating, adding to it, handling the transitions, and providing the shepherd care to make sure it all happens right. But the end result is that you build a church.

These felt-needs churches, seeker-sensitive—I'm not trying to be critical, but I meet a lot of those people that don't have the foggiest idea about Bible doctrine. That's why they are blown around by every wind of doctrine. They are entertained by skits that make some reference to the Bible. Great crowds come, but their lives are not radically changed. And they are not tied into the Bible. If we have to be forever worried about offending people because of the Bible, we're missing something.

My experience is people want to know the Bible, and the more you demand the more you get. So to me teaching and preaching is the bottom line. Everything else supports that. Teaching and preaching is the bottom line, and if they don't have that in their heads, then it won't be in their hearts.

Preaching in Unsettled Times

An Interview with Jack Graham

Since 1989 Jack Graham has been pastor of the twenty-thousand-member Prestonwood Baptist Church in Dallas, where he preaches to twelve thousand to thirteen thousand people each weekend. From 2002 to 2004 he also served as president of the Southern Baptist Convention, the nation's largest Protestant denomination. *Preaching* magazine editor Michael Duduit interviewed Graham one year after the events of September 11, 2001, and the interview appeared in the November-December 2002 issue.

Preaching: **We seem to be living in unsettled times—economically, with the threat of war, cultural upheaval. As you gauge the times in which we live, how does that impact the way you preach?**

Graham: The Scriptures always speak to crisis, and certainly our nation is in crisis. The world faces uncertain days. So it is a relatively easy thing to take Scripture —so much of which was written in a time of crisis. Certainly when you read the New Testament—the New Testament church was facing an adversarial culture and a world that was very bloody and dangerous.

We just dedicated a new wing in our facilities in Texas, and we lifted up a cross connected to the rubble at the World Trade Center. I actually held up in my hands two crosses that were forged out of the rubble and the metal from the collapse. The message of Christ and the cross rises out of the rubble of human depravity and gives us the opportunity to bring a message of hope and life to the world.

Those of us who proclaim and share the Christian faith have the most incredible opportunity and the most open door in my lifetime. 9/11 marked our generation forever, just as Pearl Harbor marked a previous generation, the "greatest generation." My prayer is that Christians in our time and our nation will rise to the occasion. We have the privilege—those of us who preach and teach—to undergird and strengthen believers in this time in order to take on the issues of life.

We have a new generation coming along. I look out at our young adults, our teenagers, and even younger, and I really feel the weight of that. I feel the responsibility of preparing our families for hard times, and I don't expect it to get any easier. So we have a message, and certainly when it's biblical it's concurrent with the times, but it also speaks to the future and the promise and the hope of tomorrow that we have in Christ.

Preaching: **The nation recently marked the first anniversary of the 9/11 events. How did you try to approach that issue in your own preaching?**

Graham: It is so important for those of us who preach Sunday after Sunday to connect to the issues of the day. I remember last year right after the actual events of 9/11, I put aside what I was doing at the time—preaching through Ephesians. I laid aside the series to deal with the particular issues we were facing. Then again this fall, in the remembrance of 9/11, I was actually able to take what I was doing. I've been preaching through Genesis this year, and the Sunday after 9/11 I preached a message on "The Genesis of Jihad." I went back into the life of Abraham and even before, to Cain and Abel, to show the hatred and hostility in the human heart, and even to Adam and Eve and the hatred that exists in the human heart, the depravity as a result of sin. Particularly I did a message on Abraham and his two sons, Ishmael and Isaac, and related that to the current problem. One of the greatest testimonies to the authenticity, authority, and accuracy of Scripture is the plan of history and the destiny of men and nations that we see there, rooted in Genesis.

Napoleon asked one of his generals if he could provide any evidence that the Bible was God's Word. The general said, "The Jew." Certainly if you look at God's dealings with the Jewish nation and the Arab world and preach to these issues, there is a tremendous response. When we actually did a service for 9/11 on the anniversary, it was an amazing service. As we lifted up that cross it gave me the opportunity to speak of our hope. While evil is very real, we also recognize that God has conquered sin and death and hell.

Preaching: Do you find that the events of 9/11 and since have created a new openness to the gospel? Are you still seeing that?

Graham: Definitely. Some are suggesting that after the initial rush to church last year, people have gone back to business as usual—that in most of the churches people are back to "normal." We prayed for a new "normal" to get back to—the way of life that we enjoy as Americans will never be the same. I can tell you from our experience and that of other pastors I know that when the church is marked by the work of the Spirit and the Word of God is taught, there has been—I don't know if you'd call it "revival," but I know that in our own church, we're at a new level in terms of volunteerism, people stepping forward to serve, certainly in decisions for Christ. Everything in our church is growing and alive, and I think there is a new sense of urgency in the lives of our people. I also think there's an openness in our community—people are asking questions, and it gives Christians an opportunity to step in. We have this wonderful message of Jesus that compared to all world religions is incomparable. We have a reason for the hope that is in us, and we can proclaim that.

I have a suspicion that where church life and Christian faith went back to business-as-usual—people went back to church and found the same-old, same-old—the church needs to change. Where there is life and the breath of the Spirit, the proclamation of Christ and his cross and the resurrection, I think in those churches you're finding a great sense of blessing, of the refreshing Spirit of God. It's very exciting where we are.

Preaching: Do you find yourself adapting your preaching ministry to capitalize on that new openness?

Graham: I do. I also think that perhaps in the last year in my own preaching ministry there's a new directness. I personally feel that the times are more urgent, and that it's not "sky-is-falling" rhetoric to preach the seriousness and soberness of our times. While obviously we have great joy in the way we live, there is for me a desire to get the message out even more quickly and straightforwardly. In my mind, in the last year my preaching has taken on a new heat, if you will. I just want to make sure that every time I preach people are hearing answers to their questions, and that they are receiving not only comfort for the times but a challenge for the times, to live full-out for God.

Preaching: In addition to anxiety about terrorism and war, there's also an economic unsettledness in the U.S. right now. In your church you have a broad range of economic conditions—from people of modest means to people of great means. How do you speak to that issue? Does that make a difference in your preaching?

Graham: In our church, regardless of economic status, everyone faces the fragility of the times economically. There are very few people who have not been touched by this, no matter where they are on their pay grade—especially in our area where there were a lot of dot-com businesses that opened and closed. At the upper end of things you've got people who are losing in the stock market daily. Regardless of a person's economic status, everyone is facing more difficult times.

Interestingly, we are in the middle of a capital campaign. We started a capital campaign for the second phase of our building program literally two weeks after 9/11—we relocated the church and are now completing that relocation. Yet—and I would attribute this to the fresh wind blowing through our church—people have responded with sacrifice. We have spoken of giving out of affluence and abundance, but also out of sacrifice in times of economic stress, and our people have responded to that.

Also, the preaching and teaching of the Word of God just leads naturally to the building of the body in people's lives who do realize that their hope is beyond the material and their strength is in Christ. So you really couldn't have a better time to be preaching the great truths of Scripture than right now. Although you don't wish for such things, to me personally it's easier to preach in hard times because people are more open and honest and more needy of the message rather than in times of affluence and pride. We've been humbled by this, and when we are humbled under the hand of God, then he moves.

Preaching: Tell me about your own preaching style.

Graham: Over the years my preaching style has not changed, from rural churches in Oklahoma to West Palm Beach to the Dallas area. It hasn't changed because I believe the most effective way of preaching is to simply take the Scripture, explain it, illustrate it, and apply it, which is biblical, expositional preaching. That kind of preaching covers every conceivable subject and matter.

At Prestonwood, I am consistently teaching a passage of Scripture—for the most part preaching through books. I'm preaching through Genesis right now. Last year I was preaching through Ephesians. Coming up next year I'll do the Sermon on the Mount, so it will be a smaller series. My preaching is somewhat typical of expositional preaching. I don't do verse-by-verse homilies. I try to take a passage and outline it, structure the sermon, and deliver it.

My preaching is very Christocentric. My goal is to introduce people to faith in Jesus Christ, so there's always an evangelistic appeal in my preaching. Each time I preach I make every effort to share the gospel—the death, burial, and resurrection of Jesus Christ. My preaching is very invitational. I would say it is somewhat confrontational—with truth—and I would say it is expositional.

Preaching: How long would a typical series run for you?

Graham: The Genesis series I started in January, and it is going to run the entire year until December, when I'll do a Christmas series. I'm actually speeding up a bit through the patriarchs; I've done the life of Joseph before, so when I come to that in a few weeks I'll speed up and just do a few messages on Joseph. I took some time on Abraham; I'll spend about four or five messages on Jacob, then Joseph about the same. The Ephesians series was about nine months.

Preaching: Do you have any problem sustaining interest in an extended series?

Graham: I believe people respond if it's interesting. I try to outline these longer series in subparts. For example, Genesis is a long series, but you have subplots. Once we finished the first eleven chapters—creation, the fall, Noah, the Tower of Babel, and all the rest—then Abraham breaks out and it is a great series on faith. I'm calling the series on Genesis "The Legacy of Faith." This happens to be the twenty-fifth year of our church's existence, and the theme of our entire year is "The Legacy of Faith." So it works beautifully not only in church life to speak of legacy, but it also gives us the opportunity to address many of the pertinent, big issues people are addressing: Who am I? Where did I come from? The rage of nations and the hostility of men. All of these are in Genesis.

So the important thing is not how long a series is. Expositional preaching should never be boring. It should be interesting, it should be inviting, and it should be dealing with subject matter that is appropriate for today. It's that old thing of the Bible in one hand and the newspaper in the other. I try to approach introductions to messages with contemporary connections.

Preaching: When you do an extended series, do you break it at certain points through the year?

Graham: Yes. When I was a younger preacher I thought I had to just stay with it. As I've gotten older and a little more mature in my preaching—just like with 9/11 last year, to be preaching on some unrelated subject at the time would have been a waste of a huge opportunity. We listen to the Holy Spirit, and we look to the issues of the times and address them.

The same goes for church life, if there's something going on in the life of the church that needs to be addressed. For example, when we came to the literal anniversary of the church, I broke out of Genesis and did a message to the church on the call of the church in our times, the ministry of the church, and how God has used Prestonwood. So we definitely need to be flexible to change as times call for it.

Preaching: How far in advance do you begin planning a sermon series?

Graham: I start with God's work in my own heart. I believe preaching should be out of the overflow of God's work in the heart and life of the preacher. It begins in my own life, my own devotions, what is God saying to me? That may be a subject, or an issue of importance; it may be a passage that is driving me. For example, I'm going to be doing a series on the Sermon on the Mount. As Southern Baptists our theme for the future is "Empowering Kingdom Growth," and I've just been living, thinking, and breathing Christ's words about the kingdom, and of course the Sermon on the Mount is the constitution of the kingdom. So I've just been living lately in the Sermon on the Mount, and I can't wait to get there. I'm going to start in January. It's still in its formative stages, but I've begun reading. That's pretty typical; I don't plan much more than three or four months out.

I sit down and outline the book in big-picture style, break out the passages, and typically come up with the various sermon titles and themes, and lay it out. That's all flexible and changeable. My sermon preparation for the week is typically that week; I don't work very far ahead. With the demands of the church I can't stay more than a day or two ahead!

Preaching: What does your week look like in terms of sermon preparation?

Graham: I give my mornings to study. By Sunday night on many weeks I'm already doing some light reading and preparation. Monday is light reading; I may get to the sermon and I may not. By Tuesday morning I want to be into sermon preparation. Tuesday, Wednesday, and Friday mornings are given to sermon preparation; if I'm not finished I'll go in Saturday morning.

The actual sermon preparation is to do my general reading on the text. The method many of us were taught is to bring your own ideas to the text first, then supplement it with commentaries and homiletic material, but for me it's always been best to read my way into the text. Typically I have a stack of books I'm working on for that particular passage, and I just read myself full—I'm underlining and making notes. Then I sit down with a blank legal pad, and hopefully, by that time I'm coming out with an outline.

My preaching style has been pretty much the same through the years— I look first to explain the text, then to apply the text, then to illustrate the text. I try to get my explanation and exegesis down where I understand the passage. The most challenging part is to apply and illustrate it; I spend a lot of time working on that.

Preaching: How much of your sermon is composed of each of those three parts?

Graham: I don't think I've ever analyzed it, but my goal would be to be about a third each. I typically preach about thirty-five to forty minutes, and I would say that a good ten to fifteen minutes of that would be dealing with the text itself; then the rest of it would be wrapped up in application and illustration, plus introduction and conclusion.

Preaching: What do you carry into the pulpit with you?

Graham: I carry handwritten sermon notes into the pulpit. The reason first is habit, but it also cuts down the time of sermon preparation for me. If I'm working on a manuscript or even typewritten notes, that's another step. I have a set of hieroglyphics in my own writing and notations with words and key thoughts. I take a sentence outline into the pulpit with key thoughts and passages, and illustrations. I rarely write out the illustrations.

One of my strengths in the pulpit is spontaneity, and I've felt through the years when I'm working with a manuscript or overly prepared notes I get too wooden in the pulpit. I do much better when I'm free-flowing, flexible with words. I rarely preach without notes, but typically my notes are pretty simple in terms of their structure. Once the sermon is preached, I have a wonderful secretary who can type my handwritten notes, and we file it. For the sake of radio and television ministry we do transcripts now.

Preaching: How much time do you normally spend in preparing a message?

Graham: That's always a hard question to answer because in sermon preparation there are times of gestation, then times of birth. I'd say anywhere from eight to ten hours, maybe eight to twelve hours. I preach three services each weekend, Saturday night and twice on Sunday, and that's the same message. Then there's typically one other preparation per week: either the midweek service or a business luncheon that we do.

There was a time when I was doing three or four preparations a week. That was a very heavy schedule. Now it's primarily one major preparation, then another preparation of some kind.

I live with the sermon. Any preacher knows that Sunday's coming. That's the challenge of being a pastor-preacher. It's not the delivery of the sermon that's the challenge or pressure for me. The challenge is the preparation. There's never a sense of completion because you're always preaching next week, so maintaining freshness and the fullness of the Spirit and your own devotional life are essential. So all week long you're living with this sermon you're preparing; you're never far away from what you're going to do.

It's like a great pitcher in baseball. A class-A minor leaguer throws the ball in much the same way as a Cy Young winner like Randy Johnson. What separates one from the other is in the delivery. Same baseball, primarily the same motion. What separates one pitcher from another is the delivery. I believe what often makes the difference in the sermon is in the delivery.

Preaching: As a preacher, what do you wish you'd known twenty years ago that you know now?

Graham: I've always believed in the impact of preaching—that it truly does make a difference. It really is an audacious thing. I wish I had known even twenty, thirty years ago what a huge difference preaching can make in people's lives. I believed it then, but I believe it even more now. Preaching truly is God's way of fleshing out the message in the lives and personalities of his people. I've never been more eager to preach.

I think all young preachers battle the issue of being yourself. We all have models, mentors when we're young. I wish I'd known in my twenties and thirties that God wants to use my personality, the way I say things, even my style—that God uses each of us. I wish I'd had that confidence of knowing that God really does want to use Jack Graham, and my experience, my gifts, and abilities. I always challenge young preachers with the idea to be your best self. Learn from others, but don't be a cheap imitation of somebody else.

Preaching: What final counsel would you share with fellow preachers?

Graham: Preaching must come out of the life of the preacher, the authenticity of the preacher's life and the character we build. There is no effective preaching without credibility in the pulpit—we've seen that many times. What I have tried to do is to build within my life the consistency of character that produces a consistency of message. The standard of biblical preaching and the call is a high call. We all fall short, yet we should aspire to preach a message that is consistent with our character and that our character will be consistent with our message. The integrity of the pulpit.

Another issue that has been important for me is the environment in which our message is preached. The worship style is different and dynamic within the context of every church. I do believe that the best preaching occurs in a context of heart-felt and warm-hearted worship—where the congregation is prepared to receive the message. When I step to the pulpit people are ready to respond, and that's due in large part to the wonderful ministers of music and worship leaders that we've had in our churches. Preaching takes place best in that context where lives are being changed—where there's an expectation that when the Word of God is opened a powerful result is going to take place.

Preaching to Engage Culture

An Interview with O. S. Hawkins

O. S. Hawkins is now president-CEO of Guidestone Financial Resources of the Southern Baptist Convention (the SBC's annuity and insurance agency for ministers), but at the time of this interview he was pastor of the largest congregation in the nation's largest Protestant denomination—the First Baptist Church of Dallas, Texas, a congregation known not only as the flagship church of Southern Baptists but also for its most famous member: Billy Graham. Hawkins came to Dallas from the First Baptist Church of Fort Lauderdale, Florida, where he became widely known for his effective preaching that featured an expository model with a distinctively contemporary flavor. This interview appeared in the January-February 1996 issue of *Preaching*.

Preaching: You came to First Baptist, Dallas—a historic church in the buckle of the Bible Belt—from Fort Lauderdale, much more of a resort community. Now you find yourself in a downtown church, with skyscrapers all around you. How has that affected your preaching? What kind of adjustments have you had to make in changing contexts?

Hawkins: We were downtown in Fort Lauderdale, too, in the middle of the city. But there's a world of difference between Fort Lauderdale and Dallas. Fort Lauderdale is virtually a new city. *Money* magazine recently said it was in one of the most transient counties in America. A third of the population moves in and out every year. Very few people move there from the Bible Belt. Everybody's from New York, New Jersey, Pennsylvania—they're mostly from the Northeast. Many of them—if they've had any church background at all—have been from a liturgical background.

And so much of what we did at First Baptist was refreshing to them because they had never heard it. I pastored there fifteen years and we never had the same Sunday schedule more than eighteen months at a time. We would constantly change because we could do that.

Here, it's a much more traditional part of the world—we're in more of the Bible Belt here. We have a tremendous pulpit heritage here for a hundred years, and the church is full of biblically literate laymen and women. So the challenge is to reach, as Stott would say, "between two worlds."

I've always been an expository preacher, but I've always fancied being expository in a contemporary way. It's been a good discipline for me to be here because I cannot wing it here like you can get away winging it at some other places. I've not noticed a tremendous difference in my own technique or style.

I think if anything it's helped me to come back to some real basics of preaching. There's a subtle danger out there among young conservative preachers; they're hearing it in some of the conferences, or it's being interpreted as such. They're very subtly being told to avoid four things. They are being told to avoid context—there's almost a pride among some of not preaching expository sermons. I heard one large church Southern Baptist pastor say he never preaches an expository sermon as though that were a badge of honor. So they are being told to avoid context almost, to market the church in such a way to find out what people want and then seek to meet their need. And if they can find a text to tag to it, fine.

Second, they're being told to avoid confessions or doctrinal truth. Young preachers are being told that people don't want to hear about doctrine, and there is a tremendous dearth of doctrinal truth being preached in the pulpit today. In my opinion, this is part of our problem with impacting the whole culture. We never hear words like "repentance" anymore. We had a couple join some time ago; they came to me and said, "You know, we have been members of another church for several years, and we cannot remember when we ever heard the blood of Christ mentioned from the pulpit." So there is this subtle thing that people are being told to avoid any type of doctrinal preaching.

Third, I think they're being told to avoid controversy. Don't deal with controversial issues. Consequently, we don't. We don't take pulpit stands anymore on matters of righteousness. Many people don't deal with current issues that are prevalent in their cities, whether it be homosexuality or the abortion issue or whatever it might be. It's absent in many, many pulpits. There's not a certain sound coming because people are told to avoid all those types of controversies if you want to reach people. I think we've gone overboard in doing that.

Finally it seems as though they are even told to avoid confrontation. Avoid confronting people with any type of decision. I'm not necessarily just talking about the public invitation, although I'm an advocate of it. There are a lot of people who confront people with the gospel without giving a public invitation. My friend Jim Kennedy, who I pastored with in Fort Lauderdale for fifteen years, doesn't give a public invitation, but he always confronts people with the claims of the gospel. So I'm not just speaking about a public invitation. I am talking about bringing a person into confrontation with the gospel of Christ.

Preaching: You spoke of expository preaching in a contemporary way. How do you approach merging those two?

Hawkins: This is an ecotonic world in which we're living. An ecotone is that place where two ecosystems come together. I pastored down in Fort Lauderdale where that salt water from the ocean comes into the intercoastal waterway and meets the fresh water from the river. Where they blend together and merge together is called an ecotone, and it's a place of tremendous possibility. Fish lay their eggs there. It's also a place of tremendous danger because certain things happen environmentally there.

That's the world we're called to preach to. We have an incredible opportunity. We are meshing and blending right now our modern world with a postmodern world. The world I was educated in, the world you were educated in, most everybody reading this article was educated in, is history—it's over. I just read the other day that all the accumulated knowledge in world history is going to double in the next five years. We are already in a postmodern world, and it's a time of great possibility for those of us who can translate the gospel in a contemporary way. It's a time of horrible problems for those who are still locked in a time warp in the 1950s or '60s, trying to translate the gospel in that manner.

We have little children who are growing up—before they even get to school—with three-dimensional computer graphics, then they're going into some Sunday school classes with flannelgraphs! So we're not connecting with them there.

I'll give you a couple of examples. I generally preach thematic series—mostly through books but I do them thematically. For example, I preached through Philemon recently. As I looked at each paragraph in Philemon, the whole book was about relationships. Relationships are so important. What I saw in Philemon is five paragraphs that had everything to do with relationships.

It talks in the first paragraph about the importance of affirmation. Paul said, "Your love has given me great hope and encouragement, you have refreshed the hearts of the saints." And so I preached that paragraph on the importance of affirming one another in the home right where you are; it has a dynamic effect. And he deals with the win-win principle and says, "Formerly he was useless to you and now is useful to me and to you." In relationships we can both win.

Paul deals with forgiveness, he deals with commitment, he deals with accountability. He closes the book by saying, "Oh, by the way, get the guestroom ready for me; I'm coming back," and this guy knows Paul's coming and he's going to hold him accountable. I took that as an issue that was prevalent out there in the world.

Everybody is looking for relationships, and I boiled it down in that book to the fact that there are only three relationships in life: the outward experience with each other, the inward experience with ourselves, and the upward experience with God. We're never properly related to each other until we're properly related to ourselves, and we're never properly related to ourselves until we're properly related to God. I developed the whole book like that.

Recently, I wanted to address this subject of the generations that are lost to the church. I typed in "Generation X" and pulled up about 85 articles. I started narrowing the search; I wanted to narrow it down to some characteristics of Generation X and these other generations lost to the church—what are they thinking and why they're outside the church. After I'd narrowed it several times, I got down to about 15 articles, and I pulled them all out. I read them and came up with five basic characteristics of this lost generation to the church.

The first one is this: they're searching for meaningful relationships in life; most of them have never known one. They're looking for a home they never had. They've been the product of massive divorce, they are afraid of commitment, and the number one characteristic of this generation is the search for meaningful relationships in life. The second characteristic was they want immediate gratification; they don't want to wait for anything. They don't invest in mutual funds because they want it and want it right now.

Third, they want it for nothing. They say give it to me but without cost or condition; they don't want to work for it. Fourth, they want guilt-free living. They have been raised in homes without any moral absolutes; 81 percent of them don't even believe there's absolute truth, but they are searching for guilt-free living. It's a real confusion and conflict within their hearts and minds. The final thing they're searching for is prosperity, yet they know they don't have much hope of attaining it. They're the first generation that will live in homes not as nice as the homes they were raised in.

So I took those five characteristics and God gave me a verse. I used my Bible almost as a computer and started narrowing the search. I found we have the answer to what they're looking for; it's in the Bible, and that's not just preacher talk. You can narrow it all down to one verse in the Bible, Ephesians 1:7: "In him we have redemption through his blood, the forgiveness of sins, in accordance with the riches of God's grace" [NIV].

The number one characteristic they're looking for is meaningful relationships in life. Paul said, "In him we have redemption through his blood." It's in a relationship we have something to offer them. They're never going to have a relationship with others until they really come into a relationship with God—that's what they're really searching for. And we have a generation out there that does not know Christ, not because of the public schools, it's not because of legislation; it's because we've not made him known. So what we are looking for is relationship. We have it there in him.

Second, they want immediate gratification. In him we have redemption—present, active, indicative, occurring in actual time. We don't have to wait for it. What they're looking for we have to offer them right now; they can have it.

Third, they want it for nothing. In him we have redemption through his blood; it's already purchased for them. They just don't know that; we've not translated it to them. They want guilt-free living. The next phrase in our verse says we can have "the forgiveness of sins."

Finally, they are looking for prosperity. Their parents were raised in a generation of economic boom; they came out of college and went into high entry level jobs and progressed through corporations. This generation got graduate degrees and are flipping hamburgers at McDonald's. But Paul says, "In him we have redemption through his blood, the forgiveness of sins, in accordance with the riches of God's grace." We've not preached much grace, and they just don't know that he who was rich for our sakes became poor that we through his poverty might become rich.

So I try to take what the world is trying to do out there, what the world is thinking, and I try to bring it back and center it in the Word of God and let a response issue out of the Word of God. And at the same time, I want to bring people into a confrontation with their sins.

There's another thing that we're being told today: that we should try to avoid any kind of second-person preaching, which by and large I adhere to. But there's a total dearth and void of it out there. Study the apostolic sermons, study Peter at Pentecost.

What did Peter say? He said, "You, with the help of wicked men, put him to death by nailing him to the cross." He brought people to accept their own personal responsibility for their sin, and that is not happening today. At least I don't see it happening in much of contemporary preaching.

There's a lost word in our Christian vocabulary out there, and it's "conviction." When Peter preached, their hearts were cut. You go into many modern churches today and you see crowds, you see excitement, you see music, you see dialogue, but you seldom see the convicting power of God that leads people to have their hearts cut, to then say, "What must I do?" as they did then.

One of the things in the church growth movement that is alarming to me is the lack of emphasis on the power of God. I've been to Ephesus one time, and it floored me. You walk through the ruins of the city of Ephesus, which has the most incredibly reconstructed ruins in the world. Walk down that corridor, see that twenty-four-thousand-seat theater, go to the library, go to the temples, go to the bathhouses. It is massive! It is incredible, and it was such a pagan culture.

And to think that Paul went into that city with just a couple of friends, engaged the culture, and transformed the culture. He didn't go door-to-door and market and see what people wanted; he didn't do any of the things we are telling people they have to do today. When you walk through that city and see it, and see how it was engaged and transformed, there's no explanation for it except the power of God. God did it. That's something that seems to be not very high on the priority list in our discussions on church growth or preaching. I think church growth is centered in leadership, and I personally think it's centered in the pulpit.

Preaching: This postmodern era in which we live seems to be one in which we will have to revive the apostolic model of preaching. So many characteristics of this era mirror those of the first century, in which Paul ministered. Perhaps our textbook for preaching in this era needs to be the book of Acts.

Hawkins: You're singing my song. The very culture in which we're living is a pagan culture not unlike the one the apostles penetrated. More and more so. For us it may be even more difficult because so much of our culture is gospel-hardened already, where theirs wasn't. Theirs was more like Fort Lauderdale; the gospel was new to many people down there. But in much of where preaching is taking place in America, people think they know it all, though they don't.

You mentioned apostolic preaching—there's a common thread running through it. Study Peter's first recorded sermon, at Pentecost in Acts 2, then study Paul's first recorded sermon, at Pisidian Antioch in Acts 13, and you'll find something very common to both. You find what Paul said in 2 Timothy 3:16, that all Scripture is given by inspiration of God, and it's profitable for four things: doctrine, reproof, correction, instruction in righteousness. When you study the apostolic sermons you find a balance in their preaching, and they did those four things: they taught doctrine, they reproved sin, they corrected false paths, they instructed in righteousness.

Look at the Pentecostal sermon—Peter taught doctrine at first; he established a biblical basis for what was happening. He opened the scroll to Joel, illustrated with a couple of Psalms, built a biblical basis, and taught about the doctrine of the resurrection. He reproved sin. He corrected false paths as he called them to repent. And he instructed in righteousness; he gave them instructions as to what to do. Paul did the same thing at Pisidian Antioch.

In Thessalonica in Acts 17 is a real model for our preaching, when it says Paul, as his custom was, went in and reasoned with them. The word means he "spoke through"—he spoke through the Scriptures. I think it was an expository message. He took the Scriptures; he spoke through it with them from the Scriptures, explaining—he laid it out to them—and demonstrating that the Christ had to suffer and rise from the dead. And some of them were persuaded. I think we do have to come back to apostolic preaching.

Some people think in order to do that you have to be archaic, you have to stand behind a big wooden pulpit somewhere and make no expressions and make no application. We're just out of balance in our preaching. We've gone from one extreme to another. We've gone from an expository extreme that was void of any application or relevancy to current issues, and we've gone to a totally opposite extreme, where we just want to put everything in that's practical and how-to and applicable without the Scripture. What's happening, though, is that we're seeing the pendulum come back a bit to more balance, where it can really be effective.

The apostles were engaging the same kind of culture we are—a godless, pagan culture. That's what America is. And they weren't trying to be cute about it. They went in, and the power of God came on them, and the power of God is what brought all of this about. When we return to that and bring back a balance into our preaching, we can see something happen.

Preaching: **As you mentioned, you are pastor of a church with many biblically literate laypeople. At the same time, you're also trying to reach a culture in which most people have little understanding of Scripture and even less sense of its authority. How do you preach to both of those audiences?**

Hawkins: Hopefully I'm relevant enough and applicable enough and interesting enough to appeal to that person whose eyes can be opened to gospel truth, while at the same time meaty enough and biblical, doctrinal enough to be able to translate to those folks.

Every Sunday I preach to W. A. Criswell, I preach to Charles Ryrie [editor of *Ryrie Study Bible*]—he never misses a service. I preach to so many professors from Dallas Seminary and our Criswell College; a lot of retired theologues and preachers are in our church. At first I wondered if this might be an intimidating factor, but it is not. It's the most helpful thing to me, because it causes me to study that much harder. And I talk to these fellows; they're my biggest asset. If I have a passage that's complicated, I talk to three or four of these guys before I preach. Most of those folks know that the future of our church is in translating this message to those who are beyond our walls. We're trying to make our decisions here at First Baptist on the basis of those who are not here yet.

Preaching's a challenge wherever you go, not just at this church.

Preaching: Tell me a bit about your own approach to preaching, particularly your planning and preparation process.

Hawkins: There are many factors that are involved in preaching, from my perspective—not simply the study time and formulation of the sermon. I bring everybody I can into my preaching. For example, we have a large prayer ministry, involving about seven hundred of our people. We have four people praying every hour, around the clock, seven days a week. Every one of those people pray for me every week. I ask them to pray for me the prayer of Ephesians 6:19 in relation to the pulpit ministry, where Paul said that he prayed that utterance might be given him that he might open his mouth boldly to proclaim the mystery of the gospel. So I ask them to pray for me each week that I might have freedom in my preaching, that utterance might be given to me.

Unction is a strange phenomenon, isn't it? We get in that pulpit, and we know when we have it and we know when we don't have it. I ask them to pray for me also that I might have fearlessness in preaching—that I might open my mouth boldly, that as I stand in that sacred desk to translate this message, I might be bold in what I do and not shy away or back off from it. It's a real temptation for pastors.

I ask them to pray for me that I might be faithful in preaching, that I might proclaim the mystery of the gospel. I want to always have the gospel there, the *kerygma*. So before I ever start my preparation, I have hundreds of people praying for me.

We also have a prayer meeting every Saturday morning in the auditorium. They pray for me at 8:00 each Saturday morning. We kneel at every seat in our auditorium, and we pray for the person who's going to be under the preaching of the Word of God there the next day. We don't know who they are, but God does.

Then when we come into the worship service, I ask those people in the prayer ministry to ask God to lead them to someone in that auditorium that they don't know, and to pray for them during the course of the message. We pray toward the pulling down of strongholds. Some people have strongholds of pride that keep them from a breakthrough. Some are in a stronghold of procrastination; they're just putting it off. Some are in a stronghold of presumption; they just presume on some decision they made years ago. So during the course of the sermon, I have people praying for those in the auditorium.

You can imagine what that does in a time of invitation, when a certain man—there's a spiritual battle going on, and people are praying—that man comes forward to that altar, and these people know they've had as much a part in that as I have or anyone. This is a very important part of my sermon preparation—having my people pray for me as I prepare.

Before I even get to the message, another important part is my personal visitation and my own personal contact with people in need of the gospel each week. For example, on Saturdays I telephone everybody who visited the Sunday before. Takes me about four hours to do it. Everybody who visits this church gets a personal call from me. What that helps me to do also is to know where people are—where they're hurting, why they came, what they're up to. Of course, in my own personal visitation I am able to sense the needs of people. This is very important to me. To be isolated from people affects our preaching ministry. So that's a big part of my sermon preparation, though it's not in my study.

Then you come down to the study of the text. I didn't keep up the languages after seminary, but about twelve years ago, in Fort Lauderdale, it dawned on me that if we have this language that it was written in, it doesn't make sense for a preacher not to know something about it, not to be able to know how to use it to translate this gospel. So I taught myself a working knowledge of the language. Every year I've gone through a different Greek text.

I think of myself as an expository preacher, and that's a difficult thing to define. For me, it means that I take a passage of Scripture, usually a paragraph in the context. I begin by doing a word study. I do a lot with the computer now; I have Logos in there. It parses all the verbs for me, and that's very helpful.

I've been fortunate, in that most of my life I've been able to think analytically. I look at the passage and ask the pertinent questions: who, what, when, where, why, how. I go through the verse, and I put an inflection on a different word; I live with that verse for a long time, reading it many, many times. If I'm not familiar with it, I'll put it on a card and carry it in my pocket; many times during the day, when I'm waiting on someone to pick up the phone, I'll pick it up and look at it, reading the verse over and over, each time putting inflection on a different word. It's amazing, once I started doing that, what I began to learn. As I read the words of Christ, I wonder how they really inflected.

An outline begins to emerge. I preach in thematic series, so I already know where I'm at thematically. From that, I then go to my library, go to all the sources I have there. I go to sermonic materials I have filed. On my computer I'll put in an introduction, the main points of my message, and a conclusion. Then I just begin to fill in different thoughts and ideas underneath those areas. I'll do maybe half a dozen pages, print it out, and then I'll go back through it and arrange it. I still pretty much go with explanation, illustration, and application under each point. Then I live with it for a few more days, and seek to preach it.

Preaching: How do you go about planning a thematic series?

Hawkins: Many times they emerge. In Fort Lauderdale I preached through books of the Bible, but always in a contemporary thematic fashion. In Dallas, I've done a few books; I just did Philemon. The most well-received series I've done since I've been here was called "Moral Earthquakes and Secret Faults." Earthquakes don't just happen; they're preceded by fault lines that run underneath the surface. And moral earthquakes don't just happen; they're preceded by secret faults—little cracks in character that occur sometimes years before. We think they're not very big things. I preached about eight messages related to that. That wasn't from a single book; it was arranged thematically. I dealt with temptation, with other issues.

I usually plan my preaching during the summers. For many years I would read *Preaching and Preachers* by Martyn Lloyd-Jones every summer; another book that really formulated my early preaching ministry was John Stott's little book *Portrait of a Preacher*—especially that chapter on us being stewards of his gospel. I read, and then I plan my preaching during the summer.

When I'm preaching through a book, for example, before I preach the first sermon I've pretty much outlined the sermons I'm going to do. I've determined the titles, the object, the basic theme of each one. I stay in every morning to study; I don't come in the office until 11:00 or 11:30. I've always done that. I'm an early riser; I get up about 5:30 or 6:00 in the morning and study in my home. I spend every morning studying, then I read at night.

I never get away from it. This is one of the things that's impossible for people to understand—how a pastor who is serious lives with it every day of his life. It never gets away from us, it hovers over us constantly, it's a part of us all the time. It's something that we live with.

Preaching: **How long is a typical series for you?**

Hawkins: It depends. In Fort Lauderdale I was over two years in James, which is too long. I've come back now to a shorter length; many people think you shouldn't go over six to eight weeks. I think it all depends on how you do it. I'm about to do Daniel here. I'm doing it from the first six chapters within the context of engaging the culture. How do we as a church really engage our culture? How do we not bow down to all the golden images that are around our culture? I'll probably do that in around ten to twelve weeks. I think my series in the past have been too long.

Preaching: **How long is an average sermon?**

Hawkins: Some of my people will probably tell you too long! At 8:15, our early service, I have about thirty minutes; at 11:00 I preach about thirty-five minutes. Probably ought to be preaching about twenty-five, but I preach thirty to thirty-five minutes. Sunday night I preach thirty-five minutes.

Preaching: **If you had the opportunity to advise young preachers starting their ministries, is there some particular advice you'd offer about preaching?**

Hawkins: My main advice would be to be a servant. I've taken as my theme Acts 13:36; there in the Pisidian Antioch sermon, Paul parenthetically mentions King David. He says that David served God's purpose in his own generation, then fell asleep. The advice I give young preachers is be a servant. Of all the things that could be said about David—great administrator, great leader, great motivator—Paul says he was a servant.

When I came here [to Dallas], I got a lot of advice. The church had gone through some heartache, some heartbreak, was pretty wounded. I had people tell me I needed to come in and get it by the throat, get right in their face, slap them down. When the committee came to me and asked me to come, it was like the Spirit of God told me, "You just live in Samuel and Kings and Chronicles." Devotionally, I just read those six books over and over, and it was incredible how God spoke to me about pastoring and preaching in this church. For example, in 1 Kings 12, Rehoboam has become king, and he's about to go see Jereboam and mend the thing before the kingdom really divides down the middle. He gets two bits of advice. One group says, "You go up there and get in his face and say, 'If you think my father was tough, his waist is like my little finger.'"

The other group said (in 1 Kings 12:7), "If you'll be a servant to them, serve them and speak good words to them, they'll be your servants forever." If you look at my telephone, you'll see that verse—it's been on there for two years. And that's what I've sought to do.

So the most important thing I can say to young preachers is be a servant. You're never more like Christ than when you're washing other people's feet.

Preaching from a Pastor's Heart

An Interview with Jim Henry

In the fantasy world of Orlando—where theme parks and holidays are the rule—how do you make an impact on the real life needs of people? As pastor of First Baptist Church since 1977, Jim Henry has preached and loved his way into the hearts of thousands. In the process, the traditional downtown church has exploded in growth, moving to an expansive suburban location, and draws people from throughout the region. In recent years Henry was elected twice to serve as president of the Southern Baptist Convention. He is also an original member of *Preaching*'s board of contributing editors. This interview appeared in the September-October 1999 issue.

Preaching: Whenever I have had the opportunity to hear you preach, there seems to be a real pastoral quality to your preaching. As you preach, you seem to have a strong connection, a bond with the people in your congregation. How do you, in your own ministry, connect those roles of pastor and preacher?

Henry: I think part of it came from the way I was raised. The first pastor that really impressed me was Dr. Powell at First Baptist Nashville. That was a big church in those days. I was just a little eight- or nine-year-old kid when I started there. In fact, he baptized me. He took an interest in me personally. He brought me bubble gum after World War II when you couldn't get good bubble gum. He gave me an autographed Bible.

I'd go by and see him on Sundays. He would say, "Go to my office; there is some King Leo stick candy." In those days it was rare to get, and I knew there would always be a piece of candy up there. He was a hero to me—he loved me. And of course, when I was called into the ministry, my pattern really had been stamped in a sense by Dr. Powell. I hadn't connected it all until recent years. I got to thinking about why do I do certain things, and I go back to Dr. Powell. I've had some other pastors, but that was an impressionable age. I heard him preach, but he pastored me, too.

I realize that in preaching if I'm not where the people are and not engaged with them, then I'm probably not going to connect with them. God has given me a love for people—to reach out to people and be reached by people. I love people. So when I became a pastor, I was engaged with the people and their families from the very beginning: hospitals, weddings, deaths, standing around afterwards shaking hands. Having coffee, eating lunch or dinner with them just was part of my routine. I did not know any better. I thought that was what you did.

Then as the churches grew that I was in, I tried to keep that connection, and it became more difficult because your leadership role changes. You become more of a vision caster; the administration piles up. The fact that you've been at a place a certain amount of time, it's kind of like a snowball. You get more people that want you to write a letter of recommendation for them, or they want to get into school. You get more of that just by being there—you get asked to do more things. But I still realize that I can't pastor or preach to these people if I don't keep doing this. So I find some other ways to try to stay connected. For instance, after the services, I'm usually the last one to leave. Not always, but usually I'll stand around on Sundays and Wednesdays just to be with the people. They know I'm there. Or I will have a reception line where people can come by. But I am going to be available. If somebody wants to tell me something or introduce family or a friend, I want to be there.

I keep a list all year long of people who have lost a close family member by death. And at Christmas I write a personal note to those people because I know this first Christmas is a little bit different without your dad or your mom or your son or daughter. It is just a little note, but it is a connecting thing. It is a pastoral thing. Whenever I see a name in the paper, members that have been promoted or received an athletic award or something, or like the kids who have been in state Bible drill recently, I write a letter and send it out to all of them to say, "I'm proud of you." I handwrite some; sometimes I dictate. I still do weddings; I don't do them all because we have so many. I still do funerals; I don't do many, but I do some. I still go to the hospital; not every week but some. If I don't live with the people where they are, then when I get up there to communicate with them I'm not going to be talking to them about where their needs are and what does God's Word have to say to them.

I have had to fight sometimes because it is easy to get caught up in other things, which are also very important. But I still continue to go out and eat lunch with our people, dinner sometimes. I have a dinner group that I meet with—in fact, two—just to stay connected in an informal way with our people. When you go in that relationship they say, "What did we sing that song for? Why are we doing that?" They talk to you. You are hearing the people. Most of these people love you and they will be honest with you, so that keeps me connected. Not always, but you can keep up a lot with what is going on in the hinterlands with the people by doing that.

So when I get ready to preach, I am sitting there and I'm looking at a passage and thinking, "OK where does this connect with this guy that this past week I talked about? Here is a GenXer, or here is somebody that is seventy-seven. They are all going to be sitting out there. What do they read in the paper? What do they hear? What did I hear about that couple getting ready to be married? What was their biggest struggle? Why did these people break up? Why did this man, this Sunday school teacher, divorce? People have told me they're concerned about him; he was such a great teacher."

So is something in that message going to connect with some of these people? Every message cannot connect with all the needs out there. But there is always something that will, and at some point I told our people if you will come and listen to me most Sundays, somewhere in the year I will hit where you are sitting because I am going to preach the Bible. And it does. And it will not only make itself applicable—it is already relevant—but I will seek to apply it to where you are. I really work at that. The amazing thing is that sometimes I have an application with some particular issue or thing in mind to go this way, but somebody will come up or write me a letter and tell me the Holy Spirit took the same passage and met another need that I hadn't even intended to meet. It is a joy as I think of preaching the Bible and the work of the Holy Spirit, which becomes more and more mysterious to me the longer I pastor and preach.

I think Phillips Brooks said it: he never went to his study and looked in the Bible that he didn't see his people's faces running across his study. When he went out to meet his people, his study would beckon and he would see the Bible. It is that tension constantly for us as pastors and preachers. But I cannot disconnect pastoring with preaching. I'm afraid I would become aloof without meaning to. I wouldn't be where they are living. I feel like they've got to know that you are real, because some of them think that you are not, that you are just in an ivory tower. Pastors are probably more connected to the real world than people think. That is a perception. But if you don't ever relate to them, they will never know that you are connected.

I've found something else. A lot of times it is not a matter of preaching what they need. You preach the truth and the Lord, and just by lifting up Christ and the truth, that need is going to come to him. They will connect back up. So you may be preaching on the majesty of the Lamb, or right now I'm doing a series on Revelation on Sunday morning, which I have never tried before. But I'm having a tremendous response to it. It is prophetic, and yet it is relating to people, I think, with their fears of the future, uncertainty. All of this is going on with people today.

In my preaching I can sometimes see the faces of those in pain, those who are dying, the disappointment of people who have had a husband or wife walk off, or a Sunday school teacher who has let them down because of infidelity. There's the joy of celebration, the emotions, the funny things that happen in life that people tell me about. I've got thirty-five minutes or so on Sunday to try to connect that up. I try, I really pray, and I ask when I pray, "Holy Spirit illuminate me to find the truth in what you are saying so on Sunday it will be real to the people sitting out there."

One other thing I do on Sunday morning: I just go and sit in the sanctuary. Nearly every Sunday morning I walk through the worship center and I pray. I just try to imagine the people sitting up here in the balcony, sitting down here, people slipping in the back. They may have lost somebody, or they have disappointed them, and they don't want to get too close to the front because they think they may start crying. Here is somebody that just got bad news about a medical report, somebody got fired. Here's somebody whose son graduated top honors—you know joy is going to be there, too. So I just pray over the lost, others who will be there. I say, "Lord, you know all of these needs," and as I am praying and walking I touch the pews. I can't touch them all because it is so big. But I pray over sections and ask the Lord to connect the preparation, the Word of God, with the guys and gals sitting in the pews.

Preaching: You mentioned that you try over a period of time to hit the different kinds of needs or concerns of varying audiences. How do you guide your preaching in such a way?

Henry: That usually arrives out of a sense as I pray. Right now I am preaching out of Revelation. That is going to take me several months to finish. What that came out of—I was looking at the year 2000 coming and the growing uncertainty of Y2K. What is going to happen in the twenty-first century? I just felt like there are people that are wondering. So Revelation seemed to be a way to go there.

A lot of times it is out of what is happening in the culture around us: what are the people thinking, what are the people reading, hearing on television? What are the things they are asking? I've started getting letters saying, "Should I take my money out of the bank? Should we have enough to take care of our neighbors? What is the church doing?" I realize, hey, this is what this guy sitting out there is thinking about, and I just can't overlook it. So that helps me in my long-term planning, to be able to say, "OK, here is a book that will deal with a whole lot that is coming in the future, that will keep us from going nuts over it and give them a balanced approach to the future."

Then as I am walking and praying and listening to people, a lot of times things will begin to come up. I'll receive a letter or something, and I begin to hear this several times, then I say, "OK, there are a lot of people thinking about this. I may need to do a series on this particular area of life." So then I may do an eight-week or a twelve-week series because of what I am hearing from my pastoral work, from the letters that I'm getting, from television, the people of the church who email me, fax me, write me.

Sometimes, it's where the church is at a particular time. Are we at a point where I need to bring this to the whole church to look at? It is dealing with the church or our witness or whatever. So that kind of dictates where I go. Sometimes I may be in a series for a year at a time. Sometimes I'm in a series, and I don't know where I am going in six to eight weeks. I say, "Lord, where am I going to go next?" I look at the calendar, I look at what I'm hearing, at my prayer life, and from there I seek to move to either a series or a book.

I have found—this is an amazing thing, at least for me—I seem to get the best results from expository preaching. I know there are a lot of definitions for expository preaching, but I seem to do better preparing, get better response, and I think in the long haul help our people more by preaching through a section or a book than I do just picking topics. But every person has got to know where they are and the people they are dealing with; that could vary from place to place. I have found, at least where I am located, that expository preaching seems to be the best. It is easier for me, in one way, to prepare. It also seems to be the most fruitful in the help the church receives from me. I feel in a sense more satisfied when I've done expository preaching.

I have done topical preaching, textual, and am still doing those. God blesses that, too. But for the long haul—I'm heading toward forty years in it—I think expository preaching has helped me. A lot of books in the Bible lend themselves to that. You know 1 Corinthians, a lot of issues that come up today—remarriage, divorce, sexual morality. You can do James and Daniel. I've done a series out of Proverbs, though not all the

Proverbs. I spent about three months in that. So I just try to stay tuned in and hope that I've heard right and then jump in. When the church was at a certain point I went through Acts, the advance of the church. It is time for the church to take a step forward, and you say, "How did the early church do it?" So I went through the book of Acts. I guess that is the way I try to do it. Sometimes, I've been a year ahead, sometimes it is three or four weeks, and I'm wondering, "Where are we going next?" But he has always been faithful.

Sometimes issues come up that force you to change in the middle of a series, like the Columbine event. I wrote that Thursday and Friday. I had already had my Revelation message, and I began to see what had happened. I was down in Palm Beach at a pastor's meeting, and I could see the gravity of that and saw what was happening. I watched the television, and I said, "Hey, come Sunday, I can't act like that did not happen. People are going to be saying, 'What's going on in our country?'" I said, "Lord, show me what you've got. But I've got to have a word from you."

So, I came to work frantically on Thursday and Friday morning, and he gave me that Isaiah 1 message. God blessed it. It seemed to provide a catharsis. It seemed to resonate with the people. It had tremendous response; in fact, it was the second highest response for tape requests we've ever had. It seems to have been used by the Holy Spirit.

I did that when the Challenger blew up; we're right here nearby [Cape Kennedy], we have people who work over there. I just couldn't say, "Well, pray for those families." Sometimes you just have to say, "What does God have to say to things that are happening?" So, I try to be sensitive to that.

Preaching: In the face of an event like the school shooting at Columbine High School, as a pastor and preacher, how do you approach something like that? How do you go about preparing that kind of sermon?

Henry: Well, there are several things. Of course, first of all, it starts with prayer. I am not a great prayer warrior. I am still a neophyte in that, but I said, "Lord, help me. I know you are speaking to this country. Where can I go, where can I start? I've just got thirty-five to forty minutes. What can I say?" And all I could think of is Isaiah. That was the impression I had: Isaiah. And so I just opened to Isaiah 1, and I read it.

Then I wondered, has anybody written on it? I pulled and checked on my commentaries and things, and there were a few things in there, and I said, "This is it. What happened in that day is what's happening in America today."

I wanted to address it on broader issues than gun control and the parents. I didn't know what the parents did and didn't do. I did not have enough information. But I thought there was a converging of things that brought about the Littleton scenario, which basically was we turned our back on God. So I gathered a lot of the material that I put together over the years on God and country; I have a file called "God and country" with moral issues and spiritual issues facing our country. I just pull out newspapers and magazines; people send me stuff. Some of the material goes back several years, where people were writing things that are coming true today. I can see the prophetic sense of what people were beginning to see in 1980 and '84, and even 1965. I could go back and look at this old stuff as well as this new stuff. I pulled all of that together.

Then I looked at the Isaiah passage and said, "Lord, give me the major points out of this." I read everything that I had, pulled out of it, and made a stack. I used two or three commentaries and pulled out a few things. I made a big stack of material, then I narrowed that down. I looked at my points, looked at the Scripture which made the points. What of this material applies to that area? I was just pulling stuff, copying and pulling, adding.

I think the other thing I preach from is passion and concern. I think sometimes—hopefully not in anger but maybe in frustration—in a sense, we have all felt we want to lash out somewhere, somehow, at the tragedy of it. There had to be some passion in it—compassion as well as passion. Folks, we've got to make some changes beginning with the household of God. It's a time to be committed, which was my final point.

Rachel Scott was one of those who stood up to be counted and say, "I do, I do." This is the time to say "I do" if you want to count for Christ. So my application was we can all say, "This is bad, this is awful." But I had to bring it back: "What is that to you sitting there? What is this to me?" This is the time to be bold in the faith. We cannot just sit by; this is the time to say, "Count me in my faith, count me in the church, count on me to give my witness. I do! I want to stand up for Christ. Live in a day of 'I do'!"

So that is how it came together, out of my own concern, my own compassion, and my passion. What I had been watching and hearing and all of that just began to filter together. Somebody said a message is usually like putting something on the stove and you cook it for a while. I think that happened on Tuesday. It was cooking from the time I got here, read the papers, watching CNN. I had a breakfast with a group of pastors that Thursday morning. I was hearing what they were saying. So the thing was cooking for really two and a half days before I got it to the study Thursday. From Tuesday to Thursday morning it had been filtering. It was a time to light up the fire, the fuse was there.

Preaching: Obviously, this message reflects an unusual situation. What would a typical week of preparation look like for you?

Henry: I don't do anything on Monday because I am shot from Sunday. I do office work, meet with the staff, do letters, phone calls—try and get that part of the week by me so I can not be detoured come Tuesday. I devote Tuesday morning, usually a good part of Tuesday afternoon and Wednesday, and Thursday morning pretty much to that Sunday morning sermon. I used to do Sunday morning and Sunday night. Most of the guys I know still do. I am grateful that I don't have to. Our associate pastor does the Sunday night one now, so I can apply a little more energy to the Sunday morning sermon.

I get in there on Tuesday, after I've had my quiet time. I get on my knees and say, "Lord, I'm getting ready to get into the Word. Holy Spirit, illuminate me. Help me with how to say it, what to say, what to leave out, what to add. Bring out the truths that are applied to our people and our church and in me and where we are."

Then I go to work. I read the passage, like I'm going through Revelation now. In Revelation, some parts you can do a few verses, and part you can do a chapter. So, I look at how much material I need to cover, what does it fit? Then I have collected and bought every book that I could get a hold of—probably got twenty to thirty books on Revelation, commentaries, etc. I have a file of messages from people that preach from Revelation. Then I pull a file that I've accumulated across the years on prophecy and the second coming. Then I go to my sermon file, where I keep just sermons preachers have preached years ago—R. G. Lee, E. J. Daniels, and people like that—to see if they had a sermon on this particular passage. So I bring this wealth of material to bear.

First, I read. I see if anything jumps out at me. Is there any general theme that runs through here? I read the ones that deal more with the wording. I'm not a scholar by any means, but I try to study after people who are. So I will try to read the study guides and commentaries that deal with words and meanings and the theological application of that verse before I get to the other part of the illustration. I read through those first, and then from that I usually sit down and say, "OK, this is the central truth here." Then I'll start to sketch. I will get a lot of extra paper out, and I will start sketching. I look at how I'm going to approach the outline. Are we going to have three points, or are we going to have six or seven? Be deductive, inductive?

After I have gotten my outline, this is my usual pattern. I finish going through it all, then I go through and say, "OK, this is my outline. I've got the theological meaning. I've got the word meaning. I can't go through it word by word because you'll dry them out. Are there any places I need to concentrate on a word? He says this word five times in this passage, so that's evidence the Holy Spirit wants to get our attention." So I'll say, "What illustrates that? Have I got anything in all of this material that illustrates what he is saying when he talks about the difference between the lion and the lamb? Is there anything about a lamb? What is a lamb; what is *the* lamb?" Then I go through, and I've gotten material on the lamb and the aspects of it. Then I'll take an application and apply it to that point.

So I've sketched a rough outline. I've gone through and said "illustrate this" or "quote from this" or whatever, and I've noted where I have got it filed—say, Walvoord—page 17—and so I make all those sketchy notes. Then I push that over to the side, and I start writing it. I go to my old seminary professors Dr. Stanfield and Dr. Taylor in New Orleans. Usually when we turned in our sermon outlines we had to have the text, the title, the introduction, and then our outline. I still find myself preparing my messages that way! So I get a clean paper out; I take a ruler and make like I am turning in a paper at school, write the text, write out the title, write out the introduction. Then I get to my outline for my headings, and I start writing.

I don't write a full manuscript, but I end up with usually five to seven pages handwritten, which I guess in one way is a full manuscript. But when I get to the illustrations, if it is something that I have clipped, rather than write it out I just say "illustration—see note on *Titanic*" or whatever that particular illustration is. Then I'll pull it out of my file, and Sandy will copy it for me. I'll attach it when I finish that page—I just put a clip on it so that when I get ready to start putting the sermon in my heart to preach it in my mind, it'll be there. I'll go through it, and I'll be reading this theological part and the word meaning and the verses, and I look at the Bible. I'll get the illustration, and I'll just pull it out and read it, get it in my mind. Then I'll stick it back on that page of notes. Usually I don't go back and rewrite. It is not something that I would publish, but for me I've got it.

Once I've finished that, which is five to seven pages, the next thing I do is a brief outline. We put it on our image magnification for our people so that they can get the major points. We throw that up while I'm preaching. Then I write out a half page of notes—which sticks in my Bible—of the major points and illustrations, things that I want to be sure that I put in. I go through that, and I highlight the major points and illustrations and quotes; I put little red circles around it so that gets my attention. When I'm preaching I can look down and say, "That is a major point; that is where I'm going next. Here's an illustration, here's an example."

I want to have that by Thursday or Friday morning; I try to finish that up because I have to have it for the image mag people before I leave for the weekend. At that point I drop it, because by Thursday or Friday I've been in it all week, and I'm mentally tired of it. I try to keep Saturday nights clear unless I have a wedding, and we try to have no weddings starting after 6:00 here. I used to go to ball games, but now I rarely go out on Saturday night. If I do, I try and get in early because I know that Sunday is coming, and that is my ballgame. That is the Super Bowl for me, a preacher.

So Saturday night I do a little prayer walk in the community where it is kind of quiet. Between 8:00 and 9:00 I walk and pray for my fellow pastors and evangelists that I know. I go back home, get my notes, lay down in bed, and I go over them: that outline and my manuscript and the text. I read all of those side by side while I'm laying in bed—usually always once, sometimes maybe two or three times if I haven't gotten it in my heart well. Go to sleep, get up about 5:00 on Sunday morning and clean up, and come in the church and have prayer time. Then I'll walk here. Go upstairs to the pastors. We pray together, and they leave. Then from about a quarter to eight until 9:00 I just walk it in, or I sit down with it.

Then I imagine myself standing out there, and sometimes I'll talk out loud like I'm doing the introduction. I just make myself stand up there, and I see the congregation, and I'll talk: "Last Saturday, when I was driving . . ." And I'll just talk out. How does this sound? And I'll walk through that thing several times; that is where I'll do my last refining. I'll say, "I believe this point A will go under this illustration or under Roman numeral II better than where I had it," so I'll make an arrow and I'll pull that out, and I'll make a final tweaking right there. I'll try to say, "How do I conclude it? Does this wrap it up? Does this sum it up?" Then I say, "OK, now, what are you going to do with it?" I try to think through how I'm going to give the invitation to the believer—"Now what does this mean to you?"—and to the person that is lost and needs to come to Christ. I try to think through the wrap-up right there. Then at 9:00 they come and get ready to go downstairs, and at 9:15 is kickoff. And after that it is the work of the Holy Spirit.

Preaching: You said you have been at this for about forty years now. Over those forty years, are there some key things that you have learned about preaching that would help young pastors early in their ministries?

Henry: I think if I had to do it over, I would have put more of a priority on preaching earlier in my ministry; I would have applied myself at being a better communicator. Even though God has given me a gift—I'm not a great communicator, but I feel like he has given me a gift of relating to people—but I think I would have worked at it and studied it, watched others and tried to hone my skills more than I did, rather than flying by the seat of my pants. Then I could have, because the churches were smaller, were not as demanding. But because I was not as disciplined, I would spend my time doing other things. I probably wasted time; in fact, I know I did. A lot of times I would study for thirty or forty minutes, then I'd be up and say I've got to do something; I'd go and write a letter. I didn't just focus in on preaching and getting ready to preach. I would watch others and hone my skills earlier; I wouldn't wait until later.

Preaching must be a priority. I mean, other than your personal walk with the Lord, it goes hand in hand with everything else you do. Even if you are a good pastor, as much as I can do one on one—as important as that is to my preaching—if I can't communicate that on Sunday, then it doesn't make any difference, in one way, what I've done all week long. For instance, I used to do a lot of counseling. If I was starting over, I wouldn't have done as much of that. I know sometimes you are the one [pastor] that's got to do a lot of that, but I did too much. I didn't realize that when I'm preaching God's Word and applying it to life, I get more done in thirty-five or forty minutes on Sunday morning than I could if I'd spent every hour five or six days a week listening to people. I've got to do some of that—there is a balance there—but I would have put more priority on preaching. Come Sunday morning, it is just like an athlete. You know, can you hit the bucket? Can you hit the golf ball?

There is a sense of people saying, "What have you produced now on Sunday morning that will help me on Monday morning?" I must realize it is a priority. I cannot make it third, fourth, fifth in the list. Next to my family and my walk with the Lord, I think it is coequal with pastoring. You have got to be careful because you can say, "Well, I've been out pastoring," and neglect your preaching. Or on the other hand you can say, "I'm preparing preaching," and neglect your people.

I think another thing is I would have begun a better system of gathering and labeling materials. I've got an extensive amount of illustrations and things. I think if I had started earlier and been better disciplined, I could have saved time looking through a lot of stuff. I'm an old duffer now, and I've got some habits to break at this stage in the game. It's too late! But if I had started earlier—like I did with my writing out my sermon and things that I got from seminary—I could have been filing and breaking those down into smaller bites of material instead of just having broad topics like "The Holy Spirit." I could have brought that down to gifts, fruits of the spirit; you could have broken them down into all kinds of things. If I had taken the time and done that, I would have saved myself a lot of time in the study. The younger guys that are probably working computers and stuff like that, they can pull stuff off, but I'm still doing it the old fashioned way. I still think it is invaluable to have that file that you have gleaned from your own reading or whatever.

The third thing—and these are not in any particular order—I would enlist my people to help me more. I've done this here. I've asked people, "If you see something or hear something that you like, if you are traveling and you are in Dallas and you have read an article that may not be in the Orlando paper, or if you get *US News and World Report* and there's a great article, send it to me. Be my eyes and my ears." Consequently I get faxes, mail, email sent to me, because my people feel, "I'm helping my pastor." I'd involve my people more than that.

Preaching: I'm sure they enjoy it when they hear you use something they've sent.

Henry: They light up. You talk to them later, and they say, "I heard you use that thing I sent you." You're involved in their lives, so it does something both ways.

Another thing I would say is how important it is to coordinate, as best you can, your preaching with your music. Plan your worship service. I used to say, "I'll preach, and you just pick out the hymns, or whatever. Just tell me when to get up." To me, at one time, those were preliminaries. I've learned since they're not preliminaries; it's all a part of the package. The most important thing I do, in one sense, is open up the Word of God, but the Holy Spirit may open his Word in another way, in some other ways in that worship experience.

I meet with the worship team every week; we meet together and pray and see where we're going, how can we lead our people to worship and praise in this experience come Sunday. I would really emphasize the teamwork and having the people together, or your minister of music. What do we need to be sharing with the people this Sunday? If you plan around that, it's amazing how much more powerful it is.

If I were doing it all over, I would start working earlier with my minister of music, and I would have also been more free to worship before I preached. I still have to work at it, but I need to feel free to trust the one who's leading the music, and trust my own preparation, so that I can feel free to worship. It's just been in recent years that I've come to that, because I was so worried about things—and I still notice things like, "Why didn't the usher let those people in?" or "Why is this kid running across here?" I was so caught up in what I was going to do when I got up that I was not worshipping. As I studied and read more about worship, I realize I can't just stand up there and preach and think that's worship; I've got to be worshipping, too. So I've focused on trying to be ready enough, or not to get too distracted because the sound system screeched—those things happen—to just say, "Lord let me worship you, let me sing to you, let me pray to you." I read something recently, to not miss the "God moments." I want to be free to worship so that I don't miss one of those God moments.

Preaching to Mend Broken Lives

An Interview with T. D. Jakes

Time magazine called him "America's Best Preacher," and there are thousands of listeners across America who wouldn't disagree. After building a strong church in South Charleston, West Virginia, T. D. Jakes led fifty families from that church to Dallas to create The Potter's House, which within five years grew to more than twenty-eight thousand members. Today Bishop Jakes is also known for his weekly national television broadcasts and his arena events held across America, as well as a string of best-selling books. Under his leadership, The Potter's House has also taken a variety of initiatives to meet human needs through ministries to the homeless, drug abusers, prison inmates, and many more. This interview appeared in the November-December 2003 issue of *Preaching*.

Preaching: One of the fascinating things about your ministry is that it has engaged the interest of women in a significant way, yet at the same time your Dallas congregation has a higher percentage of men than a typical church. How do you explain that?

Jakes: It's hard to explain it. I'm not sure that it was something we purposely set out to do. One thing is I do the "Woman, Thou Art Loosed!" (WTAL) conference, which has brought national visibility, but I also do a men's conference called "Man Power" that is growing by leaps and bounds. We had around twenty-five thousand men last year. We're expecting fifty thousand men in Atlanta this year at the Georgia Dome.

I've tried to deal with the entire perspective of the family from the woman to the man and vice versa. My ability to connect with women has come from being a counselor and a pastor over half of my life, and twenty-seven years have been behind a desk, listening to people talk about the deepest issues and area of their lives. That gives you a unique opportunity to hear and to understand and to translate that language into some order. Sometimes we really have the answer inside of ourselves but we don't put it in an order where we can really hear what's going on in our own heart.

Preaching: How did the WTAL emphasis come about?

Jakes: The WTAL started out as a Sunday school class. It was supposed to be one class for about forty women. I was inspired to do it because I had counseled so many women who were going through similar dev-astating childhood issues and scars that were affecting them in the cur-rent context of their lives. I decided to bring them together in a Sunday school class because I believe that there are biblical answers to all of the sociological ills that we face today. I thought that not only would they find encouragement from things that I had to say, but the deeper encouragement would come from them seeing that they were not alone. For them to look across the aisle and see another woman who was being touched or ministered to as well would cause them to know that there is a sense of community which is critical for our well-being.

What started out as one class—being long winded, I didn't finish and decided to carry on for a second week, and twice as many women came. By then I just added some more to it. I could have finished, but I added more. By the fourth week we had women standing outside of the door to hear me talk about this subject for which I had no name. I later called a friend of mine—the now deceased Reverend Archie Dennis—and said to him, "I am teaching this class for women, and it is growing in leaps and bounds." He said, "Why don't you come to Pittsburgh?" I was then living in Charleston, West Virginia. He said, "Why don't you come to Pittsburgh and do it in my church?" I said, "OK." He said, "What do you call it?" I said, "I don't know." I was teaching out of Luke 13, and I said, "Well, I guess we'll just call it 'Woman, thou art loosed!' That is what the Scripture said." And he said, "OK."

I think I touched a nerve where there was a need in the pews that evidently we had not touched in that way before. Now we've gone from that to our largest crowd. We had eighty-six thousand women at the Georgia Dome. I didn't plan it. It just kind of happened.

Preaching: Do you think that the response you've had reflects a reality that much of the church is not connecting or engaging in the lives of women?

Jakes: I think that we are doing a better job now than we used to, but we have not always been as sensitive as we should have been. Partially because there are so many men manning the helm of the church that we are preoccupied with men's issues, leadership issues, theological issues, and we approach ministry from our own perspective. In order for ministry to really be effective, I think it needs to be approached by what does the congregation need more than what does the pastor need to talk about.

God, when he gets ready to minister to us, does it by coming where we are. He came in the person of Jesus Christ to embrace the human experience and then offered the solution, and I think it is critical for Christian leaders that we don't lose touch with the people we serve. We have to do what Christ did. Sit where they sit, feel what they feel, and then speak out in a deep sense of compassion because we are one with the people that we seek to minister to.

Preaching: In your messages, how do you connect both with the needs of women and the needs of men?

Jakes: I think it is a challenge when you try to do it in the same message, but one of the great things about having a women's conference or a women's book, a men's book or a men's conference, is that you can focus. I think it's the difference between a general practitioner in medicine and a specialist. That specialist can be more precise in his evaluation of your condition because he's localized all of his attention to one particular area, and thereby he can do a better job. Any time ministers are afforded an opportunity to amass leaders or support groups or women's ministry or men's ministry, then we can fine-tune our text and adapt it to the concerns of the crowd that we seek to serve.

Preaching: Thinking now about your Sunday services at The Potter's House in Dallas, how do you plan or develop what you are going to do in preaching?

Jakes: I think I spend a lot of time in prayer and a lot of time in observation of the needs of our congregation. "Lord, where are we now?" I don't presume to know where we are just because I am there. God's perspective is higher and wiser than mine. "What do I need to minister?" Our services include thousands and thousands of people—we make up twenty different nationalities. We have everybody in our congregation from judges, lawyers, attorneys, and millionaires to homeless people. There is a wide range of people. It is not just a typical inner city church where it is all inner city people. It's not a suburban church where there are all people from the suburbs. I have just an amalgamation of every type of person imaginable, so I need divine intervention to know what to do.

What I have had to look for amidst that vast array of persons and personalities are common denominators. There are so many that I am shocked. There are common issues that concern both the person who's living in a shelter and the person who's living in a palatial mansion in north Dallas. The desire for betterment, the desire for emotional stability in a chaotic world, how do we deal with aging, how do we deal with loneliness, grief, depression, fear—those things have no color, they have no culture, they have no economic or sociological context.

I try to develop series that will minister as a pastor to a multiplicity of needs. Sometimes those series are born out of a message where you strike a nerve—you didn't even know there was going to be a series, and you create a series. You say, "Come back next week. I am going to talk more about this." The crowd often teaches the preacher how to preach. Their response, their reaction, how well we have affected them. So many times we walk out of the pulpit and we think we did a great job because we said something that inspired us, but if it fails to reach them . . .

Communication is not complete until the person who hears you is receiving what you have to say. It's not how well you speak; it's how well they hear what you are trying to say. When you make contact with those persons you want to continue in that vein until there is a feeling of satiety that exists both in their hearts and yours. The Bible said that the Word of the Lord would not return unto him void, but it would do that thing where unto it had been sent, so we can't stop that Word until it has accomplished that thing where unto God has sent it.

Preaching: Are there some ways that you read the congregation to determine whether you've connected or not?

Jakes: I find it difficult—and it's funny, because I am leaving here to go to a stadium full of women, some seventy thousand women—yet I find it difficult to connect with a crowd where I can't see in the eyes of at least a wide range of those persons. You read people's eyes and hearts. Preaching is really a conversation. It is not a monologue; it's a dialogue between you and the congregation. Even though it's not always that they verbally respond—they are talking back to you if you take the time to listen, to feel the atmosphere in the room, the anointing. As you speak on certain issues, it lets you know that now you've hit it. You've hit what God wants to say—now that you are through saying those first five minutes with all the things that you wanted to say—and finally you hit a sentence where you feel that push behind you, that surge that says, "Now you have dropped into the vein that God really stood you up to say." And when you hit that vein, why move? Stay right in that track and allow God to guide you. The Holy Spirit was given to us to guide us. I think that even as we minister we must be guidable and allow the Holy Spirit to influence. It doesn't matter what I have in my notes to say. It doesn't matter whether I get my favorite point in or not. It matters that I am guided by the Holy Spirit to that precise area of need in the lives of my congregation.

Preaching: **How do you go about preparing a message?**

Jakes: It can vary for me, after twenty-seven years of ministry in the gospel. Sometimes it begins with the text and I have to find the subject and the outline. Often it begins with the subject and I have to find the text that helps me to describe the subject. Many times the story of the text becomes a metaphor that points to the issues and the lives of a person. I think that sometimes when we get so engrossed in the text that we lose sight of the congregation we've lost the point, because the text is only a backdrop to help me reach the lives of the congregation. If I am so consumed in talking about Esther that I forget about Ruth or that I forget about Mary who is sitting on the third row or Elizabeth who's sitting on the fifth row, then I've lost the point. Esther is only used as a tool to help me enhance Elizabeth's life or Sister Sally's life who is sitting out there in the congregation.

I go through the Word of God looking for illustrations from a biblical perspective that will enhance the congregant's experience. I have a recipe for preaching that I have used for twenty-seven years—it's not original, I read it somewhere. I can't remember where, but it stayed with me. It is a four step process.

The first one is to *study yourself full*. Gather as much information as possible on the subject that you are going to speak. The second one—which I think is perhaps even more critical than the first—is to *think yourself clear*. If you study yourself full but don't think yourself clear, when you get up to speak you give a lot of facts but the facts have no continuity. I call it theological indigestion—you're just sputtering up information that's not put into a palatable format. The first one is study yourself full, the second one think yourself clear.

The third one is *pray yourself hot*. If you don't have a real passion about it, you can't preach effectively. If it's not hot to you, it won't be hot to them. The fourth one, which is critical, it is *let yourself go*. Don't be inhibited in the pulpit. You're just an instrument. Don't be so self-conscious that you're not God-conscious. If you will let yourself go on stage and you are relaxed, then that relaxes the congregation. If the pastor is tight, the congregation is tight. Then the whole hour, or whatever it is, is laborious because nobody is comfortable. It is like riding with somebody—if you've ever gotten into a car with a driver who is nervous, their nervousness is contagious. You can feel them holding the wheel and shaking, and you're sitting up there thinking something is wrong. That's what happens when somebody mans the pulpit who will not let themselves go. If you study yourself full, think yourself clear, pray yourself hot, and let yourself go, you have a great experience.

Preaching: When you're getting ready for next Sunday in your home church, what would be the day to day activities for you getting ready to preach?

Jakes: I'm a night stalker. I get up during the night when I am really excited about something—while everybody else is asleep—and I get on my computer, and I'll just wail it out. I used to carry around a suitcase full of books. Now thank God we got a PC you can put all of those books, and with one click of a button you can reach anything you are trying to reach. Then I study those things that I think are very, very important to me; I may spend the day thinking about those things.

My days are rapid pace: often traveling here, there, and everywhere, board meetings, dealing with issues. I'm not only pastor but I run a couple of companies besides. I can find myself in a business meeting that takes me way away from theology altogether. But in the back of my mind that message is still turning that I had during the night, and it builds, it develops. It's almost like you take a piece of meat and you marinate it for a couple of days before you cook it. I like to marinate a message—sometimes a few days and sometimes a few weeks. I've got messages in my head that have been in the back of my head for months. One of them has been in the back of my head for a year. I haven't preached it yet. I just haven't found that right time or that feeling of readiness, and I don't like to preach it until I've got the right message for the right setting.

Preaching: We recently did a survey of readers of *PreachingNow* (our email newsletter), asking who were the preachers that have really influenced them significantly. Billy Graham and Chuck Swindoll topped the list, but you were one of the top five preachers identified as influencing the lives of these current pastors and preachers. Who are the preachers who influenced you?

Jakes: It's really funny because I would like very much to be able to present some distinguished list of renowned names—and there are certainly some great ones—but I grew up in the hills of West Virginia. I had a very rural background where very few famous people ever come. The people that impacted me the most about Christ were people that nobody would ever know. I had a Sunday school teacher named Inez Strickland who lived to be 103 years old who taught me as a little boy about Jesus Christ. She was never famous. I don't think she was ever on TV or written up anywhere. She taught me to love the Lord. Sitting on the front porch drinking ice tea with Ms. Strickland left an indelible impression on my life.

There were old country preachers in the hills of West Virginia who didn't even preach with microphones because their congregations grew to the flowing mass crowd of fifty people, but they knew God in a phenomenal way. I often tell people that everybody that's famous is not great and everybody that's great is not famous. The people who meant the most to me were just real people, simple in their delivery, concise in their ideology, and passionate about their conviction. I have tried to maintain that perspective as life has carried me into situations beyond my wildest dreams.

Preaching: How has your preaching changed over the years? How have you changed?

Jakes: I don't think the preaching has changed much at all. I think the environment has changed. I think that the preaching is what it is. God fashions us in obscurity and then brings us to some visibility, and I think that it is very important that you resist the temptation to change who you are as God brings you into the light. I think God wants who he called. Sometimes when God calls us we start trying to become something that we think we ought to be, but God called who he wanted. I've tried to remain very close to what I was before. They told me that if you get on television that you need to polish up, you're too country, you're too loud, you're too wild, you're too passionate. I am going to do my thing. Either love me or hate me, America. I am who I am. I've tried to hold to that.

A lot of things have changed around us. The environment, the requirement, the demands of leadership, how we pastor has changed drastically because there is a great deal of difference between pastoring twenty-eight people and pastoring twenty-eight thousand. There's a huge difference in how we do what we do. But the core gospel message shouldn't change.

I am afraid that the church is becoming worldly in its need to come up with something new and different. Anytime something is new we either have to improve it or it deteriorates from what it was before. How can the gospel be improved? How dare we deteriorate what is already perfect? I have tried to hold it pretty close to the way God gave it to me. Everything else about it has changed—staff, needs, requirements, obstacles, enemies, adversities. All of that has changed but the core message. I could show you some tapes of me preaching in the storefront and—aside from being a whole lot smaller and a lot more hair—I was pretty much the same guy, a little younger.

Preaching: **Is there an ongoing struggle to deal with the issues of celebrity versus being a pastor, being a servant of a congregation?**

Jakes: From a perspective of arrogance it is not a struggle to me because I'm not really attracted to notoriety. I actually love normalcy. I don't enjoy being famous. I enjoy normalcy. I never set out to be well known; I set out to be effective. Being well known is something that I live with. In my prayers I ask God to teach me how to live with it, not give me more of it. I can do without it. Yet, I am willing to give up the things I love—the privacy I crave, the individuality that I still yearn for, if I can help somebody. The day that I cease to be a servant to him in that way, then please let me do like Peter. Let me go a fishin'. I would much better be in a boat with a couple of friends with a fishin' rod in my hand than to be in front of thousands of people who really don't know me.

Preaching: **As you look back over your ministry are there some things you know now that you wish you'd known when you were starting out?**

Jakes: Yes, I think if I had it to do over again, I would have done it slower. I would have moved slower. I would have taken more breaks along the way. I'm a type A workaholic sort of person. I drive straight ahead like there is not going to be a tomorrow. Twenty-seven years into it I find out there was a tomorrow, and I found out that if you don't get it all done today, it is OK. I would have forgiven myself for not finishing. That would have been something critical. I would not have charged myself such a high bill of responsibility when somebody that I was trying to win failed and blamed myself as if I were the savior of another person. That would have been different. More time with my kids, that would have been different.

There are a lot of little things that I learned along the way. I would have learned not to grieve over dreams that didn't come true, buildings that we were trying to buy and couldn't get, doors that were closed in our face, opportunities that didn't come to pass. I wouldn't have taken it all so seriously. The older I get the more I realize it really doesn't matter—that what God has for you is for you. God has a plan, and when he opens the door no man can shut it, and when he shuts the door no man can open it. Not to get in front of the door and wonder what I did wrong or right that caused it to shut or open. These are the things that experience teaches you. You learn to calm down.

The other thing that I think is very, very important is that I find that success is not complete without a successor. Many, many times people enjoy what you do but they don't learn how to do what you do, and the best thing you can do in all of your life is to pour what you do into somebody who can repeat it—who can actually do it, not just enjoy it. To work yourself out of a job—that is critical so that you will ultimately reach your destiny and not be like David. Almost lost his life killing giants in his later years, repeating what he did in his younger years. I think it is important that you kill your giants in your youth and not try to reduplicate that issue over and over again for the long run.

Preaching: If you could talk to young pastors and give them any counsel as they begin their ministries, what would you tell them?

Jakes: A young man asked me years ago, if I had to sum up in one word what a young pastor had to be in order to fulfill his dream, what would that word be? And I looked at him and said "relentless." Anybody who's ever been successful at anything—whether you are talking about somebody who's a rock star or somebody who is a successful businessman, no matter what the area—they are going to constantly be bombarded with reasons to quit. Every time you get out of bed in the morning there is always a reason not to get up out of bed. If you are a person who will accept defeat—because defeat is always on sale and it comes cheap—and if you choose to buy that, you can die at any time along the way.

But if you are relentless—if you can wipe tears and discouragement and frustration out of your face and still jump up out of bed and say, "I'm still going to do it"—you can get great things done for God. Many of the men that God called were people that we would have never touched. Men like Peter, who was just a brawler and a wild man, or David, who was lustful and lascivious. Every one of them, whether you are dealing with David or Peter or Paul or anyone else. . . . They beat Paul half to death—they thought he was dead, and he got up and went to preaching again. Anybody who ever did anything mighty for God had to be relentless.

I would say to a young minister to be sure that God called you. Have no question about it; don't let it be ego. Don't let it be your grandmother who said you have a preacher's head. Be sure that God called you. Don't let the university call you. You can know about God's Word and not be called to preach. Those are two different things. If you are sure that God called you and that your life will never be complete until you do this one thing. If when you stand up to preach and you begin to talk there is something that rises up out of your soul that says, "I was born to do this, I was absolutely born to do this," then don't let hell or high water stop you from reaching your dream. You must stay relentless.

Preaching through Pain

An Interview with David Jeremiah

David Jeremiah is one of the nation's best-known preachers. The pastor since 1981 of Shadow Mountain Community Church in southern California, Jeremiah's sermons are heard across the nation through his *Turning Point* radio and television programs. The chancellor of Christian Heritage College, he is the author of more than a dozen books and speaks regularly at major Christian conferences and events. This interview appeared in the March-April 2003 issue of *Preaching*.

Preaching: In recent years you have faced a battle with cancer two times. As pastors and preachers, we often speak to people who are dealing with serious challenges in their lives. How have you dealt with this challenge in your ministry? Has it changed your preaching?

Jeremiah: You couldn't go through what I've gone through without it affecting how you preach. Several things cross my mind. One, what I preach now about suffering and the challenges and testing of life is probably what I preached before, but now I preach it not only because it's in the Bible but because I've experienced it as true.

Someone told me that people listen to you differently when they know you've been through something. It's not that you say anything different—it's that they listen to you differently. We had an interesting illustration of that right after I came out of the stem cell transplant in 1998. We got a spate of telephone calls at *Turning Point* with people telling us they were so blessed by the teaching of the Word of God and that I was preaching with so much more passion after I had been sick. Unfortunately, what they had heard were messages I had preached before I had been sick. I chuckled at that, but then I realized I was not preaching differently—they were listening differently. And they were listening differently because they knew what I had experienced. I think that makes a major difference in how the Word of God is received and perceived by the people.

Preaching: Do you sense in yourself a new perspective on your work as a preacher?

Jeremiah: When I was coming out of this last deal with cancer, I wondered what I would preach when I got home. I had missed seven weeks in the pulpit. I realized what had been such an encouragement to me was the Psalms. So I came back and preached a series in my church called "The Encouraging Psalms." I found many psalms that were encouraging to me, but I found ten to preach on, and that became the basis for a book I did called *A Bend in the Road*. That became such a blessing to me, and I'm sure I preached those psalms with a passion that I could not have had had I not gone through what I did.

It's interesting that when you go through strong chemical treatments it causes fatigue, but if you're a speaker it causes a raspiness in the voice. I listen to those tapes now, and I sound pretty pathetic to me, but God used that series in a marvelous way, because people realized, "Our pastor, our shepherd, has been through some stuff. He's talking to us from the same Bible he's been preaching to us for twenty years, but it's different now. He's walked through that."

If you've ever been going through some difficulty in your life, and someone comes up to you and says, "I know how you feel"—and if you look at their life and it doesn't look like they've had even one tiny bump in the road, you don't have a lot of encouragement from that.

Regularly now—almost every week—someone calls me and says, "My friend has the disease you have, they have cancer. Would you call this person for me, or could you write them?"

We just learned that one of the guys on my staff found out he has melanoma. He and his wife are in their thirties. I called him on the phone and said, "I know exactly what you're going to experience. I know what you're going through. Let me help you walk through that. Let me help you know what you're going to experience. Whatever you need, I'm here to help—not as your pastor, but as a pastor who's walked down the same road you're walking. You're going to be all right; you'll make it through this—but you're going to be afraid sometimes. When you're afraid, you not only need to call on the Lord, but you have a buddy over here who cares a lot about you."

Henri Nouwen's book is called *The Wounded Healer*—I think there's truth to that. I think that when God allows you to be wounded, he tenderizes your spirit. I think of all the things people have said to me about my preaching after these experiences—it's that God has given me a tenderness. I'd like to think I've always had a tender spirit, but I know that in my younger days I was a pretty hard charger. I think God has used the illness to break my heart and tenderize my attitude toward people who suffer and toward the ministry of the Word.

Preaching: Several years ago there was a movie called *The Doctor* in which William Hurt played a surgeon who saw patients as specimens rather than as people. Then he got cancer, and he learned to see patients from a new perspective. Now that you have gone through such an experience yourself, are there insights you've gained that can help other pastors as they minister to people who are suffering?

Jeremiah: It's surprising to me the absurd things people say to you when you're going through something like this. People would come up to me and say, "You have lymphoma, right? You know, my sister had lymphoma," and then they would proceed to tell me about her suffering and how she died. That happened so consistently. Why would you feel so determined to tell someone who is going through a disease about someone else who had it and didn't recover? I got to the point where I would stop people who were starting like this, and I would say, "If this story doesn't have a happy ending, I don't want to hear it."

We were on a Christian cruise one time. It was January, and in March I was going to have this stem cell transplant. The last night they had a prayer service for me; they laid hands on me and prayed for me, that God would take me through this. My wife and I went to the Orlando airport, and a lady who had been on the cruise came up and said, "Can I talk to you? I just want you to know my husband was on a cruise like this, and they prayed for him, and a year later he died. It's not going to do any good." And she walked away. Here's a lady who's very bitter about the death of her husband, but why she would want to tell me that? I don't know. There seems to be in the hearts of some people a desire to tell someone who's suffering something that, if they thought it out, they'd realize is not going to help them.

My counsel is, I'm not even sure *what* you say to a person who's going through that is as important nearly as much as just being with them. Let them know you love them, that you'll pray for them. But I don't think there are any mantras or words you can say that will be all that important. I just know that the people who ministered to me the most were people that called me on the phone to say, "We're praying for you.

We want you to know we're standing with you." Those were people like John MacArthur and Tim LaHaye and Jim Cymbala—guys I respect.

I remember when I knew I was going to have to leave my pulpit for a while, Jim Cymbala called me—one of the busiest pastors in America—and said, "I'm going to take a Sunday off and come out and preach for you to help you during this time." And he did, and of course it was wonderful—the place was packed morning and night, and we had a great sense of revival that day. He did that for me. Did he say anything to me? No, he did something for me that he knew would mean a great deal to me during that time. That's what I think we need to do as pastors, to help one another and help our people. I can't actually tell you anything that anybody said to me, either time, that was life changing. But I can tell you about things like that which meant more to me than you can imagine.

Preaching: Serving in an era of remarkable social and cultural change, what are some of the greatest challenges you think preachers face today?

Jeremiah: I'm an expository preacher in an age when expository preaching is viewed by most architects of the church as no longer relevant. If you look at the church-growth movement and the seeker-sensitive models, expository preaching is not even in the vocabulary. I do not say for a minute these guys are all wrong; I listen to some of them on tape, because many of them have a tremendous heart for God and a love for reaching this culture. But I fear the long-term absence of the value that's involved in the expository preaching and teaching of the Word of God.

I've been doing this now for thirty years, and I do not see any waning in the power of expository preaching. What I see is a lot of guys I know who started out with that passion now giving into the cultural pressure of being relevant and cute and very topical, to the point where sometimes there's not enough Bible in the message to know it's a sermon.

I really believe with all my heart that if those of us who are committed to the application-centered preaching of the Word of God, if we will just hang in there, then people will come back. They'll realize they can't live with anything other than the bread of God's Word. The challenge for people who do what I do is to make sure we are committed to it enough to withstand the pressure that's put on us by the culture—by the religious culture even—to change and move in a different direction.

Preaching: What drew you to exposition as a primary model for preaching?

Jeremiah: I grew up in a pastor's home. My father was a preacher. My father's with the Lord now, and when he died I got all of his sermons—

boxes of them. I've looked through my dad's preaching, and as best he understood expository preaching, that's what he did. They're very well outlined; he preached through many books of the Bible.

So as I grew up, I heard him teach the Scriptures. When I went to college at Cedarville in the late '50s and early '60s, I was headed toward a career in radio. When I was a senior, I was asked to go speak at a little church, and God called me to preach. I had one year left in college to get ready. I took classes from a man named Robert Gromacki. Bob Gromacki set an example for me, in his lifestyle and in his teaching. I learned he had gone to Dallas Seminary, so immediately I wanted to go to Dallas Seminary. If I was going to be a preacher, I wanted to learn how to do it.

So I went to Dallas Seminary, and I had the privilege of being there in the "glory years." Dr. Walvoord, who just went to be with the Lord, was president. Merrill Unger was there. I had Howard Hendricks as my chief professor. Haddon Robinson was teaching expository preaching. I got there, and I got excited about learning how to preach. I took everything that Haddon Robinson taught, and Howie Hendricks—his course on inductive Bible study just riveted me. Howie motivated me; Haddon taught me and modeled for us.

So I came out of seminary, and that was all I knew how to do. Haddon Robinson exalted expository preaching to such a degree that if you thought about preaching any other way, you should turn in your degree!

Have I modified my approach to that since taking those courses? Sure, I think all of us do. We have to become who we are. We had this thing Haddon taught called the central idea, the "Big Idea." Well, there were times I was preaching expository messages but I couldn't necessarily tell you what the central idea was. I couldn't always make that work, but the discipline of it was really good.

Preaching: You mentioned earlier that your goal is "application-centered" expository preaching. Tell me about how you approach application in preaching.

Jeremiah: When I got out of seminary, some of the guys I graduated with actually had a philosophy that an expository preacher only says what the Word of God says, and he allows the Holy Spirit to make the application. I don't remember ever hearing that at Dallas Seminary, but somebody must have said it sometime because I ran into that over time.

As I look back over my preaching career, when I first got out of seminary I worked very, very diligently at the interpretation and the exposition of the text. I still do. But I work far harder now in how that is applied to people than I did in the beginning. I realize that there has to be a balance between what the Word of God says and what it means to the people. I work very diligently to find out what it says, and I work just as diligently to figure out what it means to the people.

The question of "so what?" is so important today. I don't think expository preaching suffers because it's the wrong method. I think it suffers because it's not done very well by some people who attempt it. They make it dry and boring. If that happens, it's unforgivable—how can you make the living Word of God dry and boring?

In my situation, if it's a matter of getting one more point in the message that comes from the Word of God or illustrating the points I've already done better, I'll choose the latter, because I want the people to walk away with something that's going to work in their lives. I think if we don't do that, then we ought not be preaching. It becomes more of a lecture. People don't need a better set of notes—they need to know how the Word of God is going to work in their lives.

Preaching: How do you go about developing that kind of relevant application in your sermons?

Jeremiah: I wish I could say there's a formula. There isn't a formula, but I think I've learned something that is very helpful to me. This isn't going to surprise anyone: you've just got to read your eyes out, and you can't just be reading theology.

I'm working on a book on passion, and the reason I got enamored of that is I like to read business books. I read Shultz's book on the development and growth of the Starbucks company [*Pour Your Heart into It: How Starbucks Built a Company One Cup at a Time*]. In fact, Mac Brunson [First Baptist, Dallas] gave me that book when I preached at his church last spring. I put it in my office, and recently when I was going on a trip I pulled it out, and then I couldn't put it down! Here were some people who poured their hearts into everything they did, and as a result that company became an extreme success. Of course, I've read Collins's book *Good to Great*, and I'm reading a book right now on execution by a businessperson.

What I find is that as I read this stuff, and as I'm constantly studying for messages, reading things that I'm going to preach—those two worlds come together in a way that makes it possible for me to take what I've studied over there and say, "OK, here's how it fits into this world over here." As preachers we live in an isolated world. I don't go to work in a secular environment every day. If I don't find some way to interact with that environment, then my preaching becomes irrelevant.

I'm reading everything I can get, listening to tapes. I'm always trying to get input into my life. Finding good illustrations is hard work. I work really hard at it, because illustration is the thing that nails the truth to the heart of a person.

Preaching: Are there particular places you tend to find good illustrations?

Jeremiah: Well, you don't find many in illustration books. Once in a while you'll find one there. I just think most of the good illustrations come out of things I've read somewhere, like newspaper articles. I'm pretty much a sports nut, so I like athletic illustrations. I have a son, Daniel, who works for ESPN, and he'll drop something in my lap every now and then.

Recently Daniel had a little disappointment in something he thought was going to happen and it didn't. I was worried for him because I love him and I felt bad for him. I called him one day and asked, "Are you going to be OK?"

He said, "Yeah, I'm fine. Do you remember the guy who went to Notre Dame as coach, but he was only there a week because they found out he had lied on his resume? He left, and everybody said, 'That's it. He's done. He's finished. His coaching career is over.' Well, next thing you know he shows up as an offensive line coach for an NFL team. They did a feature on him in the paper."

He said, "Dad, I cut the last two paragraphs out of the paper and hung it on my refrigerator. Basically what he said is, 'Angry people live in the past. Excited people live in the future.'"

I wrote that down. It's in my notes. I haven't had a chance to preach it yet, but that can be used to illustrate a truth of the Word of God.

Because of our exposure on the radio, people send me stuff, too. I get a lot of things. Maybe 10 percent of it is worth hanging on to, but I'm so thankful they send it. When you sensitize your heart and mind to something, you start seeing stuff you never would have seen otherwise. One of the reasons I think it's great to start preparing to preach as early as you can, get your ideas in your mind as soon as you can, is things start sticking to the ribs of your mind that you would never see otherwise.

Preaching: As you look to the remaining years of your ministry, are there some goals you'd like to accomplish?

Jeremiah: I want to make sure, first and foremost, that I finish preaching through every book of the New Testament. I'm close, and I've done the hard ones, with the exception of Hebrews—Hebrews is on my list. I'm going to finish Acts early next year, so I will have done Acts, Romans, and Revelation, both of the Corinthian epistles, Philippians, Colossians, Galatians. I've done the Gospel of John. I've got a couple of the Gospels

I want to go back to, though I probably won't go back and do strict, verse-by-verse of all of the gospels, but I want to get to all the Gospels before I'm finished.

Then I don't know how far I'll get in the Old Testament. I love narrative preaching, and I've done the life of Abraham, the life of David, Joseph, Elijah. I did a chart once, and I found you can almost preach the entire Bible narratively. I love preaching the Bible through personalities, and I find that's preaching that's easy to apply, because these are flesh-and-blood people. I finished the life of Abraham this last year, and I find people loved it. If you do Abraham and Joseph, you've gotten Genesis 12 through the rest of the book. I haven't figured out what to do with Leviticus yet, but sometime I've got to get there!

Preaching is what gets me up in the morning. I've got a lot of things on my plate, but that's what makes it all worthwhile. The preaching of the Word of God is so powerful. I marvel at that.

Preaching in the Emerging Church

An Interview with Dan Kimball

Dan Kimball is a forty-three-year-old pastor who has helped launch a national conversation about the emerging church. For a number of years he led an alternative worship service (Graceland) for Santa Cruz Bible Church, and since February 2004 he has been pastor of a newly created church (Vintage Faith Church) that is seeking to offer new models for ministry to younger adults in that California community. He is the author of *The Emerging Church*, and his newest book is *Emerging Worship*. This interview appeared in the November-December 2004 issue of *Preaching*.

Preaching: What is an "emerging church"?

Kimball: The frustrating answer is there's no definition. There are so many variations of what we're seeing emerging churches are like. Every so often in history—in American history and church history—there seems to be a rethinking of what we're about as culture changes. What I think is going on right now is a pretty widespread rethinking of church as a whole, primarily among younger leaders—many of whom have grown up and have been on staff at contemporary or traditional evangelical churches. They are rethinking, "Is this the way that we're connecting with our culture for the gospel?" So that's probably the common denominator—that most of them are rethinking the church.

Preaching: Why is it important to rethink the church right now?

Kimball: To me, it's extremely important. It's hard to make a general blanket statement—because there are churches all over the place where

God's doing things. But when you take a general look around at most churches—even the mega-churches—what you find is a drastic dropout rate from teenagers. As George Barna said in a recent book [*Real Teens*], something like two-thirds of the teenagers will be dropping out, which is a lot higher trend than normal.

We're seeing more people growing up—younger people in particular—growing up outside of church culture, and we're not seeing that many churches significantly making a difference in the emerging culture. So even successful mega-churches are responding. Willow Creek does their Access service, Saddleback's doing some sort of video café with candlelight and acoustic music. Even large churches are realizing we need to do something different if we're serious about reaching and preaching to emerging generations.

Preaching: Rather than talk about the emerging church in terms of characteristics, why not just describe what I might see if I came to your church some Sunday. What would that experience be like?

Kimball: One difference is even in using the words "go to church" to describe what we're trying to do. I actually have a chapter in *The Emerging Church* book on this. When you say, "I go to church," we are trying to reframe it and say something like, "When the church gathers on Sunday." We're trying to break out of some of the subtle, consumerist kind of thinking by trying to watch our terminology. So I'd say, "When the church gathers." We're trying to build the church out of home communities, but then we all meet together on Sunday nights.

We started the new church in February, and we have been going verse by verse through the Sermon on the Mount since then. A major part of what we do in worship is a kind of verse-by-verse teaching. We're then going to go through highlights of the book of Acts.

What you'd experience when you walk in? We start off thinking about what would create an environment for worship—that would really focus on the risen Jesus being the predominant reason we're there. We pay attention to aesthetics, not for an emotional trick. Every church, whether they are Southern Baptist or Lutheran, pays attention to aesthetics, so we're just looking at it through a different lens. And we create a space—we have a team called the sacred space team—and we try to say this is a sacred, set-apart space for worship. Last week we were teaching on the wide gate and the narrow gate in the Sermon on the Mount. So you walk in and we actually set up the entry way as a narrow gate, so as people walked in they recognized the entry way was even communicating what we were teaching about. At the end of the entry we had the Scriptures from Matthew 7 there up on the screens; you can't miss it. You walk in and there's Scripture—that's what we're talking about tonight.

Then the room is set up. We said, "How can we have the cross the predominant thing in this room?" So we built a different cross and put it dead center in the front of the room. Right now we're using the facilities of Santa Cruz Bible Church, and we put a cross right where the pastor or preacher would stand—we put the cross right in that center spot. So that is a dominant visual when you walk in.

Whatever we're teaching about, the series, we have artists who paint paintings that are all about the passages of Scripture. What we generally do is give the passages out a month or five weeks in advance, and the artists will then paint various sections of the Scripture. And so around the room you'll see people painting their expressions of what the teaching's about. One week we did a sermon on heaven, and we had someone do a huge canvas—a really kind of glorious light, a scene of light. And the next week we talked on hell; they took a roller and actually rolled all the bright to total black on this painting that's up on the stage.

The room is set up to have everyone looking up at the screens and not at the music band; the music leaders are off to the side so that they aren't coming across like a rock concert. They're not the focal point, though we still do music.

We are always thinking, "How are we communicating the Scriptures through speaking, through visuals, through people's lives?" When we were talking about heaven, we brought up a man who was just given six months to live— he's seventy-nine years old, and he has cancer. And basically he is so weak, but he has been coming and hangs out in the back and prays for me when I speak. And so we brought him up—even though it's predominantly a crowd in their twenties who are there—and he talked about what it's like facing the reality of heaven and the perspective he has. He also challenged everyone there, saying, "Most of you are in your twenties, heaven isn't just when you die you're going to go there, you need to be living out the kingdom of God and the kingdom of heaven—we have a mission here." He was trying to break the stereotype of "You said the prayer and now live however you want, because you got your ticket."

When we gather we might have a couple of songs, some visuals. Every week we have a report from one of our home communities, because every week we have one of our home communities host the night. We're constantly reminding everybody the church meeting is not about the big meeting—it's about smaller communities that are gathering together. They'll give a report of what God is doing in their groups, how are they experiencing community, and how God's changing one of them. They read the Scriptures for the night, they'll host in different ways, they'll pray for the offering. So they're involved in the larger meeting.

I'm the primary person who does the preaching. What I'm noticing with the whole emerging church movement—at least what we're doing in our context—is that we are getting deeper in the Scriptures. There are no three point outlines with acronym words—I'm not saying that's negative, I'm just saying for our context. One week I talked about what was death in the Old Testament, what did that mean, what was the word "grave," how did that change with the intertestamental viewpoint of the afterlife, what was becoming more clear when Jesus came about, what did Paul say about it, what did Revelation say about it? It's somewhat like teaching a theology class. We're specifically going into word studies; we are hitting a lot of historical context.

I think what people are looking for in our culture is depth. We talked about hell an entire night, so that's almost like the total anti-seeker model, you might say—though we're being sensitive to seekers. We walked through what different world religions and world faiths believe about hell and the afterlife—the accusation that Christianity alone has this sense of hell is actually not true. Mostly every world faith has some sort of punishment in an afterlife. So I'm trying to also connect with culture, because you can't just assume that everyone's thinking in just a Christian worldview. I know there are people coming who have different beliefs, therefore I want them to understand that I am aware of other world faiths, other ways of looking at the world, because that's the way our culture is raising people. Then I use that to move to the biblical explanation of things.

I teach thirty to forty minutes, sometimes forty-five minutes. In my opinion I have to study all the harder, because we do not water things down—if anything, we are simply giving it more depth. After the preaching we have about a thirty minute response time. Services are about one hour and forty-five minutes. We have about a half an hour where it's more contemplative music that is being played—some people choose to sing to the songs, and some people just sit.

We set up a prayer path on the side of the room, behind the curtains, and prayer stations that were interactive prayers about the Scriptures that we're teaching. One was like a table setup—and I have nothing to do with this; this is a twenty-one-year-old girl who designs these and volunteers to do this. They set up a table, and they created kind of a fork in the road, and it went in two different directions; one side was a wider road, and the other side was a narrower road. And there are little push pins, and so they're saying, "Will you take out a push pin and be praying, not saying the name of the person out loud because they might be with you, but just moving a pin over to the narrow road. Ask God to please bring them to the point of conviction where they need Jesus and choose to be on the narrow road." There's another interactive table, but they're all based around the Scripture and people. Not everybody goes to those, but people can choose to go over and have some sort of interactive prayer that is based out of the Scriptures. Scriptures are on the table. So we're teaching and giving people the opportunity to respond to it.

We set up a prayer cove, and we have a Jewish prayer shawl we set up over this little archway that you go in. We have people, a prayer team who are trained, to then pray for people at any time during that half an hour. We quite often have times when we might read; last week the music worship leader had everybody recite a passage of Scripture together that tied into the message as one of the last things they did, so everybody's all saying the Scripture together. And then we'll sometimes have open prayer.

We have about 400 or 450 people that are there right now, and we try the best we can to communicate, "How do you try to break down a larger meeting to feel a sense of community?" It's not the best logistically, but people can be praying more in community.

Preaching: Since you only gather on Sunday evenings, is this the only worship experience for most of your participants, or do many go other places on Sunday morning?

Kimball: I was at Santa Cruz Bible Church for thirteen years on staff. I was doing kind of an alternative worship gathering called Graceland; then we decided let's actually start a sister church, so we started this church plant in February. We call the new church Vintage Faith Church, and we look at it like a sister church of Santa Cruz Bible Church. And we're now actually paying rent for the building!

Preaching: Is Graceland still going on?

Kimball: No. When we decided that we were going to start a new church, Graceland folded into Santa Cruz Bible Church. We had about five months or so where we didn't do anything Sunday nights, and then we launched Vintage Faith in February.

Preaching: As you look down the road, do you anticipate, at some point, being in a separate facility and having a different kind of schedule?

Kimball: Downtown Santa Cruz is kind of a cultural hub; it's not a downtown, run-down district—it's actually a higher-end area. We're looking at purchasing a building that will be too small for our larger worship gatherings, but we want it to be a coffee house, art gallery, have midsize meetings there, a student kind of study center, and we're looking for that right now. That would be our first step, versus looking for a property to meet in for the larger meetings. We do a lot of setup; that's the only hassle—it's more than just the chairs. In the future I could see two or three or four meetings of four hundred or five hundred people and each of the meetings at different locations around Santa Cruz County, with different leaders.

Preaching: Since you began thinking and working on the idea of the emergent church, and since your first book came out, have you changed some of your thinking about this movement?

Kimball: Yes. I think one of the big things is that there is such a wide variety of theological thinking, so when you hear the words "emerging church," there's great diversity in what they look like, how they think, how they express their faith, and what they believe theologically. So it isn't like it's a denomination, or it isn't like in a purpose-driven church, though they're probably somewhat the same. But there's a great diversity among them. The more I've spoken around and do things, the broader I see that. So that makes it all the harder to categorize.

I've also seen a lot of sadness in the relationships between senior leaders in churches and the emerging leaders who have different values and different ways of thinking. I've heard such horrible stories of how leadership in churches function with one another, not allowing new things to emerge because of control issues or different things. And I've seen sad responses from emerging leaders and how they go about dealing with this. A sad part of it, to me, is a lot of tension that is caused in the body of Christ in local churches, generally due to control issues and confusion: it doesn't all fit into a nice system or nice package, or this is what a church is supposed to be or this is how a senior pastor is supposed to function. That caught me off guard, seeing how widespread that is.

I think what is really refreshing is this interest in theology again, the discussion about it, the desire for depth. I think that's a very refreshing thing that's going on right now.

Preaching: Your comment about leadership conflicts leads to the question, "Does an emerging church need to be a new church, or can the things you describe be done within the context of an existing congregation?"

Kimball: It generally depends on the senior pastor. I think there are senior pastors in existing churches who don't recognize this as kind of like starting a Korean church within your church or a Korean worship gathering and ministry. If you look at it like you're just starting a college group and one day they'll grow up and then become like you—those are the ones that end up having a lot of conflict.

Where it works, the senior pastors see this like a mission. It's not just changing the music or adding candles; it's really a rethinking holistically. It affects evangelism, it affects preaching, it affects how you view worship gatherings, it affects spiritual formation, and how you go about even small groups. For the senior pastors that have done that—there are some—I think it's great. If you're a senior pastor and you have more of a traditional view of the church and you can't get out of that, it's a disaster waiting to happen.

Preaching: In *The Emerging Church* book, you said this really isn't a generational issue so much as it is more of a philosophical or worldview approach.

Kimball: When I first started, I thought it was generational. I just thought it was an eighteen- to thirty-year-old thing or a Gen-X thing at that time period. Then the more I was listening to people and watching who became part of the community that we were starting, I recognized that there is a difference. Most of the emerging churches are generally people who are under the age of forty, but it isn't like when you hit thirty . . .

I know a church where when you hit thirty you have to change to the other part of the church. Or I know churches that still start an age-specific worship gathering and say, "Well, when you hit age thirty, you now have to shift out of how you have found yourself accustomed to wanting to worship when you're in the community and express your love and worship to God in a certain way." If I'm in my twenties and hit thirty, how I learn is already ingrained in me, and I may not want to have a business presentation of four application points to these two verses—that may totally go against my whole concept of what preaching should be. So making a big shift, I would say most of the time, won't work. And that's what I think we all realized. It is more than just an age thing.

Preaching: What can a traditional church learn from the things emerging churches are doing, even as they continue to have a traditional style?

Kimball: See, this is an interesting observation because my only experience—I didn't grow up in a church, so my only experience really was a conservative Baptist Bible Church. We were never taught the worship practices throughout church history. You'd only light a candle at Christmas Eve or something. I think that there is a desire to not go back and be the church of medieval times, but to appreciate different forms of worship. I was never even taught the liturgical calendar year. I couldn't have told you what Lent was. They never taught me in seminary, it was never mentioned in the church that I was taught in, so I'm like, "Boy, I've missed out on that richness." So if you're coming from a Baptist, conservative type church like I was, I'd say to learn to not just think in your own particular denomination or your own particular form of ministry but to search church history.

The ironic part is when I've talked to people who are coming from Episcopal churches and some Methodist churches, they may be doing some totally liturgical things but they're saying all the young people are leaving; they want to do all the pop music and break out. And for them it's like reintroducing these forms of worship, but doing it with life and meaning, and not ritually so that it becomes almost lifeless and routine. It's become so dry that many younger people are just saying, "This is not connecting at all with me." But I think there are opportunities to reintroduce it.

And I'll just say to be thinking past your denomination—respecting your denomination, honoring your denomination, but not thinking that your denomination and particular form of worship or preaching is what heaven is going to be. And I think that when we start looking outside of our own particular microcosm of church experience, it really starts changing our hearts. We should be open to different ways and approaches of how we think of our worship and church and preaching. As long as we're sticking with the Scriptures—that is the important part.

Preaching: Are there some things you're learning about preaching and communication as you go through this process?

Kimball: I would say almost everything I was taught in seminary I don't use. I do use the Bible classes and the theology, so I don't want to knock that. But breaking preaching down into an academic outline—you know, point 1a, point 2b . . . You can almost go two directions. One is to go so academic and historical that it doesn't mean anything in your life today. Then, on the other hand, many churches go so "felt-need" applicational that we are then basically throwing out much of the content and depth and history. Then we're training people in our churches to think of Christianity like one girl told me: "It feels like Tony Robbins with a Bible verse thrown in." And that's their viewpoint of Christianity and what Christian teaching is.

I think you get into some interesting dynamics of those that grew up within a church context so they just assume this is the way it is. As preachers, we have lost our voice in our culture.

I'm right now writing another book called *I Like Jesus But Not the Church*, and I'm interviewing eight non-Christians, all in their twenties and one in their thirties. And I'm just listening. They're all open to Jesus. They respect him; they haven't read the whole New Testament, but there's a respect. Almost all of them have no problem believing he was raised from the dead, which is so fascinating. If you think about this, that changes our apologetics. You don't have to say, "Here are five reasons why Jesus rose from the dead," because they practically all believe that already.

And they find it almost amusing that we argue about evolution. Because they're saying, "You know, I want to experience God and find out about him." They don't care if he created the world in six days or in six million years. It's more like, "I want to experience and know this God, and if Jesus is this teacher, what did he have to say?" But preachers are so negatively thought about because most of their exposure is TV preachers, radio preachers; depending on who you happen to watch or listen to, it's a mixed bag of what you're going to experience.

But what they really desire is dialogue. And for me, in our context you can't dialogue too well with four hundred plus people in the room. So we're setting up an open forum once a month right after the worship gathering ends. If you disagreed with me, if you have questions, if you want to challenge me on something—and I may not even have an answer, because some of this is so mysterious. But if you show that you are open to talking, to having questions asked, you don't just give your presentation and hustle off or not listen . . .

I'm amazed at how many of these younger people I'm talking to right now for this book, are all saying, "Christianity from preachers is a one way thing. They don't care what I think; all they care about is dispensing their information and forcing their belief on me, not caring what I am personally believing at this time or wanting to dialogue and interact with me." That's common. Every single person is saying that. And if we're serious, then that changes how we go about preaching, how we set up our church to be more interactive. Maybe not in the big meeting, but somehow we need to be doing this.

How do we have more trust built in us who are up on the platform? Generally—and if you're from outside the church in particular—all they know, for the most part, is abuses of power and authority. And they think people are mindless who just sit there and listen to somebody and don't challenge their thinking. I've already sensed most of this, but it's been fascinating listening.

And here's the other thing: they want to learn; I've heard this many times—if they come to church, they don't want to sit and have like a kindergarten explanation. They want to be digging deep, to know in depth; they want to be respected for their intelligence. So it isn't like you have to dumb things down at all. I don't know how that's going to impact the future of the church as a whole in our culture, but these are really fascinating observations that preachers need to pay attention to.

Preaching: Some observers have said that in order to talk to people in a post-modern environment, it requires the use of narrative and story. It sounds as if your preaching is, if not propositional, at least pretty heavy in content.

Kimball: When I talk about narrative and story, I try to set it up. When I talked about heaven, I didn't jump in and start talking about "Here are the facts about heaven." I go to try to say, "We talked last week about how God created the Garden of Eden and it was this paradise." And I go back there and tell some of the story of what occurred there and then thread through to when the thief on the cross used the word "paradise." Look in Revelation 22—possibly could heaven be a garden? What I try to do, in a narrative sense, is to be constantly piecing in where what we're talking about fits in with the grand narrative of the biblical story. So it isn't "Here's how to have a happy family, and here's three principles with three Bible verses to back up each principle." I listen to some sermons, and they're so helpful, but it's pretty much just the pastor's opinion about things.

When we did the Sermon on the Mount, we set up a great story of what was going on. We actually even projected on the walls the hills of northern Galilee, trying to get people in this setting, to really try to see who Jesus was as a rabbi. We talked about what a rabbi meant at that time, and how rabbis would find disciples. Then we talked about what was a disciple back in that particular time period and that history, and how intense they were in imitating the rabbi they followed. It colors the whole story of what's going on so it isn't just Jesus telling the facts. It was a colorful story, the narrative way of presenting this, so it made more sense, I hope, to people.

Preaching: Where do you see the emerging church going over the next decade or so?

Kimball: It's very difficult to say. I hope what will occur is that we will see a change in our culture as a result. And to me, the great test of the church is are we seeing local towns having a climate change in their spiritual and kingdom living? Where I hope it will go—no matter what form and expression emerging church communities take—is that we will see people being drawn to know Jesus as a result of Christians really living out their faith. Not that we have better preaching or not that we have better music—all that stuff is so non-important if we're not seeing any actual change in people's lives and in our towns and cities. And what I'm saying now I believe is what most emerging church leaders I know are focusing on. That's what I keep hearing over and over again.

I think it'll be non-denominational, but not a denomination itself—post-denominational in many ways—still very much attached to various denominational histories, but not focusing on that. I just see us being very passionate about mission, and I think very passionate about the Scriptures.

I think God has us all in different roles and ministries, and there isn't one that's better than another or more hip than another, or anything. The men that have made a difference, that God's used in my life, you know they had almost nothing in common with me culturally, except they were Jesus to me.

Preaching and the City

An Interview with Erwin Lutzer

Erwin Lutzer has served since 1980 as pastor of the historic Moody Church in Chicago. A native of Canada and author of more than thirty-five books, Lutzer is featured speaker on the radio programs *Moody Church Hour*, *Songs in the Night*, and *Running to Win*, which altogether are broadcast on more than seven hundred radio stations in the U.S. and around the world. This interview appeared in the March-April 1998 issue of *Preaching*.

Preaching: As pastor of the Moody Church, you serve right in the middle of a major urban area. What are some of the particular dynamics or issues that are involved in preaching in that kind of urban context?

Lutzer: I think there are a number of things that are very important when you preach in the city. You need to be able to preach to broken people. I just came back from a seminar last week at which I spoke for Exodus International, which works with homosexuals and gays, and I gave a report to the congregation on Sunday. I told them how we saw people who have given their sexuality to God, and I explained what happened at this meeting. It's interesting the number of people who came up later and thanked me because that's where they are at.

Whenever you are dealing with the city you need to be able to preach to people on a number of different levels. First of all, you think of brokenness, with broken families, sexuality, problems in terms of where people are at. Secondly, though, you are also speaking to a business community. So, you have issues of ethics, witnessing in the workplace, how to really live out your life on Monday morning. I believe that if a revival ever comes to the United States of America, it is going to have to come with a revival of the laypeople. The reason for that is because we as preachers are heard only by a very small segment of the community, mostly people who agree with us. The life lived in banks and hospitals and factories and so forth—and the integrity of the life lived in those contexts—is the way in which I believe that the gospel is able to spread in the city. So, there are two areas in which I think preaching in the city has its challenges.

But there also is the need for reconciliation. There are things that we can do as pastors to help people see that the church is bigger than our local congregation—to see the bigger picture of the body. Last year, for example, I switched pulpits for one Sunday with Wally Washington, who is pastor of a black church in the neighborhood. He came to Moody Church, and I went to his. There are things that I think can be done to help people to see that if you were to think of circles—and each circle is a local congregation—God's work in the city encompasses all of those circles of evangelical churches that preach the gospel. Those are the special challenges of the city.

Beyond that, when you think about human need, whenever I prepare a message, I usually have one or two people in mind to whom I'm preaching it. Because this helps me be realistic, this helps me to think in terms of the person in the pew rather than just the content on the desk. Human need is so universal that if you are ministering to people where they are at and showing the relevance of doctrine, then preaching in the city is not that different than preaching anywhere else.

Preaching: You mentioned the renewal of the laity and helping them live out their faith in the workplace. In many situations, clergy seem so distant from the life issues of many laypersons. How do you find yourself as a preacher and as a pastor getting in touch with the kind of needs that they have?

Lutzer: One of the things that has helped me to be in touch with the laity is we have a Moody business club—Moody Business Network we call it. Every month we bring in a speaker that comes from the workplace, and they share their testimony; they explain their faith and how they live out Christ wherever they are. What that does is, it helps me to be reminded as to the kind of issues which the laity face which I do not face. You know, at the church I work with Christians. Therefore some of the ethical dilemmas laypeople face are not really at all what I face.

The second thing is, even though I am the pastor of a large church, I do still do some counseling. And you know, I think this is so important because you are off on your own round and doing your own things, and suddenly there is somebody there and you're confronted with a reality of human need. It has a way of bringing you down to earth and reminding you that life for many, many people is difficult. And interpreting the Scriptures and trying to minister to them in their need is a tremendous challenge.

One of the things that I've always said to preachers is that if you want to be able to minister effectively, you have to know yourself well. Rembrandt painted nearly one quarter of the pictures that he painted of himself. He was not a very good-looking person, and he did not flatter himself; he did not try to touch himself up to make himself look good. People said to him, "Why is it that you paint yourself so often?" And he said, "Unless I can really paint myself the way I am, I can't paint others the way they are." So, I think that one has to know oneself really well. The struggles of my soul are the same struggles of the congregation. But there have to be those points of contact where we intersect, and I must be constantly reminded of what is happening out in the pew.

Preaching: One of the issues preachers discuss today is a hunger for application of Scripture in preaching. There is a growing interest in application of preaching to the real-life needs of laypeople. How have you tried to deal with that in your own preaching?

Lutzer: My philosophy of preaching is this: I intend to use God's Word to change people forever. That's my intention. Now, we've both preached our share of forgettable messages, but that's the goal to which I aim. I actually pray and ask God that there will be some people that will hear this message that will never, ever be the same again. Because that, I think, is the goal of preaching. It is to bring about permanent, total transformation.

In terms of application the other thing I do is this: when I prepare to preach, I usually think of someone in the congregation—someone whom I know well who I believe is committed to Christ but maybe not as committed as I'd like to see him be. I always ask myself, "Why would this message change him forever?" That gives me a sense of realism. It reminds me of the fact that the theology that I'm preaching here has to be explosive—it has to explode in the life of the listener in such a way that if it were ignited by the power of the Word and the Spirit, it would change him.

Therefore, as you think in terms of application, I believe that application should happen throughout the message and not just at the end. I do need to confess that often the last five or ten minutes is where I really do think in terms of the nitty-gritty. That's where you think in terms of illustration, where you think in terms of actually re-creating situations which people face. Because here's what I have discovered: we as preachers sometimes think that if I give somebody the general truth, they will fill in the details and apply it. That's not true. You have to give them the general truth, then you have to apply it for them. Then if you missed their particular area of application, I think they will actually fill in the details for themselves once they see it in concrete life. But application is very, very important. In fact, without it a message somehow stays in the study as an academic exercise.

Preaching: You've done some writing in the area of evangelism. And obviously in the urban setting you've been describing, evangelistic outreach is a critical concern. What do you see as the relationship between preaching and evangelism?

Lutzer: At Moody Church, because of the diversity of our congregation—visitors coming in from the neighborhood and so forth—I would like to think that every Sunday the gospel is preached. That does not mean that I preach from John 3:16 every Sunday. In fact, last Sunday's message was on David and Goliath because I'm preaching a series on David. Nevertheless, as I got to the end of the message, I talked about all of the various giants that we think are unscalable; even the greatness of our sin could be a giant. And I explained how, through Christ, these kinds of giants can be dealt with within our hearts. We usually think of giants outside of us. I talked about the fact that the giants that are within our hearts are sometimes greater than the ones that are thrown across our paths. So even there I've preached the gospel.

But here is the thing: I am not as anxious to see decisions in a particular meeting as some people think I should be. There are two reasons for this. One of them is invitations. After the message we give opportunity for people to come forward to meet a prayer partner if they so desire. So we get converted people and unconverted people together. What I often do is ask people to go home and to seek God—to actually call on God to be saved. And therefore, they do not need to come forward to be saved. That's one of the problems I have with some invitations, where there is an identification of coming forward with being saved. And actually that is not necessary.

Number one, I think that every message should contain the gospel because we should be giving people hope and pointing the way. Number two, I think we have to understand that the Holy Spirit of God sometimes takes time to work in an individual to bring him to saving faith; therefore, I think it is important not to get the chicken ahead of the egg. And number three, I think it is true that a majority of people still come to know Christ not because they heard a sermon, as important as that is, but because they saw a life. It's that personal relationship that often makes the connection.

Preaching: Let's carry on the issue of the public invitation. What are some of your convictions on that topic?

Lutzer: When I was growing up I was very shy. We used to go to services where there were long invitations—singing "Just as I Am" many, many times. And I remember saying to myself, "If I have to go forward to be saved, I'm just going to have to go to hell." Because the idea of walking forward in the presence of so many people, including my parents, their relatives, their friends, and all of my friends, was just an obstacle to me. Ever since that time—since I was then converted in my home at the age of thirteen and was delighted to know that it isn't necessary to go forward—I have thought about the area of invitations, and this is what I've concluded. I believe that it is a mistake to make an identification with coming forward and being saved for two reasons. Number one, you are talking to shy people just like I was, who think, "If I have to go forward, I can't be saved." So, that is the first mistake.

The second mistake is the impression that just because you come forward you're saved. You have all these people to say, "I've made my profession because I went forward in a Billy Graham meeting," or "I went forward in a church and I made my profession." That doesn't mean you're converted. So, the way I give an invitation at Moody Church is this: I give an invitation for those who have questions and those who are in various degrees of spiritual questioning, those who are in need. When you give an invitation like that you have Christians coming forward with non-Christians because you are not making that tight identification. And you realize that you are there to help people no matter what level of spiritual development they are at, whether they are saved or unsaved. It is a general invitation for spiritual need.

Number two, I believe in the sovereignty of God. The Bible says while Jesus was preaching many believed. So I actually conclude the message oftentimes with a prayer for those who are sitting in their seats to receive Christ right there. And we have people doing that. Then later we encourage them to tell us about the fact that they have accepted Christ as Savior. So in doing this you see what we are saying to people is, "You don't have to come forward to be saved." And also we are not making the mistake of saying, "Now that you have come forward, you are a Christian." Assurance will be granted to you by the Holy Spirit and through teaching rather than us telling you that you are saved now that you have prayed.

You really have to trust the Holy Spirit to be faithful to do his work and to give him opportunities to bring people to closure. I do not call people to the altar or to the platform, but I call them to Christ. And I think that is important.

Preaching: **You said you have the invitation for spiritual questioning and needs. Is there a point at which you have an opportunity for people to make any kind of public declaration or identify themselves with Christ?**

Lutzer: About three weeks ago in a staff meeting we talked about a time like that and I think we are going to do that a couple times a year. We have people being saved through Evangelism Explosion and visitation in the homes, and we should give these people the opportunity to make a public disclosure. However, many of these people do make a public disclosure in other ways: among their friends, their family, and so forth. But I think the idea of bringing them to the front and saying, "These are the number of people, these are people that have accepted Christ in the last six months," is a marvelous idea.

Preaching: **How do people join Moody Church?**

Lutzer: When they join Moody Church they have to attend a one day seminar. And that is held about three times a year on a Saturday. They come on a Saturday morning, and I teach them for an hour and a half; other members of the staff come and teach them. We have lunch together with them, and then we have other teachings until later in the day. Late Saturday afternoon they are interviewed by an elder or a deacon, and then their fitness to join the church is assessed. One of the things, of course, that we always seek for is whether or not they are born again of the Spirit. And if they are, that basically is the only requirement, unless they're living in some kind of sin that we would discipline them for if they were church members. Then we would not have them join.

There are some people who attend all the time who don't join; it may be their decision, it may be ours. That's the way you join the church, and then two or three weeks after that we have a special induction ceremony in the morning service.

Preaching: **Let's shift gears a bit and talk about the process of preparing to preach. How many times a week do you preach, and what is your process of preparation?**

Lutzer: I preach every Sunday morning and probably half the time Sunday evening. Sunday evening we have other things—concerts, other ministers that sometimes preach, and so forth.

When I'm in a series like I am now in the life of David, what I'm going to preach on is pretty well mapped out because I have his life mapped out. In fact, many, many years ago I preached through his life. But I know that no one will remember that because it was so long ago, so this gives me a chance to rework it. So the basic structure of content is already there.

What I do then is, of course, read the passage; you meditate in the passage, and as you do that what you are looking for is that one explosive idea that you hope people will remember. Long ago I think that we as pastors gave up on the idea that people are going to remember our sermon because we have three nice alliterated points. I do still preach propositionally with an outline, which I think is very important. My outline is very clear. It is not necessarily alliterated, but it is parallel. We can talk about the technicalities some other time. But what you are looking for is the one idea.

Let me give you an example. Yesterday I preached on David and Goliath. My one idea was this: the thing that separated David from everyone else is that he had a God-sized imagination. I got that line from Eugene Peterson, and I gave him credit in it. But, it helped encapsulate it, and as an outgrowth of that the real idea led to this statement, which is the one that I wanted them to remember: *The size of your giant is determined by the size of your God.* Big God, small giant. Small God, big giant. That was my bottom line.

When I came across that, I was faced with the issue of preaching on a topic that has two problems. I mentioned this to the congregation in my introduction. Number one, it's so familiar. People who have never picked up the Bible have heard of David and Goliath. So people say, "Ah, David and Goliath, I know this." That's number one. The second problem is misapplication. I believe that story has been misapplied because people leave saying, "Well, what I want to do is find my Goliath. You know my Goliath is the boss in my own life. And I'm going to go to him tomorrow in the name of the Lord and watch God slay him." And what we do is we choose all of these giants. The fact is, this [Goliath] is the only problem that David had that was so easily taken care of. Later on he's going to be hounded by Saul for ten long years, and God is not going to take that giant out of his life. So I have to help people with the story or else you are going to just have people go off on all kinds of things.

We have a woman at the church who has cancer, and she is dying. She won't go to the doctor because she believes that God has healed, is healing her—and maybe he still will. The point is, people will identify all of their giants, and they will say, "God, now you are obligated to take care of my giant." So I need to help people with that. The bottom line was, how do I preach this? So I agonized over it. And then the idea came to me. Why not talk about the God-sized imagination and the one idea that I hoped people left with. If you shook hands at the door and asked, "What in the world did I say?" I would like them to have said, "You told us that the size of our God determines the size of our giant." And then at the end I helped them to identify their right giant and not misapply this passage.

Preaching: How far ahead of time do you map out a series like this? Do you preach primarily in series?

Lutzer: Primarily in series, but not always in an expository series on a book. But I do a lot of theological series. For example, I just did a series of six messages on the judgment seat of Christ. When you are doing that, you are preaching on a variety of different passages. I preached a series [now published in a book] entitled "One Minute After You Die." So we talk about heaven and hell, hades and the whole bit. Again, what you are doing is selecting passages that have to do with that particular issue.

Most series can be either six, ten messages, twelve. I always prepare a series of messages in advance so that before I begin the series, I know exactly where I am going. I don't necessarily know the details, but I know where I'm going. I would hate to be embarrassed to say I'm going to preach eight messages on this and then only have material for seven. Sometimes I've had the opposite happen; I've said this is going to be seven messages, and I've regretted it because it was too short.

I usually work about two or three months in advance. And I do this not only for my benefit but also for the benefit of the music minister who is interested in coordinating music that far ahead of time. He needs to anticipate. Let me give you a specific example. In a few months I am preaching a series of messages entitled, "Seven reasons why I believe the Bible is God's Word." Actually the series is going to be eight sermons because there is going to be an introductory message. This past Saturday, I spent about four or five hours on the first message of the series, as to why I believe the Bible is God's Word. And I got that message to the point where it's kind of under control. I know now that's where I am going, I know the lay of the land. I have an idea of how this message is going to be developed. And it is there in my computer so that when I come to it I'm not just beginning from scratch. Now I'm going to go on to message number two, and number three and number four, all the way through because once I have done the essence of the study to know where I am going, then I'm OK. When I come to the series in the fall, week by week I'm going to be able to fill in the details because there is no mystery as to where I am going. And I have about maybe six or seven or eight pages on my computer that could be the essence of the message already.

Preaching: What happens when you reach the week when that message is to be preached? Walk us through that process.

Lutzer: First of all I prepare all of my messages now on a computer. That helps greatly; it also helps in writing books later, if those are edited. I prepare a message on the computer. Thursday is my day of study when I'm at home. So that message has to get down pretty well. Maybe not totally, but it has got to be pretty good by Thursday. Saturday, that's when I put the finishing touches on; that's when I take the computerized message and turn it into some notes so that I can take the notes to the pulpit. They are just handwritten notes. I always take handwritten notes to the pulpit.

Monday morning I come back, and I take the message that is in the computer and I rework it. Why? Because in the lived event, you often have new ideas that come to you. You have a new way of saying things. There is a whole new dynamic once you've preached it. So you go through and you edit it as best you can and you put it into better shape and you add the material. If it doesn't become a book someday, then it is used some other way. Because we have three radio programs, it's a constant recycling of material. If I have a series that has been mapped out and I know where I am going in this message, then that week before, I can sit down and I can prepare the message on Thursday—usually Thursday and Saturday.

Preaching: You are in what is obviously a historic congregation. How do you deal with that history—the heritage that you are a part of? Does that play a role in your preaching?

Lutzer: When I first came to Moody Church—because of its fame and because this is the church of Harry Ironside—Warren Wiersbe and I often joked together. [Wiersbe preceded Lutzer as pastor.] He said, "You know, there are still people in this day that expect the ghost of Harry Ironside to come out of the basement." I think I didn't admit this at first because I honestly didn't think this was true. But in retrospect I think it did somewhat intimidate me, and therefore I don't think I felt as free in preaching as I do today. Now when I look at some of my sermons from the past I can see this, because as I listen to them they are all very prim and proper. But I was limited in off-handed remarks and dramatic expression of ideas. So, I think it has affected me.

Now that I've been there eighteen years, I'm much more relaxed. I'm much less hampered by the fact that this is the *Moody* Church. So I feel a great debt and a wonderful honor to be the pastor there. The other thing that you need to remember, too, is that it hasn't been as difficult as you might think it is, because most of the people who remember Harry Ironside and those days, they have gone on to glory. We have a tremendous amount of turnaround at the Moody Church, and because of that most of our people are a generation who knew not its past. Therefore, I don't feel like there is something there that I need to necessarily live up to, although I want to do my best for the glory of God.

Preaching: Are the majority of your sermons expository in style?

Lutzer: Yes, the majority are expository, but they are what I would call topical expositions. When you have a topic, that is the best kind of preaching, because it zeroes in like a laser beam to a certain topic. I do not do exposition in the older sense of the word, where you take the passage and kind of make comments all the way through and then you say, "Oh, it's time to quit, we'll pick up here next time." Every one of my sermons is an independent unit. It will stand alone so that if it is played over the *Moody Church Hour* [radio program], while I may refer to a previous message—because obviously there is a connection and a context—they each stand alone.

The best kind of preaching, it seems to me, is topical exposition. Topical exposition means you take a passage, you find its topic, and then once you find its topic you leave out everything that doesn't contribute to it. Since it is fresh in my mind from yesterday, let's use David and Goliath as an example. My idea was that the size of your God determines the size of your giant. There is so much of the story that I had to leave out. I just strictly summarized it—brought the people up to the issue, painted the picture, told the story. I zeroed in on the verse that David said, "You come against me with sword and spear and javelin, but I come against you in the name of the LORD Almighty" [1 Sam. 17:45 NIV]. I got my idea across, told how it ended, and then I summarized it at the end. So this was not exposition in the usual sense. I did not feel I had to begin in verse one, to expound and comment on all of the verses. No, you summarize; you do all that you can to get that one idea across, and that is all you can do.

Preaching: What makes some preaching soar while other sermons sink?

Lutzer: The thing I would like to talk about is heart. You may ask the question, "Why is one minister effective in preaching a sermon which may be very poor homiletically, and yet is very, very motivating and life changing? And here you have somebody else who is a great homiletician. He has got it all down, and it is really nicely done, yet it doesn't go anywhere. What is the difference between the two?" I think it has to do with passion. I believe that when we stand behind the pulpit, we should believe very, very deeply in this, and we should wait on God until we sense the absolute importance of what we are saying. We must not be casual in it. Now there are some people who teach in a very casual way; in fact, I do too, and those can be very effective. But I think that when it comes to preaching there has to be a sense of urgency. Who was it that said, "Preachers must feel deeply, think clearly, and enable their congregations to do the same"? And I believe that's the thing that motivates people.

We are living in a day and age when preaching often is not highly valued. We went through a period of time, I think, where small groups were the thing. You know, everybody's in small groups. Now I think there is a greater emphasis on preaching. I still think that at the end of the day—with all the technology and everything—there is no substitute for a man of God, saturated with the Word of God and filled with the Spirit of God, conveying his soul and his mind and his heart to the congregation. And so I would like to affirm the primacy of preaching even in a very, very confusing technological age.

A Passion for Exposition

An Interview with John MacArthur

John MacArthur Jr. is president of The Master's Seminary and pastor-teacher at Grace Community Church in Sun Valley, California. A renowned champion of biblical inspiration and authority, MacArthur has written many books and served as editor of *The MacArthur Study Bible*, which had just been published prior to this interview. He is widely known through his national radio ministry, *Grace to You*. This interview appeared in the November-December 1998 issue of *Preaching*.

Preaching: Since you are now the editor of a major study Bible, let's start by talking about that Bible project. I'd be curious about what led you to get involved in a project like that.

MacArthur: In all honesty there was a time when I thought about the possibility of doing that because my passion is exposition of Scripture. My passion is to make the Word of God clear to people. And I thought the commentary series would sort of suffice, which is like a thirty year project—or turning out to be nearly that! But the guys on my staff came to me one day—and the guys that are around me know me best—and they said, "John, you need to think about someday getting all of your stuff condensed down into a single volume and maybe think about a study Bible." I basically said, "I will never do that."

Then some people at Word Books came to me with this proposal at about the same time the guys were saying, "This is something that you ought to think about." And if I had really known what was involved, I probably would have said no, because I had no idea what was going to happen when we said yes. Once they presented it to me I thought, "Well, everybody feels I should do this. I have a seminary faculty here I can run all of this through," and I said yes.

I had a guy who was going to edit a lot of my New Testament material. He did none of it and handed it back to me six months later. I just got swept up in the thing. In the end I am really thrilled for the privilege of having done it.

Preaching: **As a preacher, an expositor, what kind of unique perspective does that give you as you are going into a project like this?**

MacArthur: I'm not primarily concerned with getting entangled in systems, and I wasn't concerned with getting entangled with critical things. I didn't want it to be superficial. I just really wanted to clarify the meaning of the text and the flow of the book. I was thinking more of not just a practical application, but of understanding its applicability. I stopped short in writing a study Bible of application. But I hope I got at least to the point of comprehension and understanding so the person says, "I understand what that is saying. I understand what that means." Not only in the individual sense of this text, but by cross-referencing and cross-referencing footnotes. I can see it in the bigger context and the bigger picture.

My goal was to make the Word of God understandable. And that's what I really do every week of my life, basically. The challenge here was I can do it in a paragraph a lot easier than I can do it in two short sentences. You are battling this need to summarize and condense and choose your words very carefully, and when you are doing twenty-five thousand like that the process gets very burdensome. That was really a challenge. But I didn't want any theological system imposed on it. I just wanted to let the Word of God speak. The word "dispensations" is in there only once, and it's in the Bible text. I tried to avoid anything that would look like a shadow from outside the Scripture sort of cast over it. So I just let it speak in the flow of the argument of the book. It is very important to establish introductory material at the front of every book which was honest and legitimate; once you've done that, then you have established a certain theme, a certain flow. As a pastor I was thinking of how my people will be able to understand the meaning of the Scripture in a way that could be applicable.

Preaching: **You mentioned last night in your message—somewhat facetiously—that having gone through all of these passages and gathered** all this information, you are inundating your people with new pieces of information.

MacArthur: It is leaking out all over the place!

Preaching: Do you sense any changes in your preaching—anything that you might be doing differently having gone through this project? How has your preaching been impacted?

MacArthur: I think my preaching has been impacted because my mind has been so immensely enriched with the biblical data that I wasn't as familiar with. You know as you go through years preaching, you build a sort of base of familiar stuff. And all of a sudden I was flooded with unfamiliar stuff, so there was a newness and richness. I was using illustrations out of the Old Testament that I had never used, and still am. I was tapping into principles and insights that I never had before. And I think that was the richness for me, not only for the people.

People told me there is a totally new joy in my preaching, a new sense of adventure that they can sense even in the way that I preach and the passion of it. It is all fresh because it's been informed with fresh new insights and also because I'm speaking my convictions with greater passion because I've had to test them from Genesis 1:1 clear to the end of Revelation 22. And so what it is that I'm still holding on to, I'm really holding on to. The people are catching some of this joy. They listen not only to what I say but they pick up the passion with which I say it. And you transfer to them not only an understanding of the Scriptures but an enthusiasm and excitement about it, too.

Preaching: How do you go about planning your preaching? What does the planning process look like for you?

MacArthur: I'm probably not a really good guy to answer that question because my plan is to preach a book. Before I begin that book, I read a whole lot of introductory material because I really want to take advantage of the best that is available. This sends me into introductory material as well as commentaries where I can expose myself to everything: outlines, themes, variations, issues of backgrounds, and all this kind of stuff. I get a feel for the book, and I start poking around in it, and I start developing an outline in a general flow of where I will go. And that is as far as I go. I never break it down at that point, because I find myself constantly going behind the barriers that I establish for myself.

I find that the science of preaching sort of gives way to the passion. I'll take a passage. Eventually when I start the series I'll break up the first part of it in imaginable paragraphs in my own mind. And I'll start with the first unit and I'll say, "OK, this is a sermon unit here." As often as not, I'll go into the pulpit assuming I'll preach a sermon on that and wind up with a four-week series. That is because I get into something, and what starts out as a well-designed sermon with an introduction, conclusion, points that all work together and wrap up fine—a well-constructed sermon—becomes a very poorly constructed series. And the people are very used to that here, and because I'm coming back next week, it is sort of like link sausage—you can cut anywhere and you get the whole deal. So, I'm not really a very good model of homiletics!

In fact, I was doing a pastor's conference in Montreal, and we had several hundred young, new pastors in the French Canadian evangelical movement, which is a first generation church—the only one in the western world. They are all first generation men; they have never been trained. So I did a seminar on preaching for five days, through simultaneous translation, and at the end we had questions. The first guy got upset: "Dr. MacArthur, we appreciate what you have taught us, and we've been listening to your tapes, and we want to know why you don't do what you have just taught us." That was an honest question, and I just scratched my head and said, "I don't know why, it's just foolishness on my part."

I find there is a certain adventure to preaching; there's a certain captivating element. I'm not into homiletics as such. I don't worry too much about alliteration. If it is there, it is there; if it's not, it is not. I'm not into the cleverness of the outline. So I do tend to spill over when I don't necessarily plan to do that. But that is kind of how it goes, and when I finish that unit however that works, I just start the next one and work my way through. I always want to stay consistent with themes; I don't want to interpret something in chapter 1 that is going to collide with chapter 4. So I have to be ahead of myself in terms of having already thought all that through. There is a certain level of interpretation I've done at the front.

There is a certain unknown in my preaching process. So I can't plan a year preaching or sequence unless I'm doing a special series. I just did a special series on Romans 8. Just took that one chapter and broke it down into a series of things and gave that sequence on Sunday night. But if I'm going through a book, I find it very difficult.

Preaching: How do you choose which books to preach?

MacArthur: Honestly, early on it was something that I really worked on as thoughtfully as I could, as prayerfully as I could, and trying to assess where the church was and what was most needful. But in the process of trying to complete the whole of the New Testament, I'm running out of reasons why I'm making choices. I'm now down to the fact that I've only got two books left. So, I can either choose Luke or Mark. You know, eventually I sort of run out of viable options! But typically it had to do with the life of the church—where I thought the church was.

I'm doing one expositional series on Sunday morning and another one on Sunday night. I always wanted one of them focused primarily on the person of Christ. I never wanted to be so into theology or some aspect of theology or church life or whatever that the real focus of the Christian experience, the person of Christ, somehow got left behind. So I always wanted to have one of those books be one that featured the Lord Jesus Christ. I love the Gospels because it is Christ every Sunday. Lifting him up is still what we do.

Preaching: **Having done this Bible project, are there any Old Testament books that you are now eager to go into?**

MacArthur: I have preached through some: Daniel, Zechariah, some of the Minor Prophets; I've given them bits and pieces of Isaiah and Jeremiah. Of course my people are living in sheer terror that I might start Genesis and try to get to all the chapters in their lifetime! Or anything else that long. I just fell in love with the book of Ezekiel, which is a very difficult book. I think I worked harder on the notes on that than any other book. I fell in love with the book of Job, which I have done bits and pieces and would love to go all the way through now that I have a greater grasp for that book. I'm going to do a series on Genesis 1–3—the richness of those beginnings that I think will really be stimulating for the people. But as far as just taking one book and just marching through it, my style might make that a very long process. So I think I'll just pick sections of the Old Testament that are most notable and work my way through those.

Preaching: **What do you actually carry into the pulpit with you when you are going to preach?**

MacArthur: Of course my Bible, and inserted in my Bible I carry some sheets of paper that will be about the size of the Bible page. Depending on my familiarity with the material and the structure of all that, I can have anywhere from three or four up to ten of those. And they would just be my own handwritten notes. I mark them up in a certain way to draw attention to them, and I don't have to refer to them except maybe to quote a Scripture or read a quote—just to sort of locate myself so I don't go off somewhere and I can't find my way back. I don't memorize my sermons. I'm not particularly interested in preaching without notes.

Preaching long sermons for many years in the same place demands that you say things in a new way—that you stay fresh—and it's very important to craft things. I'm not a great orator by any means, but I don't want to say things that sound so familiar.

Familiarity inevitably breeds contempt. You are teaching the same truths over a long period of time again and again. You have to be aware of forgetfulness—they do forget—but you also have be aware of familiarity. You can't keep repeating things in the same way. Certainly the Scriptures do this. There are great truths repeated in Scripture in many places but with insights and illustrations and analogies that are new all the time. You sort of work on that; at least I do.

Preaching: How long is a typical sermon for you?

MacArthur: Fifty minutes. It's almost predictable. If I didn't have a clock, I would almost hit that.

The issue is not the length of anything. The issue is what's there. I mean, the Gettysburg Address didn't need to be any longer than it was. I think if you make an issue out of length, you make a major mistake. I don't ever want to tell another preacher you need to preach at least fifty minutes. They may not be able to do that effectively. You do need to have time enough to frame your message so that it comes with biblical impact. And that means a certain amount of re-creating. A certain amount of that is necessary.

Look at the Promise Keepers rallies. These guys are going in there and listening to hour-long messages, four or five of them in a day. Of course you can't just put anybody up there to do that. But there are people who can sustain that kind of thing. I mean, Adrian Rogers, nobody complains. Tony Evans, nobody complains. They would all be in the forty-five to fifty minute category. I don't know why that is. I think the issue is what a man has to say and the power with which he says it and the way he handles the Scripture and the way he handles his audience.

Preaching: You have said that a preacher's authority comes when he speaks the Word of God. One of the things that we were talking about earlier was the fact that churches that are growing today are churches where solid, biblical preaching is going on. How do you relate those observations?

MacArthur: God honors his Word, and I think if you get beyond that, you're messing around in human analysis. I mean, what am I going to talk about? Marketing strategies or technique? I don't want to do that. I really believe that God does honor his Word and it is sharper than any two-edged sword and it is able to penetrate and cut and wound, and then heal, restore, and rebuild like nothing else. The other common denominator in growing churches is not just the Word but it is men who are skilled at handling it.

I think God blesses his truth. You know, I think in the breadth of evangelicalism there is a love for the truth and there is an honoring of the truth of God. You see it here when the Word of God is opened and it comes to life and it penetrates. We don't have to get a polemicist up there to demand that all of these people accept the veracity of Scripture. It is conviction, I think, that is planted in the heart by the Spirit of God in the life of a true believer. The love of the truth. I just think when they hear this powerfully and clearly presented to them, it has its effect, it does its work. It is powerful, and you will believe.

We all know as well that leadership is predominantly verbal. And so, leaders who can clearly articulate truth tend to be those who can motivate and who can mobilize people. And so around that strong proclamation of the Word of God these men are also able to energize and ennoble the people around them, who then put their shoulder to the wheel and generate ministry. I do think it is the blessing of God and honor of his Word.

Preaching: You've commented that one of the things you have to work at so hard is to get your own presuppositions out of the message. How do you do that and yet allow the divinely inspired personality of the preacher to still have its place?

MacArthur: I think the answer to that is you get yourself out of the interpretation; you don't get yourself out of the proclamation. I want to be out of the interpretation and in the proclamation. There's a clear line there for me.

I remember having a conversation with a prominent Christian leader. He said, "What do you think of the exception clause in Matthew 5: except for the clause of fornication that the man divorce his wife and she remarries she commits adultery."

I said, "What do you mean, what do I think of it? It is there, so it is an exception. If there is fornication, then there are grounds for divorce." He says it can't be true. And we were walking through this area where there was a pen of Canada geese, and he said, "See those geese, we clipped their wings, we keep them here." He said, "One day there was a hole in the fence. They all tried to get out. That's why there can't be an exception clause." He was dead serious.

I said, "Tell me this: what does Matthew 5 mean if there are no geese?" He went blank. Sort of theology by analogy. You can always find the analogy. But I think the challenge in the interpretation process is to get yourself out of it, and that is where the scholarship comes in, that is where your hard work comes in.

That's why I read probably twelve to fifteen commentaries on every passage that I preach on. I really do want to be fair with it. That's the challenge, and once I get into the proclamation, then that's just me. I hope that people don't ever think that you are up there trying to present your opinion. Sometimes when you are forceful they assume that. Hopefully that is not true.

Preaching to Postmoderns

An Interview with Brian McLaren

After a number of years teaching English at the University of Maryland and other colleges, Brian McLaren became founding pastor of Cedar Ridge Community Church in Spencerville, Maryland. In his writing and speaking, he has become a central figure and mentor to the emerging church movement. McLaren is often cited in discussions about ministry to postmoderns. This interview appeared in the May-June 2001 issue of *Preaching*.

Preaching: In your book, *Church on the Other Side*, you talk about doing ministry on the other side of the modern/postmodern transition. How do you describe that transition? What is going on culturally that is making an impact?

McLaren: One of the best ways to frame it, I think, is to look back in history at other major transitions. We talk about pre-history, which is before people have the ability to write. Generally we put that about 2500 B.C. Then people talk about the ancient world, which was the world of a number of significant civilizations: the Sumerian, the Egyptian, Greek, Roman empires—that brings us from about 2500 B.C. to about 500 A.D. That is really a period during which the whole Bible takes place except creation. Then there's the medieval period from about 500 A.D. to about 1500 A.D., and the modern period from 1500 to the present. For us, modern tends to just mean now, but if we think of it as a period, we realize that someday it is going to end and something else will take its place, if past history is any model.

What would it look like if the modern world came to an end and something new took its place? We would expect there to be a change in philosophy; we would expect there to be a change in economy, a change in organizing structures, a change perhaps in lifestyles of people. A lot of us believe that we have this fascinating convergence of change in all of those areas going on right about now. That is very, very analogous to that last major change around 1500 when you had Columbus and the new world opening up. You had the decay of the feudal economic system, the rise of the modern capitalist system. You had the rise of the nation-state, which didn't exist before 1500, the rise of the industrial regime and technology. There were no complex machines before 1500. The printing press, huge new communication technologies—we can take every one of those changes in 1500 and find their counterparts today, which then creates this moment of cultural transformation.

There's change in communication technology—just as the printing press made literacy much more widespread, which changed Christianity. In some ways, Protestantism is a form of Christianity that could only exist after the printing press because you couldn't have literacy because you couldn't have books in large numbers.

Well, what happens when we become a screen-based world rather than a paper-based world? What happens when the primary modes of communication are electronic rather than through books? Huge change. Change in the way people think. Change in the way they process information. Change in the way we've got to preach to them. So there is a huge area.

Another huge area is the way we look at people who are different than us. For five hundred years the world has been getting smaller, but now we are in a place where the world gets ever smaller, ever faster, because the whole world becomes linked through the Internet and television, radio and airplanes. That changes the way we think about people from other cultures. It is not so easy to create caricatures of them; it is not so easy to see them as bad and us as good. So it changes the way that we think about other religions as well; it creates new challenges for us in the whole area of pluralism.

In the modern world we believed that we could have certainty. We could have certainty as individuals, and we could have certainty through our own rational processes. We really believe in certainty. Probably most of your readers would agree with that statement: certainty is possible for human beings. Although we might agree that there are some gray areas around the edges, there's this core of real absolute certainty that we believe.

If we went before 1500 in the medieval period, people wouldn't have believed that they could have that kind of certainty. They would have understood that much of what they know is based on what their authorities have told them, so they had faith in their authority figures over them. Whatever they would call certainty was really based on faith. In the ancient world, people were aware that there was so much that they didn't know; they lived with a sense of swimming in mystery. But in the modern world we believe that mystery is going to be removed through rational processes, analysis, science. In the scientific world we have made a lot of progress in that.

In the theological world we applied the same rationalistic process to the Bible and felt that we were getting the whole thing systematized and figured out. Our preaching and our knowing have been about certainty. It has been about principles; it has been about abstract concepts and propositions. That has really worked. People loved to come to church for the last fifty years of high modernity where they could take notes and add to their knowledge base.

Yet as we move into a postmodern world, we reenter a world of mystery and we reenter a world where people are skeptical of those overblown claims to certainty. So there is a radical rethinking of epistemology. Now there are some extremes of this in some of the postmodern philosophers, where you get the feeling that they are saying you don't know anything and can't know anything. The irony is that they are writing books about this, which makes you think they are trying to convince people of something that they would to some degree know. They are certain that they can't be certain about anything!

I think that this has a huge impact for us as Christians. I think in the long run it is a huge gain for us as Christians because the whole world becomes a little more honest that we all live by faith. I talk about this more in my second book, *Finding Faith*, that we all live by faith. I think it is going to be hard for a lot of us as preachers because we have postured ourselves in a modern posture, as the experts who dispense certainty and knowledge, rather than a more ancient view of the spiritual leader as people who guide others into mystery. Very different.

Preaching: **How has your own identity as a preacher changed as you grappled with some of these ideas about postmodernity?**

McLaren: I remember getting a feeling in the early and mid '90s that something I was doing was counterproductive to really getting through to the more postmodern people who were coming through our doors. First of all, most churches have no postmodern people coming through their doors because we give so many messages to tell them, "You are not wanted" or "You would not be interested in what we are doing here" because it has such a modern feel. When we started having some postmodern folks coming through our doors, I just felt that something wasn't working and a change was going to be in order.

I was hearing other people talk about this a little bit. They were talking about the importance of returning to narrative. So, I started thinking, "What does that mean?" It doesn't just mean telling more cute stories, bringing stories and illustrations into our sermons. One thing I started realizing is that if we understand truth to be always human and contextual, then the way I quote the Bible changes.

For example, I was just working on my sermon for this Sunday, and I am going to quote Jesus in John 7 when he says, "If anyone wills to do God's will he will know my teaching whether it is from God." I was just going to quote that, but then I thought I should reroute this in the story, because what that sentence means, the nuances and fullness of that, will come out as people see the conversation he is in with the Jewish leaders in John 7. So, it is an awareness that the whole New Testament is contextual, and the Old Testament—every statement takes place in a story. So trying to reroute the statements in a story moves us away from proof texting. It moves us back into always giving the narrative framework. Those are always inherently interesting—so much drama to all of this. John 7, what incredible drama is going on there. So that would be a big change.

Another change would be to take the posture not of the expert but of the lead scout in an expedition. So it's not like I have been there and I have it all figured out and I am bringing it back to other people, telling them what's out there. But we are all on a journey together. I am out in front a little bit, but I am trying to give them a guided tour of the new territory. It is a different posture.

Preaching: You talked about reshaping the framework into a more narrative format. How would you do that differently?

McLaren: I think before I would have just quoted the statement and treated it as a bit of disembodied information or as an abstract principle. I certainly think there is a principle going on there. I am not trying to deny that. But I would have been more propositional, more interested in just what is going on in the abstract. Then when I look at this in context: the Jewish leaders sitting there are marveling saying, "How does this man become learned having never been educated?" We have a traditional idea of how people get knowledge. People get knowledge by getting educated, by the authorities. So Jesus says it is not just getting educated by sitting in classrooms or by sitting at the feet of rabbis and listening to them. There is a heart attitude toward this thing, too. There is an experiential attitude. You are going to know my teaching; you are really going to understand it and know its validity when you try it and when you obey God's will.

In fact, it's a very postmodern passage when you think about it. It is saying that knowledge isn't about just gaining abstract information. There is a moral dimension to the gaining of knowledge. I suppose it is the biblical idea of being wise versus being a fool. You can be an educated fool. Jesus is saying "follow me" to people who don't understand that—knowing that the best way that they will understand it is by following him. They will behave themselves into a better way of believing before they will understand themselves into a better way of believing.

What I am trying to do very much is to get people in that same framework, where it's not that I am going to give them the full explanation of everything in a rational, abstract, and intellectual way, but I'm going to help them get this combination of understanding and experience and experimentation that's going to guide them into deeper understanding of the gospel.

Preaching: Not only in terms of the shaping of the message—are there other changes in your own preaching that you have been making?

McLaren: In addition to being more narrative, when we get into this we become more conversational. I think modern preaching is analytical, and I define analysis as taking a whole and breaking it down into its parts, or taking an effect and breaking it down into its causes—tracing it back to its causes. My sermons in the past were very analytical: take a passage and break it down; take a word and break it down. Everything is about breaking it down. Outlining is analysis. It's breaking things down into its parts.

Conversations don't work that way. Conversations take interesting little dog legs—the question gets raised, you go off on a little tangent, then you go off on the main point. I've found that the more my preaching mirrors the flow of a conversation, the more people connect with it. The more I try to do abstract analysis, the more it feels like something is being imposed on them. That might be just a reflection of me and this congregation. But if there is a generalization, I would say there is this conversational kind of flow. Maybe I make a statement. I have to say, "What are people thinking right now? What question would they be asking?" Well, that is where I need to go. I need to let the question that I think is naturally arising in their mind be the direction for me—not the analytical outline, the five Ps or the six Js or whatever it is. That so much dominated modern thinking—we like that because it gave us the feeling of being orderly. It's structure.

Preaching: Do you serve a fairly young congregation?

McLaren: It used to be fairly young! Then the older I got, the older they got. Ironically a lot of our younger people have brought their parents, so our diversity has really increased in the last few years.

Preaching: Many pastors struggle with this issue of how you preach to postmoderns. At the same time, in most of our congregations, we are not just preaching to twenty- to thirtysomethings. We are preaching to forties, to fifties, sixties. We are preaching to congregations that span worldviews. How do you deal with that diversity of perspective?

McLaren: That is an extremely tough issue. In the public speaking that I am doing around the country, there is an awful lot of pain clustering around that issue. The first thing is, the fact that we have that pain is a good sign. It's a sign that we are in a situation more like the first century church, because you had Jews and Gentiles having to be brought together—people on the same planet who live in different universes having to be brought together. I think we have an analogous situation. I think we've got people on the same planet who live in different universes.

I think that there are certain things that are impossible to do. For example, this problem isn't just a matter of modern and postmodern. It is a matter of religious taste. Some people have developed religious taste in a modern framework—like an acquired taste in food. You are not going to take somebody who hates Indian food and get them to like it. It is just a taste that they haven't acquired. I think for people who are highly churched and have a very strong acquired taste for a certain kind of preaching, to ask them to change their taste is like asking them to change their preference in music or food or anything else. I don't think it is a matter of biblical or unbiblical. I think it would be honest to just say it is a matter of taste.

Then I think it is a compassionate thing to say that if some people are very set in their ways, we are probably going to have to keep meeting their needs in the language and style that they are more used to. It would be nice if we could change them. Maybe a few would change, but we have to recognize the limitations of human beings. What we have to do is not let ourselves be held captive to those tastes. We need to create new venues. A lot of churches create alternative services. I think that is one way of dealing with it. Keep meeting the needs of people; as Lyle Schaller says, "Bring change by addition not subtraction." But add to that some new options.

Preaching: Regarding the alternative service: many pastors have come to the conclusion that in a single worship service they cannot deal with twenties and sixties in terms of just the worldview change; the perspective is just so different. Is it possible to do it within the same church? If you use alternative services, what are the advantages and disadvantages?

McLaren: First of all, this modern/postmodern thing isn't strictly a matter of age groups. What a lot of us find out is when we start communicating the gospel in a postmodern context, a lot of older people suddenly come out of the woodwork. They weren't coming to church before. For example, two of the really innovative churches exploring this area are in Minneapolis. One is called Spirit Garage, and the other is called Solomon's Porch. The Spirit Garage is a subcongregation of a Lutheran church, and Solomon's Porch is a church on its own—a new church plant. But if you go there, you will find a whole range of ages because there are older people who have been waiting for something like this.

Doug Pagitt, who is the pastor for Solomon's Porch, has a wonderful metaphor for this. He says, "Do you work on the metaphor of a tree or the metaphor of a garden?" A tree has one root system, and you could see an additional service as a branch coming out of the trunk of that tree. The problem is, whatever grows on that branch has to be the same ultimately—it is just more of the same. But if you have the metaphor of a garden and you say as a church, "We used to only grow green beans, but now we are going to plow up a little additional territory and grow some strawberries. We are all one church, we are all one garden plot here, but now we have two crops. Then we may add a third crop. And over time, the balance of those different crops will change. But we are not in the green bean business; we are in the gardening business." I think that is a much better way to see it.

So here right now we have three different types of services. We have our Sunday celebrations on Sunday morning. We have a much more interactive service on Sunday nights that we call Emerge. We have a Thursday night contemplative service that we call Intermission. But those three services are intended to be primary worship experiences for different people. So people come Thursdays that don't come Sundays, and Sunday nights that don't come Sunday mornings.

Preaching: Does your preaching style change between those services?

McLaren: Well, I don't speak in the other services. In one I've never spoken, and in the other, very seldom. My style probably wouldn't change a lot because all three of those in our context are more or less working in a postmodern framework. But, if I were in a more traditional setting, yes, I would have to change. The problem is, I think, when people start crossing over to the other side of this transition they find it harder and harder to go back.

Preaching: Do you see anybody out there that is doing this effectively—operating effectively on both sides of the divide, whether there are alternate services or something different?

McLaren: In every case I'm aware of, if the senior pastor or dominant leader of the church is strongly modern, he hires someone else to communicate with the postmodern audience. Where the modern senior pastor learns to transition, he finds out there is so much need in a postmodern world that he tends to let somebody else do the modern work, and he goes on to do the postmodern work. So I don't see many that remain amphibious very long. I think I was amphibious five or seven years ago. But I have been going in this direction. Interestingly our church leaders eventually said we want to go that way. We feel that this is new territory. It is a little scary but needs to be explored.

Preaching: In your book you talk about the need to design a new apologetic. What role does apologetics play in a postmodern setting? What shape does that take, and what role does preaching play in that?

McLaren: In a modern context, apologetics is about rational evidence and rational proof and rational argument. In a postmodern setting, it is not that we are abandoning rationality but that we are realizing that as soon as we get into argument in any kind of hostile way, we seem to invalidate our message to postmodern hearers. I think there are a number of reasons for this. Some of it is very cultural in America. I think 1968, Kent State, the Vietnam war—the baby boomer culture reached a point where we thought bitter argument is so dangerous and people get hurt and people die because of it. I think in our hearts we sort of moved to being somewhat repulsed by that kind of head-to-head argument.

I think for the younger generation that is even more true. Younger people who have grown up with the Balkans in the news and have grown up with Islamic fundamentalism in the news—they say if we don't learn how to get along in spite of our disagreements, the world is going to blow up. So this sense that head-to-head argument—Christianity versus Buddhism, Christianity versus Hinduism, Christianity versus atheism—that "versus" mentality sets them off right away. So instead of coming like a football game—where we are going to call the play and see who is standing at the end—I think that we move into a much more conversational and friendly mode of discourse about religion and our differences and about the gospel.

I also think that showing and listening become as important as telling and convincing. I think one of the things we start to realize is that the Holy Spirit is so active out there. If we listen to people, before long they are going to start telling us where the Holy Spirit is already active in their lives, and then we can start fanning that flame, building that spark into something. Because the Holy Spirit seems to be so active in so many people's lives, the listening becomes very important and the showing becomes very important.

I think Lesslie Newbigin, the theologian who died in the '90s, had so much to say about this. He said the greatest hermeneutic of the gospel, the greatest explanation of the gospel, is a community that lives by it. I think the importance of demonstrating the gospel at work in our lives becomes more and more important, because the gospel is no longer a disembodied message; it is a message embodied in a community.

Ironically that doesn't mean that we have to show ourselves a whole lot better than we used to be. It means that we have to make the struggle that we are having about living by the gospel ourselves more overt. We have got to show the pain. We have got to be honest about our failures, present and past. That way apologetics has a lot more to do with apology—apologizing for our failures. I mean here in America, here we had this incredible Christian heritage, and it hasn't helped us work out our problems between blacks and whites. It didn't help us treat the Native Americans very well. It hasn't made us be good stewards of the environment. We have any number of embarrassments that are part of our history that postmodern apologetics means we say, "We're really sorry; we blew it. We are just human beings, we are struggling with this. But we are still trying to learn, and we feel that the gospel is calling us to do better in these areas." That becomes a very winsome apologetic when we talk that way.

Preaching: We are seeing two major social/cultural trends: one is pluralism and another is relativism. How do you bring the gospel to bear in an environment or in a context in which you basically are speaking to people who have learned to see the world through pluralistic, relativistic eyes?

McLaren: First of all, from the far side of the transition, I think that people look back and say modern people just learn to see the world through absolutistic and non-relativistic eyes. They would say that the absolutist view of modern people is every bit as much a construct as that of a relativist. I think it is very important for us to really sit with that for a while—to really see that.

I would say that the dominant thing that we have to prove to a spiritually seeking non-Christian in a postmodern world is not that Christianity is true. We have to prove that it is good and beautiful. And if they are convinced that it's good and beautiful, they will be open to it being true. But to just say that we are going to convince them that it's true and not worry about it being good or beautiful, I think won't get us very far. Ironically that seems to resonate more with Jesus's own teaching: by their fruits you will know them, not by their water-tight, systematic arguments will you know them. So the goodness of what we're about becomes incredibly important. Then again, I don't think goodness necessarily means perfection, but it at least means honesty and humility about our imperfections.

Preaching: Let me push a little bit on that. There are postmodern folks who basically say, "You know what's true for you is good, but that may not be true for me." At what point do you have to, for the sake of the gospel, draw a line and say there *are* some things that are true and some things that are false?

McLaren: First of all I think that there is so much sloppy thinking among relativistic people, and some of it is just downright silly. I think it's appropriate for us in a very gentle, humble way to point out some of that silliness. I try to do this in my second book, *Finding Faith*, where I say that if all religions are equally true, then God must like some religions better than others, because he told some people they could convert with the sword and told other people to turn the other cheek. Well he's definitely giving some people the earthly advantage there! Just to point out to people if they say, "You can't know anything," and then you say, "Well, are you sure of that? Do you know that you can't know anything? Then you have just contradicted yourself." So there are all kinds of contradiction. I think that we can gently point this out to people, but in the long run I don't think that is the best approach to take.

I think that the best approach is to try to be sympathetic to why they are telling you that everything is equally true. This isn't really an intellectual statement. This is really a social statement. It is saying that we can't go around condemning other people or judging other people or shutting other people up because we disagree with them. I think if we could be sympathetic to that statement—which we are as Christians—then we could just move beyond it and start demonstrating the gospel to them. Then I think we start helping them consider what their current beliefs are and where their current beliefs don't take into account what's really out there.

There is a very important book just out by Stan Grenz and John Franke called *Beyond Foundationalism*. It is a book about theological method, and in the book they define theology in a very interesting way. They say theology is not just about God. Theology is a human attempt to create models of the universe based on beliefs about God. This is what is really at stake when we are talking to people about the gospel. We are not just talking about different beliefs about God; we are talking about different models of the universe.

So in a sense, then, what we do with people is we say, "Let's look at your model of the universe and hold it up against reality. Does it really take reality into account?" We can sort of join them in looking at that. If they are willing to say, "You know, I don't think my view of reality, my model, really does take all of reality into account," then we can say, "Well, let me show you how mine works. Let's see if mine takes reality into account." And we are going to both be sure that there are modifications needed because none of us has a perfect view of the universe. But there becomes a more of a collaborative process there, and it becomes an ongoing conversation with a potential for influence. So I think we are going to help people come to Christ through influence rather than coercion by argument.

I really think our modern apologetics ended up being about coercion by argument. I love what Søren Kierkegaard said about this way back in the early 1800s. He talked about why the indirect approach to truth is better than the direct approach. He said if I make a direct approach and say I am right and you are wrong, I am forcing you to, in a sense, lose face in front of me and surrender to me. But if instead I present to you, "Here's how I see things, and why don't you think about it and compare it to how you see things," then I allow you to go off in private and figure this out, and before God you can make your changes. That way I am asking you to humble yourself before God, not before me. It is like childbirth. It has got to be done very gently. It has got to let the process be at work.

Preaching: **You talk about the need to learn a new rhetoric. Obviously part of rhetoric is language. Have you sensed that your use of language has changed?**

McLaren: This is so important. Here is a place where I think the whole seeker movement and church growth movement really helped us, because they reminded us that we have so much insider jargon. Very often people are turned away from our message not because they disagree with it but because they just feel overwhelmed with jargon that they don't understand.

I got some insight into this a few years ago. A friend of mine is a committed Buddhist, and I figured I couldn't carry on a lot of extended conversation with him unless I understood a little bit more about Buddhism. So he gave me a bunch of Buddhist literature, and I just felt inundated with all of these Hindi or Sanskrit terms. I just felt, "If you people are really trying to help me understand Buddhism, why don't you translate this into English for me, or why don't you give me a nice glossary to let me know why you are using these terms?"

I think we have a similar challenge in the words we use—finding ways to make things clear. Of course Jesus exemplifies this with his telling stories. This is not the difference between modern and postmodern. I think in the modern world we really believe that truth can reside in isolated words. But I think in a postmodern world we have more confidence in truth residing in stories such as parables than just in isolated, technical words. The whole idea of technical terminology is a very modern idea—important in the modern world and important in the science and technical world permanently. So words are tremendously important. I think our methods of argument are really important. I think the postmodern culture requires us to be more gentle and respectful, which has a certain resonance in 1 Peter 3, "Always be ready to give a reason and do it with gentleness and respect." I think we have to do that. We have to be more biblical now in that way.

I think in a world where we are bombarded by print, television, radio, Internet, the importance of beauty in communication increases. In the old world, you could just be louder, and the louder you were, the more you would be heard. I think now the softer we speak, the more likely we'll be heard. If we speak with some beauty and passion and intensity, people are drawn in. Sort of abrasive, loud language got people's attention. Now abrasive, loud language makes people think that someone is mentally ill or someone is trying to cause a fight.

Preaching: The use of story and narrative has been a major trend in homiletics. How do you integrate these things in your preaching? Do you see yourself as a narrative preacher? Do you use story within another framework?

McLaren: The first thing that comes to my mind is that I struggle with that. I was born and raised on propositional preaching rather than narrative, so I think that I have always struggled. I am much less prone to quote the Bible with just a verse. I've got to tell the story around it. I've got to tell who said it. I've got to tell when he said it. I've got to tell what is going on when he said it and what context it fit in.

Very often I think my sermons will develop around a larger story—the story of how I am struggling with something in my own life, the story of how the Christian community as a whole is struggling with something. For example, this week I am going to speak on the spiritual practice of secrecy. Here is an example of a word change. We used to call these spiritual disciplines, but I don't think that "discipline" communicates the right connotation, so I am using the term spiritual "practice." I want to talk about this from the angle of two problems that we as Christians have struggled with. One is the problem of authenticity. We don't seem real. We have a lot of talk. We don't imitate the iceberg, which is one-tenth visible and nine-tenths non-visible. I think Jesus, when he teaches about secrecy, is telling us to be authentic. You have to have more going on under the surface that nobody knows about. This is a problem in the church, and everybody is aware of it. All the hypocrisy in the church and how superficial and shallow we feel and how little effect we have.

Then the other problem is our effectiveness. We make up some significant proportion of our population, but we don't seem to be having an impact, so we seem kind of lightweight. Again I think this problem is related to the fact that we're all on the surface; we don't have enough going on in secret that nobody knows about. So talking about the issue comes in the context of the larger story of what is going on in the church today and tomorrow.

Preaching: How did you come to establish this church?

McLaren: I think that I have some kind of a gift of evangelism from the spiritual womb so to speak. When I was a teenager and I began to follow Christ, I started a little Bible study. Nobody told me to, I just did. I didn't even think of inviting Christians; I invited non-Christians. That ended up growing to eighty to ninety kids in my high school. When I was a graduate student and an instructor at University of Maryland, my wife and I started a little fellowship in our home that grew to fifty to sixty people. Again, my tendency was to invite non-Christians to that.

I never thought of being a pastor. I really loved the idea of being a college English teacher. In 1985 I heard Rick Warren speak. It was the first time in my life that I heard anybody talk about church work as being evangelistic work. For me, the church was really important, really necessary, but it sort of got in the way of evangelism. But when I heard Rick speak, I thought I could be a pastor in the way he was talking about—if my work as a pastor was evangelistic work. Now I think I tend to see evangelism and nurture under the broader heading of disciple making, so it is much more holistic for me. In 1985 that is when I first thought, "This is something that I really could do." That precipitated a beginning. Meanwhile we had started a little house group that eventually grew into

Cedar Ridge. I started putting more and more of my effort into working with that group starting in 1986.

Preaching: Tell me about your church. What is a typical Sunday morning like for you?

McLaren: We are not any great model. We are just a church that is trying to be true to the gospel and reach our community—to be disciples and make disciples. When people ask about our service I often jokingly say it is a cross between Willow Creek, Vineyard, and an Episcopal service! The first forty or forty-five minutes of our service will be very much like a Willow Creek service. We have one song and some announcements. Very often we will have a drama that leads us into the theme of the sermon. I end the sermon with a prayer, and the prayer is always an invitation for response. Not that we call people forward but that the prayer that I will lead will be in response to what has been said.

Then right after that we have communion every Sunday, and we do that in more of an Episcopal style where we actually use the liturgy out of the prayer book and people come forward to take communion. I think that works here because Maryland is a very Catholic state, so for a lot of people if they haven't had communion, they don't feel like they have really come to church. I also think it is important in a postmodern context because I think we are going to see a resurgence of the value of ritual, ceremony, and liturgy. We'll include confession of sin. Very often we will include a creed, reciting the creed as preparation for communion. Then we have communion, and as people come forward then we will have twenty minutes or so of worship, singing. It might be a little more like a Vineyard kind of thing with contemporary music. That becomes a very experiential time because there are people coming forward and there are people back in the seats singing, and there is a lot to see as well as to hear what is going on.

The whole service is seventy-five minutes, so that leaves me thirty, maybe thirty-five minutes for the sermon.

Preaching: As you preach, how far out do you plan? Do you use series?

McLaren: We use series, and I generally plan about six months out. Part of that is because of the coordination we need for people getting drama scripts developed and all the rest, so we have to keep planning out pretty far in advance. We tend to use four to six week series. Generally in the summer we'll do a longer series. Last summer, for example, we gave an overview of the whole Bible in fourteen weeks, which was really fun and really helpful for people—to try to get the big historical sweep. In general the summer season we really will concentrate on being a little more expository. We did the Sermon on the Mount one summer. So we really take a passage much more in depth then. We tend to see the springtime as sort of our strongest outreach season. I typically do a series that we call "God in the Movies" where we will do four, five, or six sermons where we'll focus on a movie each week that is popular and look for some spiritual themes. Show a few clips from them.

Preaching: **What about the use of audio, video, or other technology in support of preaching? You said you do use video clips from films. Are there other things that you use?**

McLaren: We project our Scriptures on the screen. If there is a particularly interesting quote from an author—I think this week I have a clip from Dallas Willard that we are going to put up. Helping people with visuals like that seems important.

Preaching: **When you are not preaching using a movie theme, do you still use video clips as illustrative material?**

McLaren: Yes, quite often we will do that. Actually this week I am also using a popular song, so we will play the song and project the lyrics and talk about how that relates to the theme.

I think whenever we do anything with popular culture in a positive way they feel responsive. It is very easy to be negative about stuff in popular culture. There's no shortage of stuff to complain about! But when we can find some shred of goodness out there, I think that affirms and teaches them to look for some good out there, not just bad. I think that we are pretty good at teaching people to look for bad. But to find some redemptive theme of a song—I think it is helpful.

Preaching: **You talked about how your preaching has changed. As you look out five to ten years from now, can you anticipate additional changes that you may be making?**

McLaren: When I do public speaking not in a Sunday morning sermon context, I am finding that the Q & A times become incredibly important. I often wonder how we could create more opportunity for dialogue in our services. There are a million logistical problems in this. For that to happen you really need a pretty good chunk of time, and then you have got to balance out with having children and Sunday school classes and all the rest. I wonder if we don't need to create opportunities where there would be much more dialogue, Q & A, that kind of thing. I also think about this not just on our sermons and formal worship service but just in our teaching ministry in general. One of the things that Dallas Willard says in *The Divine Conspiracy* that is very important is that intensity is an essential element of discipleship. In other words, it is different to be exposed to something for one hour a week for eight weeks than being exposed to it for eight hours on one Saturday. I wouldn't be surprised if we moved more of our energy away from weekly one hour events to a really intense weekend retreat, for example. So we could do teaching and have dialogue and really engage much more deeply in the material.

Preaching: Any closing observations?

McLaren: You know something related back to rhetoric. I was an English instructor before going into the ministry. The genre of literature that pays the most attention to every word and interplay of words is poetry. I think it is so interesting that so much of the Bible is written in poetry. The prophets were poets as well as the Psalms. I think that there are huge resources available to us in poetry and helping people rediscover a few well-chosen words rather than a barrage of journalistic words that just flow out without much attention to diction.

Preaching: So when you go back to the sermon as three points and a poem, hold the points?

McLaren: Make the sermon pointless! [Laughing.] Of course people really need to be taught this. It is not that they are coming in with a huge appreciation of poetry already, but I think when we help they appreciate it; something in them resonates. Everybody is so busy; they are moving so fast—it's good for us to help them slow down. I think that part of our challenge is turning the sermon experience into a spiritual practice. So we are not just giving information. We are creating a spiritual experience, and we are guiding people in a group meditation. So that it is not just about telling people what to do out there. It is letting something happen right here. I think that's a huge new territory for us.

For some people, especially in the early stages of their spiritual search, putting aside an hour and a half to come and be in a place is a major commitment. I think that we need to honor that and help something important happen for them here. Hopefully it won't stop there. But we can't take that for granted anymore. The act of coming is pretty significant.

Leading through Preaching

An Interview with John Maxwell

John Maxwell is one of the contemporary church's leading authorities on leadership. For many years a senior pastor in California, today Maxwell focuses on writing and teaching about leadership through his organization Injoy. He is author of dozens of books and is a widely sought conference speaker. This section combines interviews which appeared in the January-February 1998 and January-February 2004 issues of *Preaching*.

Preaching: Your ministry focus has become leadership and leadership gifts. You are also a preacher and a former pastor. What do you see as the links between preaching and leadership? In what ways do you see the preaching task as a leadership task within the church?

Maxwell: All great leaders are effective communicators. It is the vehicle for the vision. For me to know where I want to take a group of people and not have the ability to cast that dream, preach that message, communicate that heart, makes the dream impossible. The vision won't be accomplished.

So one of the reasons I have committed so much time, not only in teaching leadership but communication, is I think they are so compatible. You show me a great leader, and I'll show you a person that became a great leader because of his or her ability to communicate effectively. You can be a good preacher and not a good leader, but you cannot be a good leader without being a good preacher or a good communicator. You have to be able to communicate the vision. What I love about it is that they all do it differently; there is not a certain style or a certain method. But they all have the ability to get their heart into the heart of their people. And that is always done through preaching and through communication.

Preaching: What are some of the particular approaches or methods in preaching that tend to strengthen our work in leadership?

Maxwell: I think the style is determined by the culture as far as effectiveness. You and I both know that in the United States you can go to seven or eight different areas and based on the culture you have to have a different style to be able to communicate effectively. I think the best example I can give you is my own life.

I grew up in Ohio and the Midwest. When I pastored in Ohio, I built a fairly substantial church there. The preaching was exhortation—a lot of exhorting. People migrated to it because it gave them, I think, assurance and security. When I moved to southern California that style didn't work. I had to learn to relate, be relevant, ask questions, speak in more of an open manner. Less telling, more sharing. A little bit more transparency. A little bit more vulnerability. I couldn't rely upon tradition there, so I had to adapt. What I have found is that great communicators can do that.

I'm now living in Atlanta; I've just moved here. I'm not pastoring here, but if I was to communicate here, I would do it even differently here than I did in Ohio or would have done it in San Diego. So I think that culture determines the style. The great communicators understand that and have the ability to adapt to that culture and to relate to the people on the level where they are.

As I look at communicators with different styles, different methods, they all have one thing in common. I've seen this, I've watched it, I've observed it. All great communicators have the ability to connect. They can connect with their audience. You know, when I was a kid, I used to love to go down to the railroad tracks and watch them switch train cars. They back the engine up, and you know how they bang the cars and they have a little ripple effect if there are seven or eight cars. But I learned early just because you bang the cars, it didn't mean you couple with it. You could bang a car and that old engine could pull out without the cars; you had to couple it.

A lot of preaching is banging with the people. You're banging them, and you are hitting them. A lot of pastors think when they have done that then they have communicated—I've told them, I've told them. But they never connected with it. They never had that relational, emotional, spiritual connection with it. All great communicators, regardless of style or method, understand the connecting principle; they have the ability to connect with people, know where they are and connect there.

In leadership I do a lesson called the five levels of leadership. It is a very interesting lesson. It talks about the different levels that a leader is on with the organization which he or she leads. Very simply, the bottom level is what I call the *position* level—you come to a church, you have a title, you have an office, you have a job, you have a senior pastor. But it's the lowest level of connecting or relating. The second level is the *permission* level. On that level, you not only have a position, or a title, but they begin to like you, and they begin to give you permission to enter into their lives and enter into their walk with God.

Then there is the *production* level. The permission level is built on the relationships, while the production level is built on results. After you have been effective with the people for a period of time they will say, "Well, you know I was saved under his ministry" or "I came to Christ or I was baptized in that church while he was there." And that is a whole different level. Then there is another level which is a production level, which you reproduce yourself in the lives of the people; you develop people—it is a personal development type of level. You have people in your church on all five of these levels. So, therefore when they hear me speak, they relate to my message, not on what I said but based on what level they are on. That's why pastors will go out and preach a message and one person will shake your hand and say, "Greatest message I've ever heard, pastor, changed my life. We're going to help you support the building program or whatever." Somebody else walks out, and they are not coming back. "All the guy wants is money."

They received the same message by the same man, the same time, the same words, the same place. What happened? Different levels. In communication, in preaching, it is very important for the communicator to understand when he or she walks up in front of people that they have these different stations in life. So in my communication as a pastor I always made sure that I had levels of communication based on where the people were so that I could connect with every person there, based on not where I was or where the message was but where the people were.

One more thought on that: the great preachers, the great communicators, when they come out and speak, they understand that their first job is not to take the message and deliver it. The first job is to find out where the people are. Because the message can't be delivered if nobody is at home.

I love communication. I love studying it, I love preaching, I love going out and trying to connect with the audience. I know what it's like to connect with them; I know what it's like not to connect with them. I know what it's like to look out there and to say, "There's nobody home," but I also know what it's like for them to look at me and to say, "Nobody's home." When both of us are not at home then we are in trouble!

Preaching: You talked about vision, communicating with vision. How essential is vision for pastors—having the vision or articulating the vision?

Maxwell: For the pastor to not have a vision—it's a huge problem. Without it the people perish. In my book, *Developing the Leader Within You*, I have a chapter that says that a vision is the indispensable requirement for every leader. I've never known a leader that didn't have a vision. Really haven't. Now, I've known people that have had visions that weren't leaders. They had too much buttermilk and onions before they went to bed last night. But I've never known a leader that didn't have a vision. So when a pastor comes to me and says, "Could you give me a vision for my church?" I tell them two things, "First, no, I can't. Number two is you're in trouble. You are in trouble because you can't lead people without a vision." So they are probably not a leader; they are probably making a statement about themselves more than they are about their church or who they are leading.

Let's talk about the pastor who has the vision but doesn't seem to have the ability to cast that vision, and I've seen that. One of the greatest mistakes in working with pastors I find is this: they think that one sermon will solve every problem they've ever had. So they put all their marbles in one bag and wonder why they didn't achieve. In other words, they get up on Sunday morning and they have this red hot message. Something they want to do or somewhere they want to go; and they'll preach it and they will teach it, and the people, it is hitting them cold. I mean some of them miss it, again, based on the level, the five levels. The people in the top level, they've never even heard the vision, but they will buy into it because they buy into the pastor. People on levels one, two, and three, they don't. So what I tell pastors is, let me take you through the process.

Number one, your job is not to sell your vision; your job is to sell yourself. People don't buy into vision until they buy into the leader. So the first step is, if they have bought into you, if you have integrity with those people, if you have a proven track record with those people, if they trust you, they'll buy into your vision. So your first job is to sell yourself, not your vision.

The second thing to do is not to preach that message too early. Most visions are aborted because, again, pastors overestimate the event and underestimate the process. They think, "Sunday morning, that's the time I'll preach this vision message. Everybody get on board, and away we go!" No. What they need to do is they need to begin working through the influencers of that congregation by sitting down with them like you and I are right now. Having a lunch, having a breakfast, beginning to share their heart, getting input from them. Let the influencers not only hear the vision, but help mold the vision. Nothing happens until there is ownership. Whenever there gets to be ownership with the influencers—you don't need to do this with the whole congregation—but if there is ownership with the influencers when you cast the vision, you're not the only person there.

Whoever said it's lonely at the top wasn't a leader. Have you ever thought of this? Think about it. Leaders are not alone. How do you define a leader? You define a leader by the type of people that are around them. The only people that I know that have been lonely at the top are people that have decided to take a trip without anybody. And so what you do in your vision casting is, you bring these people around you. You include the people until it is a "we" issue. What is great is the influencers will bring the rest of the people along. But never cast the vision in a message until you have given process time with that vision to the influencers.

Two things will happen: ownership and maturity. I have never had an idea that when I shared it, that the person I shared it with didn't compliment that idea and make it better. For me to go to the pulpit with a vision that I've just held between God and me, that is naive. I want to go with the vision with God and me and key players who have the heart for this church. Now you've got a mature vision as such.

Preaching: There is a difference between a boss and a leader.

Maxwell: I believe that. I think that is exactly right. A boss is trying to drive people. You define leadership with people around you.

Preaching: What do you enjoy most about preaching?

Maxwell: Lives are changed. I live for that. The thing I love about pastoring is you get to live with the people. And the greatest joy I had on Sunday morning is looking out in the congregation and there is Joe. Joe is in there worshiping with his wife. Four years ago, Joe wasn't a believer, marriage was on the rocks. Now Joe is a layperson, using his spiritual gifts for God. The growth of the people is what I love the most.

That is what I miss the most. When people say, "Now that you are not pastoring what do you miss the most?" Very simple. I don't get to see people grow. They write me letters, but I don't get to see the growth like you can see when you live with them from day to day. So, the growth of the people is the reason I did it.

Preaching to me is not an end in itself. I believe that for the great communicators, their whole perspective of communicating is to change lives and to move people from one point to the other with the assistance of God. People that are speakers, their goal is to look good. There is a world of difference between those two. A speaker, when he or she is done, their whole issue is, "How did I sound, did people like me?" A communicator preacher, their whole perspective is, "Did it change a life?" Communicators are other focused; speakers are inward focused.

And I think because of that, the results are totally different, too. If you preach to change lives, the odds are there will be lives changed. If you preach to impress people, the odds are you will impress people. So what are you in there for?

Preaching: What is the toughest thing about preaching for you?

Maxwell: The accountability. I had a guy one time tell me, he said, "John, it must be fun to speak to Promise Keepers or at the Southern Baptist Convention. And that just must be a real kick." I said, "You don't know what I have to go through before I do that. To whom much is given, much is to be required."

There are times when I feel the weight of not taking myself too seriously. I don't do that. But there are just so many people out there that are going to touch lives—because I deal with leaders all the time, I'm always dealing in what I call the multiplying factor. If I'm teaching the leadership conference and I have a thousand leaders out there, I'm not dealing with a thousand people; I'm probably dealing with a hundred thousand people. And so I feel the responsibility of that, the accountability to know that I'll answer for that some day and that I'd better give it my best shot.

When I left Skyline [Wesleyan Church] two years ago, I could look that congregation in the eye and I could say with great integrity, "I never shortcut you on a sermon." I wrote all of them out, studied, prepared, prayed. Now, I didn't always preach good messages because I'm human; I'm not good all the time. But I never shortcutted the people. I always give it my best shot.

When I was done, I could say there are a lot of other guys who could have done better than I. But I did the best that I can. I didn't play golf each week and goof off and give those "simple sermons" and write down three points and wing it. I am aware of the accountability and responsibility of speaking, not only to the listeners but to the people who bring me in. Think of their risk factor. People who bring you in are standing up there and introducing you and saying, "I'm betting my life on this guy that he's good, that he will help you." So I feel a tremendous responsibility to God to the person who brought me in. The greatest compliment I ever get is from the person who invited me in, who arranged the expense of it, the planning of it. And they come and say, "John, you did exactly what I was wanting to see happen." It just came off right, and

I say, "Yes!" You know what I mean. So I never want to shortcut God, don't want to shortcut the person who brings me in. And I don't want to shortcut the people.

Preaching: You can't talk about leadership without being a student of culture. What trends do you think are taking place in terms of communication, and particularly in preaching, as we move into the next century?

Maxwell: We deal with a culture that is just not going to sit in the pew and accept what we're saying. Biblically it is illiterate. It has many more options in life than my generation had, a lot more than what my father's generation had. No longer does the pastor have the esteemed role in the community that at one time he or she would have had, nor does the church.

I think communicators and preachers today have to be better than they had to be two generations ago. Here's why. A generation or two ago you could get up and you could preach and you could basically say, "The Word of God says," and you were off running. Ninety-five percent of that audience bought into the foundation which you were building that message on. Today that is not true. Today, before you can sell the congregation on the integrity of the Bible, you have to sell the congregation on the integrity of your life. Preachers today have to first carry it in their actions and in their life, in their character, in their conduct. If that audience buys into that, then they say, "Okay, now I'm willing to look into the Bible." That used to not happen. So, I think it behooves us to live a more godly, holy life.

There has been a moral fallout in clergy in the last ten to twelve years. One of the few good things that has come out of it is that it has caused all of us to not be as arrogant, probably "scared" is a better word—more humble, probably much slower to allow anyone to put us up on a pedestal. There's less role playing today.

Here's the transition that I'm seeing. Here's what really excites me. I was over at Randy Pope's church [Perimeter Presbyterian] Sunday because we are now in Atlanta. He's got over three or four thousand people. Here's this guy who is very cerebral, good thinker. Tremendous character and integrity in his life. I watched him very carefully unfold the Word. I am very proud of this young man who with real integrity carefully weighs his words to this congregation. And the reason he does is because he knows that there is a questioning spirit out there, so he must be right on. So there are some differences, some major differences. But I think it makes preaching better; we are communicating better.

One more thing: if the message isn't relevant, people will not have a passion to pursue it. At one time people were drawn to passion alone.

Now they are drawn to passion—they get passionate hearts for God—only when they see the relevance of it. Pastors should trust themselves outside of the church environment a little bit more. We need to pick up what's happening and where culture is. I'd like the world to be able to step into the church and feel comfortable, not because the message is compromised but because it is relevant and there is passion that comes from relevance—the hearts that will be stirred and moved and the conviction that happens is based on the fact that it connects. It connects to the people.

Now that I'm not pastoring, I go to churches and hear preaching more than I used to hear. And I think I was a little naive. I thought preaching was a little better than it is. And when I'm listening to these pastors a lot of times I want to stand up and say, "Stop for a moment, who are you talking to? You are not connecting, but you have a great message here. Let's back up for a moment. How are we going to take what you are saying and connect it with Joe over here?" There is just a little lack of awareness, I think, of where people are in their journey and what's happening to them.

Truth, coupled with relevance, makes a message hot. Relevance without truth has no conviction or changing power. Truth without relevance just doesn't connect. So, I would just really encourage pastors to spend more time with the world. Not to become worldly but to spend more time in the world to know who we are trying to reach with this good message that we have.

Preaching: How does the preacher effectively make that connection with Joe—to move from the biblical text to make the connection with the world in which Joe lives?

Maxwell: I think the main reason we don't make connections is because it is a world we are not comfortable with. And I think it takes time. When I was pastoring, I had unsaved friends, non-churched friends that I would connect with continually. Find out where they are, what they were thinking, ask them to come to church. The greatest critique that I could receive from them is that they understood it and it helped them. They'd say, "You know, I understood what you were saying."

I think communicators and preachers are too complex. We need to go back to simplicity. I've always said that a communicator takes something complicated and makes it simple. An educator takes something simple and makes it complicated. I think we need to relate and get down to where the people are, and simplicity is good. Simplicity has tremendous power.

I graduated from college in 1969. This will blow your mind—it took me from '69 to 1977 to know how to connect. The reason it took me that long was because I had no mentors; I had nobody to teach me. So I had to kind of grope and do trial and error. When I would listen to somebody speak I would ask myself a question. "Are they connecting?" And if they were connecting with me, I would ask myself, "Why? What are they doing, what are they saying that connects with me?"

I quickly learned how to discern the difference between a person who connects because of a subject and a person who connects because of their ability to communicate. The best way I can explain that is it's not a subject issue—it's the person that is the communicator. So you say, "Give me a subject that I can really communicate to people." My whole thing is if you're a good communicator, just about any subject will do. If you are a bad communicator, there is no subject that will help.

So I began to study the communicators, once I understood that the key to communication was connection. I am amazed at guys who go up and communicate and nobody's home and they don't have a clue—they walk off just happy as clams, and I'm sitting there saying, "Do you know how bad you were? If I were to interrupt you halfway in your message and looked at the people and said, 'Do we want to take a vote?' they would have found a gong, and the trapdoor would have opened, and you would be gone. Do you know what I am sayin'?" They don't have a clue.

The great communicators connect, regardless of style, personality, background, subject—it doesn't matter. There is nothing I love better than to hear somebody speak and evaluate. I can tell you if they've connected, I can tell you when they connected, I can tell you why they connected. You know I love to play golf, but if you don't understand what a proper swing feels like and looks like, you can practice 'til Jesus comes and you are still going to be bad. Practice doesn't make perfect—it makes permanent. So people who don't understand that connection is the key for a communicator—they can do their preaching, do all their study and the whole process, and they're still going to be boring until they understand that.

And how do you connect? You connect through authenticity. You connect by being yourself and not trying to be someone else. You know what I'm saying? Stay in your strengths zone.

Preaching: **Among preachers, who are some that you learned from as connecters?**

Maxwell: I saw that Chuck Swindoll connected through humor. He loved to laugh. Loved to laugh with people, laugh at himself. I saw John MacArthur absolutely communicate, connect through confidence. John

MacArthur, when you got done you were just convinced that he knew the right way. This is the way that I ought to go. I just studied these guys, and I watched them.

You know the great African-American preachers understand it so much better than the white preachers. They understand that they get on a subject and they stay there until they connect. Here's the difference between a white preacher and an African-American preacher: the white preacher has to finish the outline. A black preacher, once he finds his connection point he never leaves; he never leaves. He never finishes his message. Never does the outline right. But he stays right there. He understands that when you find the bait you stay there. So I watched and I observed—how long does it take a person to connect?

Jack Hayford was a classic example. It took him almost a whole message. He's more warm-up than anybody I have ever heard. You know what I'm saying? But I always stayed with him because he would connect. It took him forty minutes, but he would connect. And it was worth it. He could land that plane every time.

So I began to appreciate people for how they connected and when they connected and understood the process of what helped them to connect. Let me tell you something about the great communicators: there is also the type of preacher who can communicate in his setting because he knows his setting, but you take him out of that setting and he can't do that. So they are very strong in creating an environment where they are comfortable, and they connect there. But because they are not really great communicators—they just are good leaders that set an environment for connection in their setting—when you pull them out of that you say, "What happened?" What happened is that they weren't pure communicators. A pure communicator reads the situation, adapts himself or herself to that situation. Figures out what the connecting link is and moves into that. It sometimes takes a little while, but it ultimately makes that connection.

Preaching: In your book *Thinking for a Change*, you've got this statement: "If your thinking is limited, so is your potential." How do you think that plays out in the life of the church?

Maxwell: I think it is everything in the life of the church. First of all, where there is no vision people perish. From our biblical roots we understand that the size of your vision or the ability to have big thinking or big dreaming is going to determine the size of your congregation. The greatest limiting factor in a person's life is their thinking. If I don't think or if I don't think good thoughts, I am only going to be a recipient of what is given to me.

John Cotter has written some great change books in leadership. We were talking about some of this stuff, and he said, "John, the vast majority of people don't make their life—they accept their life." And I thought this is so true. People with no thinking skills or limited thinking skills, they just take what is handed to them. They have no other option. When I limit my thinking, the smallness of my thinking is going to always determine what I receive from it.

Preaching: If you were talking to young pastors, how would you advise them to become big thinkers?

Maxwell: I had to do it myself. First of all I grew up in a small denomination of 225 churches. The largest church would have been five hundred. Very negative, very legalistic, hypercritical; most of the churches didn't have one professional in the congregation. That was my environment. I very quickly assessed my situation and said, "I'm in prison here. How am I going to get out?"

What I did back in 1971 to '73 is I got a list of the pastors of the ten largest churches in America. That was the first awareness for me that there are some churches that are huge. In fact, I think in '72 the tenth largest church in America was Charles Blair's church in Denver, Colorado; if I am not mistaken he either had eighteen hundred or two thousand. The tenth largest church. Today there are ten churches in Orlando alone that are made up of two thousand.

I called these pastors up and said, "You don't know me, but I really want to learn, and I'll give you a hundred dollars for thirty minutes of your time." That was back in '72 when I made fourteen thousand dollars. I did that because I knew that there was no way they would ever give me an audience. I had to show them that I was going to be different than the average person that was passionate. Over the next three years I interviewed them. How does a young pastor get out of his limited thinking? They took me out of it. I exposed myself to a world that I did not know. I exposed myself to a world that I wasn't comfortable with. But I knew the only way for me to ever get big is to get away from that small-thinking pettiness and hang around with people who think big. They all have the same effect on me.

People ask me often, "Well, what questions did you ask?" I had like five pages of questions and a tape recorder. I had more questions than I could ever ask in a half hour. I only had a half hour—I wanted it clean. What happened was not questions that I asked or answers that they gave—there was an empowerment that happened that day. When I went back out in that empty parking lot at that church, I would lay my head against that steering wheel, and I would bawl like a baby and say, "Oh, God, if you can do that for him, you can do that for me." And I was empowered.

In fact it is interesting—I can only remember one answer to any one question that I asked of all those people. I went down to Jacksonville, Florida, and talked to Bob Grey. Our church building was full, and I asked Bob Grey if we should go to two services. We were packed out. We were so packed out we would put them in the balcony, then we would seat them on the steps going down the balcony, then we would fill the chairs clear out to the last door. When you dismiss, the last people had to get out first. The Fire Marshall would have had a heyday. I asked Bob Grey if I should go to two services and he said, "Oh, don't you do that, Johnny. It would be a huge mistake." He said, "I have played pastor in two congregations." Which is terrible advice. Because of that I had to plateau for two years while I was building a new sanctuary. Terrible advice. Terrible answer.

But the value from all of them—including Bob Grey—is that I came out of there so empowered that it lifted me out of this small thinking, "can't be done" prison that I was in, and very quickly. The first thing I noticed when I would go back to my church, when I would go back to my denomination, was that I was no longer what these people were. I knew it was only a matter of time 'til I'd have to leave because there was no connection. So I would tell a pastor to go talk to a visionary, go talk to a big thinker. They'll lift you out. They'll empower you out.

Preaching: One of the hot buttons for so many pastors is dealing with the whole issue of change. In the book you talk about the fact that reaching goals always involves change. That's a struggle for many pastors with churches that are resistant to change. How did you as a pastor get people within the church ready for change?

Maxwell: First of all let's start with pastor. Thirty years ago when I taught leadership I would have said wrongly that leaders like change and are out there paving the way, and followers dislike change. That followers are the drag and the resistance to it. I no longer think that. I think most leaders dislike change as much as followers do, *unless it's their idea*. In fact I think when change does not occur in an organization or church, it is not because the followers resist a change—it is because leaders resist a change.

Followers by and large have no influence and pretty much fall in line to what everyone else is going to do anyway. That's why they call them followers. So when change does not occur it's almost always because it was sabotaged. There is a leader to sabotage the change, not a follower. Pastors do not need to worry about the people. The pastors need to have an honest date with themselves. When churches don't change it is not a follower problem, it's a leader problem almost always.

Now that being said, I want to be very careful to say that I do not advocate or admire change in itself. I know a lot of people just want change because they get restless. I don't think that's a good change. I think growth, true, legitimate growth, necessitates change. You can't grow over a period of time without making major changes. So I think growth means change. I don't think that change means growth. Somebody says, "Well I'm making some changes," and I am saying, "That doesn't make it better." I know people who have made changes and got worse.

So let's not glorify change. Let's glorify growth. If growth occurs, a person will change, and what I have discovered is when growth occurs change is received much more positively. My challenge is not to change churches or change pastors; my challenge is to grow churches and grow pastors. If I truly get them on a growth pattern, they'll have momentum to make the changes they need to have. Because remember this: to change without growth is to change without momentum. That is very difficult. It only takes a strong degree of discipline, but you have so many nay-sayers that it's much easier to grow and then make changes than it is to change to have growth. I think a lot of times you get the cart before the horse. I would tell pastors they're responsible for the change. But really what I want them to do is not change—what I really want them to do is grow and then change.

Preaching to the Powerful

An Interview with Lloyd John Ogilvie

Lloyd John Ogilvie served from 1995 to 2003 as chaplain of the United States Senate, a role in which he opened each Senate session in prayer and led an active schedule of Bible studies and counseling for Senators and their staffs. He came to Washington from Hollywood, California, where he had served as pastor of First Presbyterian Church and hosted a national television ministry. Now retired, he is author of more than a dozen books and continues to be a popular speaker and preacher. This interview appeared in the May-June 2002 issue of *Preaching*.

Preaching: As we conduct this interview, we are sitting in the U.S. Capitol building, a place that is a symbol of political power. As you have made the transition from the pastorate of a local church to chaplain of the Senate in this place that literally brims with power, how has it influenced your approach to ministry?

Ogilvie: It has had an influence. I've had to discover ways to help people who have immense secular power learn how to find the power of God for their work. The transition that must be made is to help persons realize that the riverbed is the flow of God's power, not the river—to help them be recipients of supernatural power, instead of simply the power of talents. For instance, any Senator, to be elected, must have talents of articulation, clear thinking, organization, a lodestar kind of leadership that attracts others. However, once in office, a person needs the gifts of the Holy Spirit to be the kind of leader the nation needs—gifts of wisdom, knowledge, discernment, prophetic vision, and then empowered articulation that's really the result of knowing God personally and yielding the role of leadership to him to receive the empowerment for the task.

So our work here is around the motto, "Without God, we can't; without us, he won't." And when we get that into perspective, great leaders can be born and nurtured to recognize that apart from the Lord's power we can't move at a supernatural level. God has so created the way he moves providentially in history that he works through people. Where he wants to be he invests a person; when he wants something to occur in a particular society, he puts his people to discover and do his will. And to get leaders to be open to that call is the important thing.

Preaching: **You use your ministry of preaching and teaching not only to lead but to build leaders. How would you translate that into the local church setting for the pastor who is trying to build leaders among the laity?**

Ogilvie: I think there has to be a fundamental reevaluation of the biblical idea of the meaning of the laity. To be in Christ is to be in the ministry, so every member of a congregation is a minister. The question is, "What kind of a ministry does he or she have?" So I think our task is to be a coach of the ministers, which puts preaching and teaching, counseling and administration in an entirely different focus.

I used to ask basic questions in a church: "What kind of people do we want to put into the world?" "What kind of church will make that quality of person possible?" "What kind of church officer will make that kind of church possible?" And lastly, "What kind of pastor will be an enabler of that quality of laity?" Once we make the basic decision that we don't do ministry on behalf of the congregation but we equip them to do their ministry, then everything else falls into place. If, however, we think that we do ministry for people, and as professional clergy accomplish the work of the church, then our people are simply observers of the game we play as leaders.

I like to picture a big stadium with all the seats filled, and two teams seated on both sides of the field, with blankets, huddling in the cold. Then the coaches of both teams are running up and down the field, playing the game for everyone to see. That's the picture of the contemporary church: the clergy—highly trained and honed in their skills—doing ministry on behalf of the people rather than equipping them. Once you get an understanding that our task is equipping the saints for the work of ministry, then preaching with power becomes the task of inciting enthusiasm and excitement for ministry of the laity and the adventure of following Christ in the secular realm. Then you can reevaluate the nature of the church's program: is it accomplishing the task of putting the people into the world to accomplish that work?

Preaching: **As a pastor, what kind of preaching did you find best accomplished that purpose of equipping the congregation for ministry?**

Ogilvie: I think there's a great hunger in our time for biblically rooted, Christ-centered, Holy Spirit–empowered preaching. Great preaching comes from exposition. An understanding of the original languages is very important, so that the messenger has a message that arises out of a study of the text. Then the whole question is application to the contemporary scene—the explanation of the text, the illustration of the text, and the application of the text becomes the task of the pastor.

If you live in the text, eventually it will grip you to the place where it becomes like a banked fire, just waiting for the bellows of the Holy Spirit to be placed on it, to set it aflame to warm the minds and hearts of the people. If it happens to us, it then can happen through us, so the text must become very real to us.

Then I think we've got to have Richard Baxter's rule, "I preach as a dying man to dying men, as if never to preach again." So every sermon ought to be preached with vigor as if we will never have another chance. That kind of enthusiasm and passion is what is needed in the church in America today—and all over the world, for that matter. I call it preaching with passion, and that kind of preaching is an understanding, an appreciation, and an acceptance of the passion of Christ, the suffering of Christ for us, and then an identification with the suffering of human beings, so that we really feel what is going on inside of people. We want to bring the two together in an enthusiastic, heartfelt, but intellectually healthy presentation.

Preaching: **You talk about living with a text. I recall that as a pastor you would live with a text for more than a year before preaching it. Tell me about that process.**

Ogilvie: I would use a three-year process. I would spend a year with a portion of Scripture as a devotional exercise. If I was going to plan to preach from the book of James, I would use that book as my devotional literature for the first year. The next year I would do an in-depth expositional study and a reading of the great minds—to study the expositors, the great preachers through the ages.

In the actual year of the preaching, I would take the time in my study leave to outline the presentation for a whole period of time, a portion of the year, then prepare a manila folder for each Sunday of that series, then publish a preaching guide for that period of time. I would do forty-five Sundays a year in the parish, and I would come out of my study leave with forty-five outlines of sermons, forty-five manila folders, ready to receive the illustrative material that would go into each of them as I read, gathering illustrative materials from everyday life, and as I talked with people. Then, as I got to the week of actually preaching a sermon, there was the devotional year's resource, the intensive study scholarship, then the practical gathering of material. Then the actual writing of the sermon—it is very important that the writing of the sermon be fresh, not dependent on well-worn phrases and hackneyed language. After the sermon is written it takes about a day of memorization, repeating it until it becomes a part of the preacher, then preaching it with as few notes as possible.

Preaching: What was the nature of the preaching guide you published?

Ogilvie: There would be a single page for each week. I would list out the title, the text, and the development. I would actually write three clear, concise, distilled paragraphs explaining what it is that I wanted to do with that particular text. That would be sent to the director of music, and he would take that and prepare all of the music to fit with the particular theme of that Sunday. So from the beginning note of the prelude to the last note of the postlude, one central theme in all of the hymns, Scripture readings, responses—all would augment that one central theme.

Often I would add another page actually outlining the sermon as I envisioned it. Once I got to the week of the preaching of that sermon, the folder would be full of illustrative material that I had gathered through the year.

Preaching: Was most of your preaching in the form of series?

Ogilvie: Yes, I would take books of the Scripture for themes. The book of James I did a series on *Making Stress Work for You*. I did a series on the "He is able" statements of the epistles; that became the book *Lord of the Loose Ends*. Then I did one on the book of Acts that was entitled *The Bush Is Still Burning*. I did one on the "I am" statements of Christ.

Preaching: How long was a typical series for you?

Ogilvie: Usually three months, so I'd do three major series in a year. I found that that brought continuity and unity to the preaching. I tried to vary them so we would cover the whole of Scripture.

Preaching: I recall sitting in your congregation and marveling that you communicated so effectively with apparently no notes at all. Many preachers struggle with that.

Ogilvie: I learned that from James Stewart, my professor at New College [in Edinburgh]. His method was to outline clearly, then to memorize the outline as you worked with it, then to write the sermon from that outline. Then that outline would be clearly focused in your mind so that you could move through it without hesitation. So the outlining becomes very important.

Actually the church in Hollywood had a round balcony, and I would often picture the title of the separate sections of the sermon around the balcony, and I would picture them in my mind. I often used alliteration to help me remember the development of the text. All of those things would help me to retain eye contact. However I found that in lecturing or in giving long messages, we ought to be able to use notes unashamedly. But the sermon itself is a different article.

Preaching: And you spent a full day getting it into your memory?

Ogilvie: Yes, I would speak it aloud ten times, and then it would be in me and could be communicated without total dependence on notes.

Preaching: What's the most important thing you've learned about preaching over the years?

Ogilvie: Nothing can happen through you that hasn't happened to you. I feel a person's relationship with the living Lord is the most important aspect of preaching, and a growing relationship with the Lord is essential to powerful preaching. When we realize that we've been given the privilege of communicating the love, peace, power of the living Lord, then it's very important to maintain a growing relationship with the Lord so that we have something fresh to share with the people.

Preaching: Clearly James Stewart was a great influence in your life. In what way did he influence your ministry?

Ogilvie: He was a great expositor and loved the Scriptures. He was an intense preacher—he had hurricane force. I've written a great deal about him and given lectures on him. To me, he was the greatest preacher of the twentieth century. The chance to study with him meant a great deal to me. He was a good friend long after I finished my theological education. I would go back in the summers and renew our friendship.

We would often review what I was going to preach on in the coming year, and he would always have new insights. He was the most thorough scholar-preacher I have ever met.

Preaching: If you were starting over, is there anything you'd do differently as a preacher?

Ogilvie: I came to the commitment of a schedule that allowed for intensive study each week later in my ministry. I would start earlier allowing for two full days for study and preparation of the sermon. The commitment of one hour in the study for each minute in the pulpit is one I would apply sooner in my ministry. I think the temptation when you are starting in ministry is to say, "When I move to a larger church I'll really concentrate on study." I think you move to the larger church because you *have* concentrated on study. So the commitment of time to study and prepare is to me the most important aspect.

Then the pastor's own prayer life and commitment to an honest and growing relationship with the Lord and his accountability to a small group is very important. I would meet with a group of elders every Sunday prior to preaching, and usually one was elected to say, "Are you ready to preach? Is there anything we can pray for?"

The renewal of the church will rise or fall on the quality of its preaching, and I think it will depend on preachers who make preaching the central priority in their allocation of time and energy. To do that we will need an understanding of the officers of the church and the membership—to allow their pastor to take the time to be ready to preach is absolutely essential.

It's been a great adventure. It still is.

Expository Preaching in a Narrative World

An Interview with Haddon Robinson

Haddon Robinson is one of the most influential persons in the homiletical world. The author of the immensely popular textbook *Biblical Preaching*, he has influenced thousands of evangelical preachers through his writing and through his former students who now teach homiletics. A former professor of homiletics at Dallas Seminary and former president of Denver Seminary, in 1991 he became the Harold John Ockenga Distinguished Professor of Preaching at Gordon-Conwell Theological Seminary and is also codirector of the Doctor of Ministry program at Gordon-Conwell. Robinson was named one of the twelve most effective preachers in the English-speaking world in a 1996 Baylor University poll. He is one of the hosts for *Discover the Word* (formerly *Radio Bible Class*), a daily radio program of RBC Ministries in Grand Rapids, Michigan, which is broadcast six hundred times a day on stations around the world. He is a senior consulting editor of *Preaching* magazine. This interview appeared in the July-August 2001 issue.

Preaching: One could say that through your book *Biblical Preaching*, you literally wrote the book on expository preaching. It has been such a pivotal book in shaping our understanding of expository preaching in so many of today's churches. Since you first wrote that book, how have your views on expository preaching changed?

Robinson: I have just finished revamping the book for the new edition. My basic understanding of expository preaching has stayed the same. I think within the book itself I've spent more time talking about narrative—narrative literature, narrative preaching.

I've come clearer to seeing that when you talk about expository preaching, you're not primarily talking about the form of the sermon. You are really talking about a philosophy. Do you bend your thought to the text, or do you bend the text to fit your thought? How a person in all honesty answers that would say a lot about whether or not that person really is an expository preacher.

Another thing that has come into better focus is the reason for expository preaching—that is, laying before people the biblical text is for the authority it gives. In looking at the sermons of the past, I think it would be accurate to say that even for those who were orthodox, the authority for the sermon rested in the preacher. When Spurgeon and men of that sort preached, the people in the congregation believed that he had studied the text—that he was orthodox—therefore he could be trusted. So when you examine their sermons, you don't find in most of those sermons anything that I would look at and say that is clearly an expository sermon—it opens up the biblical passage, it's formed according to the lines of the passage, and it has the purpose of the passage in view. They are in a sense topical, but they are orthodox. You'd have a hard time in most of them just from listening, reading through the sermons, saying, "I understand the biblical text that is behind it."

So if you ask, "Why is expository preaching more important today?" it is that we don't have the authority that preachers had in the past. The truth is that—aside from people that have grown up in the church—the average person in our society does not give high grades to preachers as being intellectual or even moral leaders. Twenty years ago it would have been almost impossible to bring a case to court against a minister. Today a lawyer that's defending a minister will do everything that he can to keep the people in the jury from thinking of him as a minister. So we have lost a lot of the base, for a lot of different reasons. What we are really trying to say is, "OK, if I can get people to study the Bible and to see the text, I believe that the Bible is self-authenticating." If I can get you to really read it, to look at it, to hear it, to understand it, it has its own power to convince and to convict and to change people.

Therefore in a postmodern age one reason that we work with the biblical text is to have the authority of the text—and behind that the authority of God—behind what we say. I've always believed that, but it has become clearer to me now than it has been in the past. That is not to say that the person in the pew has to accept my view of inspiration. It is simply to say that if the Bible is what I believe it to be—the Word of God—and that the Spirit of God answers to the Word, then if I can lay that out before them in a relevant fashion, it has the power to do what my authority today can't do.

Preaching: You mentioned that expository preaching is less a form than a philosophy. Does form still play a role, and how important is that in terms of the nature of the sermon?

Robinson: I think form is important. The question is, "Where does it come from?" One answer is that the form of the sermon, it seems to me, needs to reflect the form of the text. By that I mean if I am working with a parable of Jesus, it is not the form of the parable to say, "There are three lessons about God's mercy that we learn from this story." If God had wanted to give us three lessons, he was perfectly capable, and the biblical writer was perfectly capable, of saying there are three lessons. So I had to say to myself, "Why, when God wanted to tell me about the seeking love of God—say in Luke 15, the prodigal son—why in the world did he use this story?" When the religious scholar says to Jesus, "Who is my neighbor?" in Luke 10, Jesus tells them a story.

It seems to me that if you and I were talking, and you said to me, "Who is your neighbor?" And I said, "Well, once upon a time there was a guy going from Boston down to Providence, and he got into a wreck on the highway." You'd say to me, "Wait a minute, what is this telling me a story? I asked you a straight question, 'Who is my neighbor?' I wanted a definition." But Jesus doesn't do that. So if in my sermon I suddenly come up with a didactic definition, then the form of the sermon is not the form of the passage.

I think that you could make a good argument that not only should the sermon reflect the idea of a biblical text but it should be influenced by the form. So if you are dealing with narrative literature in the Old Testament, then there ought to be about the sermon some element of story. Or if you are dealing with a psalm—the psalm isn't given to teach us things as much as it is to direct people how to worship. So I have to wrestle with that literature, not only in what the psalm is conveying but how I can have a poetic element about my preaching. That is out of the philosophy that when God communicates his truth he chooses certain forms and therefore my sermon needs to reflect that.

Preaching: As pastors deal with these narrative passages of Scripture, how would you suggest they approach them for preaching? They want to be faithful to the text, they want to be expository, and yet they want to be faithful to the narrative shape of the passage. How do you suggest they deal with such passages?

Robinson: There is a small body of literature in how to interpret the biblical narrative. Robert Alter has a book on the art of biblical narrative. He emphasizes that when you study a biblical text you need to study it in its context—not just this story but the stories before and after—and ask the question, "Why did the biblical writer put this in here?" You also have to recognize that the biblical writers give us very little description. You have this long section in the Bible about David and about Moses, but we don't know what they looked like. The writers just don't seem to tell us. They put some emphasis on action, the most emphasis on dialogue. So looking at ways of coming at narrative, I am trying to find out what the idea of this is—that is, what is the biblical writer telling this for?

I think it is a help to people to understand that behind the biblical narratives there is theology. There's a tendency to think that God gave us those stories so that we would have something to tell our kids before they went to bed. But the stories are a way of telling us about God. So as we look at the story and see it in its context and then its broader context, I have to ask, "How does this writer through the dialogue, through the action of these characters, get across his idea?" Think about any stories. One of the things you have in any good story is detail. Detail helps to make things visual, so that if I tell you about the ghetto of New York where I grew up, I can describe it: the smell of urine in the halls, the look of the garbage in the street, glass on the sidewalks. Good stories have detail. But if you have only detail without a principle, the whole thing falls flat.

So I read the details of the story in terms of its dialogue, its action, but I also have to find the principle. If I don't find the principle, I just sort of recite the story. Two dangers: One is it will fall flat. The second danger is I can make the biblical narrative say what I think I want it to say rather than to look at the narrative and say, "What is the narrator trying to get across?" There is more and more literature now on narrative. Really the whole thing started basically thirty years ago. You don't have much literature on narrative in the past, and I think it's because we live in a story culture and we suddenly recognize how much of the Bible is a story.

Preaching: There is a lot of literature on interpreting narrative. One of the frustrations pastors face is that we may know how to approach and study a narrative passage but not how to turn around and put it into a homiletical form. How do you make the transition from interpreting the narrative passage to preaching the passage in a narrative form?

Robinson: Yeah, it is a struggle. One advantage we have today is that a modern audience doesn't know those stories. I was chatting with a young woman two weeks ago who is a graduate of a major university. She has recently come into the faith. In the course of the conversation I said something about 1 Corinthians 13, and she stopped me and said,

"What is 1 Corinthians 13?" I said that it's a chapter in the Bible about love, and she said, "Is that the New Testament or the Old Testament?" I suddenly realized this lady hasn't got a ghost of a notion about those stories! I think that today one of the things that we can do is simply to tell a narrative—tell it in an effective fashion, help people to reexperience it. That is one reason for a minister to read novels, to be aware how storytellers craft their stories in order to get across not just the story but some ideas behind it.

In the past—at least when I was in seminary—the great emphasis was on the left brain. You know, analyzing. I am convinced that you don't really interpret the Bible unless you also use your imagination, especially with narrative literature. You have got to enter into that—not by cold analysis, but you have got to say, "Can I put myself back into those days, can I relive what David was feeling when he escaped from Saul?" If I can do that, then I can tell the story in a vivid way. In fact one way you can do a narrative is the first person narrative. My son, Torrey, is writing his thesis for a D.Min. degree on how to study for and to preach first person narratives. There you have to get into the mind of the character. A lot of the story preaching is not biblical; it's interesting but not very biblical—that's its great danger. But you can take that story from the point of view of one of the characters and tell it. You don't have to be a great actor. It's amazing how interesting it is for people to hear somebody who as a character relives that story. In our day it can make a great impact.

Preaching: You use the term "experience." To what extent does preaching need to be experiential versus intellectual?

Robinson: I don't think you really understand truth unless you can experience it. I think truth in the Bible is never like mathematical theory—something that you can put up on a blackboard and analyze. I think that truth in the Bible always intersects life. Therefore while I have to think in order to understand, I also have to experience in order for that truth to really make a difference. I'm not saying that I have got to move people's emotions by some tricks, but I am convinced that the Bible is never given in order to simply satisfy our curiosity.

I think that it can be a great satisfaction in having a curiosity met. I think that there are people who enjoy Bible study the same way that other people enjoy filling out crossword puzzles. Get all the parts and get the thing completed—they find satisfaction. I think there are people that study the Bible that way. They can see how it relates to its context and how its details work to get across the concept. But if it never gets into your life, if it never really touches your experience, I doubt seriously that you can call it a study of biblical truth, because I think God's truth is always designed to challenge us and change us.

Preaching: One of the critical issues so important to preaching is the whole area of applying biblical truth. How do we better make that transition from the context of the biblical world into "What does this mean for me on Tuesday morning?"

Robinson: It's a perceptive question. In fact if I have a serious book left in me, it would be on application. I think in many of our circles, more evangelical circles perhaps but liberal as well, the great heresies are not primarily in the doctrine—though they can be there—but in the application. By that I mean, I can study a text and I can understand what the text means, as a preacher. Thus if I really understand what this text means, I can preach that idea, that abstraction from the text, with the authority that says, "Thus saith the Lord." But the big question is, "When I apply it in a specific way, can I have the authority of the Scriptures behind the application?"

If it's a *necessary* implication—that is, if as Paul would say in 1 Corinthians 9, "There is one God," it's a necessary implication. There can't be five Gods. So if A is true, B must be true. But there aren't *that* many necessary implications. The next level would be a *probable* implication—it's important, but it doesn't quite have the "Thus saith the Lord." Others are a *possible* implication, I guess *improbable*, and finally an *impossible* implication. But how you take a truth from the ancient world in a different context from ours and bring it over with the authority of Scripture, I think is the thing we battle with. But on the other hand, you have to apply the text and you have to do it, I think, in specific ways, for people to get it and to put it into their lives.

There's a danger of legalism here. You can have an abstract concept, a concept that says, "You shall honor your father and mother"—it's clear that's what you're supposed to do. Then I apply it: it has to do with my aging parents. And I can tell you a story out of my own life, when my father came to live with us the last years of his life in Dallas. He lost touch with reality, and we had to put him in the nursing home. It cost me half of my salary, and I went to visit him every day, hated to put him in there because he didn't like to be there. When my wife's mother came to the end of her life, we kept her in our home and my wife took care of her. In both cases I was trying to honor my parents. Different situation—the kids were gone when Bonnie's mother was ill. But it is very easy to come to the conclusion that if you are going to honor your parents, then you must keep them in your home when they get old. Then what happens is that *that* application has all the force of the principle. But you can honor your parents in a number of different ways because of different situations. So I see legalism as the application of a principle and the application has all the force of the principle and it doesn't deserve it. So there is a theological danger in the way that we apply.

There has got to be some thought given so that what I am saying to the people today accurately reflects the dynamic of its original situation as well as the concept that comes out of it. That takes more thought than most of us have given it in the past. I think often therefore we fill people with guilt because they don't do what we say this text says we *could* do; we really say the text says this is what you *must* do. If you put a "Thus saith the Lord" by it, you have all kinds of power over people who take God seriously.

On another level just on application, I think it is a good thing for a pastor to make a grid of his congregation. Make the grid any way that you want it, but on the one side put down different age groupings in your church—the boomers, the busters, the millennials. Then come across the other side and have single living with parents, married with no children, married, and divorced. You can have a number of those grids. Then look at those grids and say, "If what I am saying today is God's truth, and I believe it is, how would it apply to a young person who is eighteen, living at home single? Does it have anything to say to the young woman who is out in the business world of living with a roommate?" If I have that grid, and when I look at those boxes, things will come to mind and I will say, "Yeah, if that person was sitting in my office and they said to me, "How do you cope with a difficult roommate," or "How do you handle frustration of having a boss that is always on your back?" Does this text have anything to say to that person? Sometimes you say yes it does. So it enables you to think of your audience—to take them more seriously because you can see individuals or groups of individuals more clearly.

Preaching: It seems like this area of application may be one of the greatest places where you need some sanctified imagination, mixed with a large dose of humility.

Robinson: That is the great advantage that a pastor has over someone like myself at a seminary. I am sometimes asked, "Who are the great preachers of our day?" and my wife says, "It is one less than you think." I really do believe the great preachers are pastors of congregations at Sixth and Main of some town who know their people. He takes the biblical text and relates it to those people's lives because he knows them and knows them well. So the pastoral side of ministry fuses relevant preaching that applies to life. In fact, often the big problem that kind of preacher has is he knows the people so well that if he applies this, Aunt

Milly in the church will be absolutely sure he is talking about her. But someone said that the mark of a great sermon is that the person in the pew wonders "how in the world the pastor knew that about me." So you learn a lot just by living among people and being perceptive. That is a great advantage when it comes to applying the truth.

Preaching: What are some of the best things that are happening in preaching today?

Robinson: I think a move away from preaching as lecture to preaching as extended conversation—a move where the preacher is talking *with* the congregation rather than *at* the congregation. I think that's healthy. It means that the preacher—though he or she is doing a monologue—isn't monological because you've thought about these people you're talking to.

I think a second thing that's going on in preaching is that there is more self-revelation. We don't, I hope, preach our experiences, but we have to experience what we preach, or at least see how this truth intersects with our lives. It doesn't necessarily mean at all that I have a catharsis experience with the congregation to talk about my deepest strivings. But there is in the audience today—especially the younger audiences—a desire to know who you are personally. In fact I'd put it the other way: I don't think you can connect with audiences under fifty unless they relate to you. I don't think today you can listen to an effective preacher six weeks and not know quite a bit about him. I think in the past—in my growing up years—you could listen to somebody for six years and not necessarily know anything about him. I think it's healthy, provided the preacher does not use himself as the best example or even the worst example. I want to sense that he or she has struggled with life. I also want to believe that they have won some victories. I'm not very impressed with a preacher that stands up and basically says, "I am a loser in this area. I can't tell you any more than I know myself." I don't want to listen to a loser. I want to listen to somebody that has struggled but has found a way through this struggle to find some equilibrium in life.

I think a third positive trend is preachers are more conscious of the need for story in their sermon. I don't mean anecdotes but this sense that a good sermon can be like a story. In the past I would go to my study and I would come out and I would deliver to the people what the results of my study would be. Today, there is a greater tendency to let the congregation in on your study. So it leads to induction rather than deduction, which is another trend. You sort of take the listener along on the journey with you. I think there is more of that being done, and I think it is a good trend because I think we live inductively. We have experiences, and out of the experiences we draw conclusions. Only in lectures in seminary and college or some pulpits do you get some sort of deductive arrangement where you state a proposition and then explain or prove it or apply it. That is a trend.

Certainly I see a greater emphasis of women in ministry today—in denominations ordaining women. Even in the denominations that don't ordain women, many of them really have come to appreciate the great contribution a woman can make as she studies the Scriptures. I am convinced that a woman reads the Bible differently from a man. Women as a group tend to be much more relational and ask relational questions. I think that more and more people recognize the contribution that women make and can make and genuinely appreciate what they do. Twenty years ago that was not the case.

Preaching: Over the next ten to twenty years what do you think are going to be some of the greatest challenges preachers will face?

Robinson: We are in a much more secular culture. In fact it's not just the post-Christian culture; it's almost a pre-Christian culture. When Paul went into a community, he had the advantage of going into a synagogue and teaching and preaching to reach some people, and then he went into the marketplace. I think that we are going to find ourselves—if we're serious about our business—just in the marketplace. That is good, and it is also difficult. I think we are going to find it much more difficult to proclaim the central doctrines of the Christian faith. To preach the uniqueness of Jesus Christ in a multifaceted culture in which you insist Jesus Christ is the only way to God—the response of people sitting in front of you is that you are a bigot. It's an emotional response. So people are willing to say yes to Jesus certainly, even to say he is the Savior. But the number of people in our churches who would say that he is the only Savior, the only way to God, is less and less.

I think it is going to be much more difficult for people who have been raised in a religious tradition to speak effectively to the secular culture. I think many of the things that church people—and I mean this in a positive sense of what church people like myself do—we often use the jargon of the faith without realizing we are using it. If you've grown up in certain traditions where you think that preaching is yelling—you try to face a secular audience today and yell at them, and you've lost them. The things that you sort of took by osmosis growing up will be less and less effective. I think the great challenge that we are going to face is not just how to preach to these people, but how do we reach them in order to preach to them? How do you get them inside the church; how do you get them to sit and to listen? I think we are going to see a declining church enrollment. We are seeing it now, but I think it is going to get worse.

I think we are also going to find that when we take a stand on moral issues we will do it at a cost. If you're pro-life, you are going to find more and more people in this culture who look at that position as deviant. The series of ads that are being run by the National Organization of Women put a great emphasis on the right to choose as a fundamental right, the freedom to choose. They are warm, and they are glowing. But they don't ask the next question: freedom to choose what? Since it is an abortion, it's freedom to choose to kill a fetus that a woman carries. They don't spell that out, but they are winning. At the confirmation hearings for members of Mr. Bush's cabinet, you heard the harshness of the rhetoric, the sense that you cannot possibly have somebody who is sincerely pro-life in that position. Conversely, that a person commits adultery—it seems to people today, well so what? What you do in the privacy of your bedroom, whose business is it? So you start to preach the Ten Commandments, and you discover people have already made up their minds that probably three of the ten don't apply anymore. So I think that we are going to find in the years to come we are going to have a whole strategy in the best sense how we get to that secular culture. I don't have the answer to it at all, but I worry about it a lot.

I sit in an airport and I watch these people come by, and if I could stand up on this bench and preach to them and tell them about Jesus Christ, I would do it. I know if I stood on this bench and preached to them, they would take me out and put me in jail. How do you reach them—these people, these different secular people who see the church and thus God as an enemy?

Preaching: Are there any pastors out there right now in churches that you observe reaching that kind of audience?

Robinson: I think you have the elements in many of the churches like Willow Creek—they have done well to attract a certain level of non-Christians. Very few of us in our churches reach beyond the circle. There aren't that many churches reaching the Muslims, the Hindus in our culture. I think there are African-American congregations that seem to be making inroads and are doing it with a faithfulness to the gospel and to its preaching. I think of someone like Tony Evans in Dallas in a large, thriving church in which they don't hedge. The pastor of the largest Methodist church in Houston, Kirbyjon Caldwell, is an evangelical and seems to be doing a better job in reaching the African-American community than we are reaching the Caucasian. But there are a number of thriving churches. Rick Warren has a significant number of people in his congregation who are new to the faith. He is in tune with southern California. It is just what they are doing today. Ten years from now, if they still have the goal of reaching the non-churched person, a lot is going to change then.

It is always easy—relatively easy—to reach people provided you don't cross them. So there are churches that are growing that would call themselves evangelical, but there are things that they would not preach because they have said that if they preach that, people won't come back. It has been years, years since I have heard a sermon on hell. Because in this culture how do you preach this today, if you are trying to reach out to people? They can't imagine it.

Preaching: **A few issues ago we had an interview with Adrian Rogers, and he made reference to that issue. Knowing he is very conservative, people think he would preach frequently on hell, but he doesn't often because it does not make for an effective evangelistic sermon. People do not respond.**

Robinson. Several years ago, I went through the Gospels, and just out of curiosity, I went through the Gospel of Matthew and the Gospel of Luke. I put a line next to passages. I put an "S" where soft passage was, "H" for hard passage, and "I" for in-between. You come to the end of that, there are far more hard passages than you are going to have soft passages. Jesus said things that got him crucified. It is that kind of faithfulness, the desire to be faithful to that—I can't really with integrity pick and choose in the Gospel of Luke or Matthew only passages where I think I'll have a soft landing with my audience. On the other hand, it is a reality that if I preach this, clearly there are going to be people that are going to respond to me—and thus to the gospel—as though this can't be Christian because Christianity is always love and grace. The term "bigot" is thrown around.

There is a lot in the Bible that is just not politically correct. And people who are schooled in being politically correct in our universities, in society—there are certain things that you say that turn them off. Because fundamental to their thinking is that political correctness somehow came down from the mountain along with Moses. That's why it's so hard to preach the biblical text to the outsider. Within the construct of faith, believers will be more patient with you. You can preach it, but I am also convinced that the person in the eighth row, four seats in, who's been a Christian fifteen years, will often sort through what biblical truth they will accept. They don't accept everything I say—that speaks to their credit—but there is also biblical truth they won't accept because it's just tough truth.

Preaching: You're in a setting where you are training the next generation of preachers. Are there particular things you try to do with these future preachers to get them ready for the task they face?

Robinson: Teaching seminary students to preach resembles teaching people to swim who have never been near water! So you have a lecture or two on "That's water." We have a large number of students here—which I think is true of most seminaries—who have not been to church that much. They became Christians in college, and so this whole thing is new. Or we have people who have grown up in the church but have no experience with people in the marketplace and therefore really do not know people. They may know the Bible but do not know people. These other people know people but know less of the Bible.

The tendency going through seminary is to believe that if you took your exegesis notes from a New Testament class into the pulpit and read them to people, there would be a great stirring of God. So sometimes the sermons you get are pedantic; probably true to the text but not true to people, to life. Perhaps you could say that people who have been out for four, five, or six years may have more difficulty being true to the text because they face people every Sunday and they're much more aware of life. But that's what you struggle with in teaching preaching.

I find that it really doesn't help just to teach a method. In fact, I sometimes say to our students, "It would be helpful if you never thought about preaching a sermon in your life." Because a sermon brings a certain form. The first thing after I study this text is to understand it. And then, having understood it, have a whole second phase in which you have to ask, "What is the best way to communicate this to my congregation?" And any form that will take the biblical text and be honest and true to it, and communicate it to a modern audience, I think is legitimate, provided the audience will accept it. There are certain forms I might think about, but I know the people in the First Episcobapterian Church will flinch. They wouldn't accept it. But if it will get it across in an effective way and touch people's lives, then that's where—in the best sense—you can use your creativity to communicate.

Preaching: Those young preachers are going to have some very different cultural challenges in the next few years.

Robinson: Sometimes when I'm thinking about preaching I think I've gotten hold of the hem of the garment, but I can't always sustain the grasp. That's because audiences change. What was effective twenty years ago is just not effective today. Preaching to an older audience, the builders—they grew up learning to listen. You can have a sustained argument with them. The younger audiences, they don't follow it. It's not their way of getting information.

We do less and less reading. Often when you ask a pastor, "What do you have to do to develop as a Christian?" one of the first things he'll say is "Well, you have to study the Bible." But the Bible is a tough read. The generation that I grew up in really valued reading, and I think the past is valued. But I think that today a person who wants to be an effective communicator has to have an awareness of visual media—movies, what goes on in television, because that's the way people get their information. The average person spends about two hundred hours a year reading the newspaper, about two hundred hours a year looking at magazines, thirteen hundred hours a year watching TV. When people are asked what is their major source of news they say "television." Fifty-five percent say it's their only source of news. So they're being shaped by a media that is visual, that tells stories, and yet for people at seminary, we get our information by reading.

That really is the world as it is. I think it would be helpful if we could take time in theological education to study how movies and television convey ideas that actually do shape us—moral values, theological values. We watch television, watch soap operas, watch the evening drama. People get murdered, robbed, raped, they never pray. They never seek out a preacher, priest, or rabbi. We live in a world in which God doesn't exist. And then folks come to church an hour, two hours a week, and you try to say to them, "God is central to your life." You're preaching within a context in which people very effectively are getting the idea that you don't call in God; fix it yourself. So it seems to me that a pastor has to have an awareness, not only of what's going on out there in terms of what the messages are, but how that message is shaped by media. I don't think we're that skilled in media, and I'm not talking about using clips of films, though that's fine. I'm really just talking about a whole awareness of how these people sitting out there are shaped and molded by a philosophy that is neutral to God or often very hostile.

It's tough to stay culturally aware, because you live—as a preacher—within a culture that's religious. And the people around you—on your board, that you work with, near voices—support what you are and what you're saying generally. It's hard to get to the distant voices and hear them. You can hear the distant voices and preach to them, but they're not my congregation on Sunday. So I have to make my people, who are committed to Christ, aware of what is going on out there.

Preaching and Church Growth

An Interview with Adrian Rogers

For more than a quarter century, Adrian Rogers was pastor of the historic Bellevue Baptist Church in Memphis, Tennessee. A church that had become a major force in the Southern Baptist Convention, the congregation had been in decline for two decades before Rogers's arrival. Today it is one of the largest churches in the nation, and Rogers is heard daily on radio and television around the world through his Love Worth Finding ministry. He retired as senior pastor of Bellevue in March 2005 and died in November 2005. This interview was published in the May-June 2000 issue of *Preaching*.

Preaching: Obviously God has blessed this church in an incredible way. It was a great church when you came here, but what an amazing growth it has had in reaching thousands of people. What do you see as the place of preaching in the process of growing a great church?

Rogers: I think it is central, and not because I happen to be the preacher. I believe that the message, preaching, is the stackpole around which everything else is built. My psychology is always if I develop the message, God develops the ministry. All that we see here, all that has happened here, I think is a response to a message. I'm not necessarily talking about homiletical structure or oratory, but truth and conviction. I believe that your zeal is never any greater than your conviction over a long period of time. I think that conviction comes out of truth and that the pastor and the pulpit articulate that truth.

Preaching: You've been here now twenty-seven years. Has your preaching changed?

Rogers: Hopefully it has gotten better! I look back at some of my sermons that I preached prior to coming here and some in my early days here. The structure was simpler. That may have been better as I analyze it, but the structure was simpler. I think my messages today are a little more packed with illustrations and information than they were in the earlier days.

Somebody asked me the other day if preaching has gotten easier through the years. If anything, it is a little harder because I take sermon preparation a little more seriously. I have not changed in doctrine I build upon my basic theological presuppositions and underpinnings, but I have not changed in doctrine since I began preaching as a nineteen-year-old boy. I have strengthened some beliefs, understood some things. But there have been no radical changes or paradigm shifts, so I have been on a steady continuum there.

I really have not changed the style of preaching much. I hope that my preaching has been enriched but not necessarily changed. I am a propositional preacher, and I preach a pretty structured message. I use an old-fashioned alliterative form a lot. That is the way I started preaching, and I don't think I'll change in these days. But I have not changed structure that much from the old thing of having a proposition to begin with—I may not state the proposition in the beginning of the message, but I may. I have a proposition, I take a passage of Scripture, analyze it, organize it, illustrate it, apply it, and preach it, driving toward a conclusion that implies a decision. I have done it for so long I wouldn't know how to do anything else.

Preaching: One of the things that characterizes your preaching is it is focused on decision, on response. How do you see the interplay or relationship of preaching with evangelism, with reaching people?

Rogers: Well, I think that everything I do is evangelism. I don't think there is any preaching that is not evangelism. I don't think there is anything that I do—if I am walking in the Spirit—that is not evangelism. So many times people have the idea that evangelism is getting lost people saved. In a large sense it is. But if you took the worst sinner that ever lived and put him on one side of a continuum, and the best saint that ever lived and put him on the other side, you and I and everybody else that we meet would be in between those two bookends. If we drew a line right in the center between the very worst and the very best and call that point salvation, when that man leaves the realm of darkness and steps over into the realm of light, just before he steps over that line, he is an almost Christian. When he steps over that line he is a baby Christian.

Now go to the far negative side where he is steeped in sin and God hating, the worst sinner that ever lived. If I meet a man there, I want to move him up that line just a little bit toward that center line. If I can move him a millimeter, fine; if I can move him a mile, fine. But I want to move him towards coming to know Jesus Christ. Someone, myself or someone else, may bring him over that line into the kingdom by the grace of God. At that moment I still want to keep moving him because he is an unfinished product. Now I am moving him toward that ultimate sainthood.

So everything is evangelism—every person that I meet I'm just moving up that line if I am doing it correctly, whether he be saved or lost. I may be the one who brings him across that line, or somebody else may. But even after he crosses that line and I am helping him to be a better Christian, that is also evangelism because I am teaching him to go back and move somebody else up that line.

So all preaching is evangelistic preaching if it's good preaching. If it is not evangelistic, there is something desperately, inherently wrong with it. So it is not just preaching hell hot, heaven sweet, sin black, judgment sure, Jesus saves. If I have a saint and I am making him a better saint, that is evangelism because he becomes an evangelizer; I am teaching him to observe all things whatsoever Jesus commanded, which is evangelism. Yes, I am preaching for a decision, but I am not always preaching for a conversion in the immediate sense.

As a matter of fact, probably nothing will ultimately kill a church more than raw evangelistic preaching in the classic sense, Sunday after Sunday, because you get shallow saints. Your preaching is predictable, the saints get tired of it, and the sinners won't come. So that is not the way to grow a church!

The way to grow a church is to grow Christians. That is not to say that a wise preacher should not, whatever he does, at the close of his message give an invitation for people to come to Christ. I believe in calling for a decision. If I preach on tithing, I would say at the end of the message, "When I am talking about tithing and God blessing stewardship, I am talking to a child of God. If you are not a child of God, that is where you need to start today, by giving your heart to Christ." And I will transition right into an invitation. If I am preaching on heaven to the saints, I say at the close, "In order to go to heaven, you've got to give your heart to Christ."

There is no competition there. I think every message ultimately ought to have an evangelistic appeal—but the evangelistic appeal is only part of it. The message ought to have another purpose, whatever it is: if I preach on tithing, the purpose is to get people to tithe. If I am preaching on prayer, it is to get them to pray. If I am preaching on faith, it is to get them to have faith. If I am preaching on love, I want them to love. I am not just filling a bucket, I am lighting a torch. I am trying to get them to do something, whatever it is.

That is the difference, in my mind, between preaching and teaching. In teaching you may be disseminating truth. In preaching you are moving hearts. You have got to have truth in it, but you are moving hearts. So yes, my preaching is decisional. Yes, it is evangelistic in a broad sense, though not just in preaching how to be saved in every service. But in every service, somewhere, somehow, sometime, I am going to tell people how to be saved.

Almost in every service somewhere, you are going to bring the gospel in. I have found out that a lot of people who call themselves gospel preachers are not gospel preachers. They believe and preach about the love of God and stand up and say, "Come to Christ." But that is not the gospel. The gospel is that Christ died for our sins, that he was buried and rose again. And when I lead people, for example, at the close of the service in a prayer, I say, "If you want to be saved, pray this prayer if you can: 'God, I know that you love me and that you want to save me. I confess that I am a sinner and my sin deserves judgment and I need to be saved. You promised to save me. Jesus, you died to save me and promised to save me if I would trust you. I do trust you. I believe you are the Son of God. I believe that you paid for my sin with your blood on the cross. I believe that God raised you from the dead, and I now, by faith, receive you as my Lord and Savior once and for all, now and forever. Come into my heart, forgive my sin, and save me.'" So if nothing else, I have given the gospel as the death, burial, and resurrection of Jesus Christ. I didn't just preach a sermon and then say, "Come to Jesus."

I think that has a very strong evangelistic appeal also. If you and I and ten other people are sitting around a table, and the table is loaded and groaning with food, and we are not eating that food—we are just sitting there singing songs—and a stranger comes into the door, and we say, "Come on in friend, sit down and eat. You need this food, it is good, it is wonderful. This is what you need." If none around that table is eating, he is going to say, "There is something strange here." But if we are sitting there feasting, and we say, "Come and sit down and join us," that is inviting to him. I think that God's people ought to be feasting on the Word every Sunday and then say to the man that comes in, "Hey, come on and join us," rather than saying, "Hey, we are all here to tell you that you need something though we are not enjoying it ourselves."

Preaching: **When you were called as pastor of Bellevue, you came to a church that had a tradition of outstanding preaching. Certainly, R. G. Lee was one of the best-known preachers in America in his day. As pastor of such a church, how did you handle that sense of tradition?**

Rogers: This is a wonderful church. When I came I was handed this legacy. I had a group of people (A) who love one another; (B) who believe the Bible is the Word of God; (C) who believe that the pastor is God's appointed and anointed leader. What more could a man ask? Now, Bellevue had been in decline for twenty years. From 1952 to 1972, every year attendance had been less than the prior year, for twenty straight years. It had gone from an average attendance in Sunday School of twenty-seven hundred in 1952—which was the apex, the highest year—down to less than thirteen hundred in Sunday school in 1972. So they were ready for God to do something.

The town, the demographics of the city, had changed. The building was run down. Parking was woefully inadequate. But that was not altogether bad from the perspective of building and growing a church. These people just welcomed me from day one with open arms.

God gave me the hearts of the people. They didn't love me for who I was; they did not know me. I was the recipient of God's grace. They loved me and accepted me, and I never tried to be Dr. Lee. Nobody could or should. Number one, his preaching was for a different day. He was an orator. Oratory is not the order of the day. People say, "How are you going to fill his shoes?" I said I'm not trying to fill his shoes; I am going to stand on his shoulders and thank God for the legacy. But he preached differently than I do. And Dr. [Ramsey] Pollard, who was my immediate predecessor, preached differently. Pollard was more of a topical preacher, and Dr. Lee was more of an orator. I am kind of a teacher-preacher doing more exposition.

Preaching: **Your life had intersected with Dr. Lee's prior to coming to Bellevue.**

Rogers: Yes, he was a great friend, and I did his funeral. He had a warm sense of humor, a great heart of love. One time I said to him when he was ill, "Dr. Lee, before you go to heaven, couldn't we take your brain and put it into my head?" He said, "My boy, that would be like putting a grand piano in a closet." He had a twinkle in his eyes, but I'm not sure if he was serious or not! He was a great man, and I loved Dr. Lee. I did both his and Dr. Pollard's funerals. They were both members of this church at the same time. I had a warm relationship with both of them. They were both supporters and prayer warriors.

Preaching: You tend to preach in series most of the time. How do you go about the process of planning your preaching calendar?

Rogers: Not as well as I ought. A lot of my preaching is reactionary as I see a need out in the congregation. For example, I am doing a little four Sunday series on building the body. Last Sunday, I preached on everybody is somebody in his [God's] body—finding the right place in his body. This Sunday, I am going to talk about unwrapping your spiritual gift and finding out what your part in the body is. Next Sunday I am going to speak on loyalty to the body—not forsaking the assembling of ourselves together. The next Sunday, I'm going to speak on spiritual maturity, how to grow up, to learn how to develop your spiritual gifts.

Sometimes I will just fall in love with a book in the Bible that I am reading, and I will say, "Man, this is good stuff. I believe I am going to preach through this." And for no reason at all except that I just enjoy this book of the Bible, it's blessed me, and I want to bless the people.

Preaching: How much of your preaching would you say is in book series?

Rogers: Probably 50 percent. Fifty percent would be book series, 25 percent would be biblical but topical series—a biblical approach to a topic like stewardship, or something like that. Then maybe 25 percent would be a potpourri—stand-alone sermons, no series at all. I don't have a real scientific way of planning preaching here. I just don't; I am not confident that I have enough of whatever it takes to project that far out in the future as to the needs of the people. I want to be able to react more quickly to the tenor of the times.

For example just before the new year [2000], I preached a series on eternity, because everybody was thinking about eternity with Y2K. I preached a series "On the Edge of Eternity." We are always living on the edge of eternity. It is not like eternity is out there like the Grand Canyon, a thousand miles from here and we are heading toward it. No, we are already there, walking along the edge. It's always the last days. From the time of the apostles we are on the edge of eternity—not that some event has to happen. So I preached a series, and it was biblical, but it was not just taken from one book of the Bible.

Preaching: How far out would you typically say that you know the direction of a series?

Rogers: That meanders until I get locked in! Recently I decided to start preaching through Romans—only God knows how far out I am to getting finished! As to when I might start the book of Romans, that all depends. I already know, for example, that I am going to do this series on building the body; then I know that we are going to do three Sundays on world missions.

Then, contrary to my former statement about preaching raw evangelism, I have decided to preach seven sermons in a row on Sunday on pure, raw, "Come to Jesus" evangelism. I'm calling it the Seven Salvation Sundays. I'm going to preach the themes that I have found through the years that reap more than other themes. And there are themes that reap more than others.

For example, hell is not a good evangelistic subject. I preach on hell; I think we ought to preach on hell more than we do because that is almost a forgotten note in the modern church. But don't expect a lot of decisions for Christ when you preach on hell, not immediately. A sermon on hell has a delayed detonation. But it's a negative thing when you are preaching, and most negative things don't receive a positive response, although sometimes it may. That doesn't mean you shouldn't preach on hell.

So how far out do I plan? It is like preparing a sermon. Somebody says, "Well, how long did it take to prepare that sermon?" I might say thirty years. Or I might say some sermons I can do in several hours; some I might take a couple days. I don't have a scientific way to say what I am going to determine as a series. A lot of that is observation, where my mind is going at a particular time, in a particular book.

Preaching: Take a typical kind of week in your ministry as you are preparing a message. What does your week look like as you move toward Sunday?

Rogers: Monday, I begin to think and pull out materials. Monday afternoon, I generally come to church and work on my desk, from after lunch to maybe 3:00 or 4:00 in the afternoon. Tuesday, almost all day I am in staff; I do very little studying other than my personal devotion time. Wednesday, I will be at my desk—my study is at home—preparing for Wednesday night and also preparing for Sunday morning and Sunday night. Thursday, I'll be home studying; Thursday afternoon, I'll be here at the church for appointments and counseling. Friday, I'll be pretty much at my desk all day long and try to have everything racked up on Friday. Saturday is family time. Sunday, I'm in the pulpit.

I preach a lot. I preach far more than the average pastor. I preach twice Sunday morning. I preach again Sunday night. I preach again on Wednesday. I preach again on Thursday for a business luncheon. All are separate, individual sermons except for Sunday morning, when I preach the same thing twice.

I have no pretense of any sermon being a literary gem. Every sermon is picked before it is ripe. You know if you are going to preach, you have to get off of the runway before you hit the pine trees. Here I come, ready or not. In my preaching I am more of a mechanic than an artist. I am just building it, over and over again. I don't think that any of my sermons are jewels; I think of them more as nails and boards. The main thing that you are trying to do is not mesmerize people, but to help them. That's what I try to do.

Preaching: **When you step into the pulpit, apart from your Bible, how much do you take with you in terms of notes?**

Rogers: I take a very full set of notes, but I don't need them. When I do my notes, I will outline a message, and I believe in a strong outline. The strong outline is helpful both to me and to my hearers. But I want my outline to follow the Scripture as much as possible. I will write out a full introduction. I will have all of my points and even subpoints, illustrations.

For example, last Sunday I used an illustration about a family that had a dog that they loved very much because that dog had been the pet of their son, and their son died. They promised their son they would take care of the dog. So they loved the dog because the son loved the dog. The point was I love the church because Jesus loves it. Well, in my notes, I would not put down "dog" or "little boy's dog." I would write that out fully, so I could pick it up ten years from now and know what I'd said then. It is that full. If you put connectives and transitional sentences into my notes, you would turn them into manuscripts.

The reason I do it that way is to save my research, to keep me from being repetitive, to see what I preached when I preached the last time on this particular text. Also I can take a sermon that I preached ten years ago, put it in a microwave, and preach it again by looking at my notes; by a ten minutes cursory glance I can know pretty much what I preached before. So when I go into the pulpit, I have a good memory. I could preach without notes—it would take more effort. As many times as I preach, I have concluded that the value gained is not commensurate with the work done, because I can preach with notes so that the average person may not even know that I use notes.

Also, I can take the fuller notes that I preach and reduce them to a skeleton outline, but I see no need to do that. Nobody looks at it but me. What I do is I take my notes, and with a pencil I draw a circle around one word, another word, and another word. When I see that one word, that whole thought explodes in my mind. I know what that one word is symbolic of or what it engenders. So I might just circle a word "dog." But that whole story then is in my mind. So I've got my outline there just by glancing at those little circles as I go down through the thing. I certainly admire people that can memorize it all, but in my own preaching I have not felt that there is enough value gained for me personally because I feel so much freedom the way I use my notes. I never feel tied to my notes.

Preaching: You mentioned that you do a lot more now in terms of illustration than you once did. As you are preparing a message, do you have an illustration file that you keep for yourself? Where do you find the best illustrations?

Rogers: A living, breathing, thinking person is drowning in illustrations if he will just open his eyes. In this morning's paper is a picture of a church, and the title underneath it is "Cathedral of ice." It was a church, a beautiful gothic structure that caught on fire in subzero weather, and the firemen had come and put out the fire; now it is sheathed in ice. You know, what an illustration is there! Some people look at that and never see it.

I think the secret of good illustrations is knowing ahead of time what you are going to preach. Somebody said it's like having a wire stretched across a stream. If you have a wire stretched across the stream, it will catch little bits of grass, and before long there will be a wad of grass on that wire. If there is no wire there, all of that grass goes on down the stream. Knowing what you are going to preach ahead of time is that wire. It is stretched across the stream, and those illustrations collect on that wire. So I'll be sitting there listening to whatever, and I will say, "Man, that is what I'm going to preach on Sunday." I will whip out a pen, and I will write it down, or I will read and rip magazines and papers, everything. Read widely, think, listen—I think good illustrations come from just being alive, being interested.

I do have extensive files. I've had a filing system since I was a kid preacher, and I have filing cabinets crammed with stuff. I don't even know what all is in there, but I have material filed by text and I have material filed by topic. I can go to a text file and find material, and I can go to a topic file and find material. By a combination of being alive today and having material filed by topic and having material filed by text, that all comes together.

Preaching: How long is a typical sermon for you?

Rogers: A typical sermon on Sunday morning would be thirty-five minutes. Sunday night would be forty minutes. People may argue with you about that! They think that by the time you finish the invitation you are still preaching.

Preaching: At least for Sunday morning, isn't that a little shorter than you used to preach?

Rogers: Yes. We are on a forced march around here on Sunday morning because we are on television. I have to get finished in order to get one congregation out and get another congregation in. Also we are on some seven hundred radio stations daily. The radio message has to be only twenty-seven minutes or less—probably more like twenty-five minutes. I have to be careful that I don't preach too long, and preaching too long is counterproductive.

In today's world we live by sound bites. There are times if you are teaching or if you are in a Bible conference that obviously people have nowhere to go; you can go longer. I used to preach longer, and I think that probably allowed for more extended illustrations.

On Sunday morning here, we try to appear relaxed and at ease, but everything is pretty well programmed down to the minute. We know how long this song is going to take and that song, how long for the welcome period, when the song service is to be ended and when I start preaching, when we move into the invitation. It is a shame, but that is the world we live in.

Preaching: Apart from timing, do you see ways in which television and radio have flavored your preaching?

Rogers: Absolutely. Preaching is a miracle that you ever really do anything with such a diverse audience. You can say on Sunday mornings, "I'm preaching to young and old. I'm preaching to saved and lost. I'm preaching to educated and illiterate. I'm preaching to spiritual and to carnal." All at the same time. Trying to connect with all those people, it is a wonder that you really connect at all.

Now take that and enlarge it by the television audience. Right now it is a frightening thing. When I preach on Sunday morning out there, that message that I preach this Sunday morning will literally go around the world. The sun on Sunday will never set on Love Worth Finding ministries. We are on satellite, covering Europe, Asia, Africa, South America; it goes all around the globe in different languages. You say, "How can that connect with all of those people?" Two things prove the inspiration of the Scripture to me: one is that it has stood up under so much shoddy preaching! The other is that the Word of God connects, and when you are really preaching in the Spirit, you are saying more than you are saying. The Holy Spirit of God will take that Word and all those different ethnic backgrounds and sociological backgrounds and bring it home to human hearts.

With that in mind, I want to be politically sensitive. I don't want to say anything derogatory about a nation or country. I want to be ethnically sensitive. I don't want to have a shade of anything that sounds like any kind of racism. I want to be legally sensitive. For example, some movie star may have been married many times, but I have no right to call her a harlot. You have to be very careful about what you say about someone. I might use a particular athlete for an illustration. I would not want to say anything about him if he should happen to tune into the service and by chance it would cause him not to come to Christ. There are a lot of people out there, and you don't know who is listening.

And it is a thrill. We get letters from Israel, from Italy, from whomever, wherever. This is the marvel of this day and age—that the sermon I am preparing for this week will go to all these places. Dale Evans Rogers was given an award at a meeting I was at. I walked out and said, "Dale, I just want to tell you we love you."

"Adrian," she said, "Roy and I just enjoy your preaching so much, we listen to you every Sunday." I thought, "Well, good night, there is Roy Rogers listening to me preach!" You know, when you are on television you are going down through the roofs of apartment houses. When you are on the radio, you are coming down through the skin of an automobile right in there to the front seat with an individual. It is a thrill. It is amazing. You have to think, "This is precious." I have to be careful that I don't misspeak or just waste time because right now by God's grace we are on more than seven hundred radio stations here in the United States every weekday and more than twenty thousand cable systems and land-based TV stations on weekends. It is a stewardship, and it is a sobering thought because you don't want to waste that opportunity.

Preaching: As you look back over your years of ministry in preaching, what would you say are the most important lessons that you have learned, the most important things about preaching?

Rogers: I have learned that you can't divorce the message from the man. Preaching is just incarnational truth. Young preachers come to me and say, "Get me a word, get me a word." Like you are walking down a hallway and dispense all of this wisdom! But I am about down to one word, which is "integrity." Handle the Word with integrity, live with integrity, pray with integrity. Be real. I've learned that lesson, not that I think I am the paragon of anything that I am talking about, but I've learned that.

I've learned also the power of the Word of God. The Word of God is indeed powerful as the Scripture says it is. God says that his Word is like a hammer; it breaks the rock in pieces. You take the hardest rock and keep tapping on it, and it breaks. I have seen over the years the incredible power of the Word of God to bring people to Christ, to hold the church together.

This is such a happy church. If we have any problems in this church, I don't know what they are, and I don't want to know. I've been here for twenty-seven years, and we have grown every year, and we are at an all-time high right now, as I speak to you, in Sunday school attendance, in baptisms, in giving, in spirit. It is wonderful. I say, "Is that the personality of a man? Is that my organizational genius?" Well, certainly not. What is it? I think our people truly love the Lord. They love the Lord because they have heard about him through the Word, and the Holy Spirit is going to witness through that. And I think that there is a holy fear.

I think that this church could fragment and come apart if it were not for the glue that holds it together. It isn't organization; it isn't purpose. It is a love for God and a fear of God. I think people fear God. On the other hand, I love God too much to cause any problems. So a lot of things are grounded in the river of love that might cause difficulty in the average church. It goes back to what I said earlier: your zeal is no greater than your convictions, and your long-term convictions come out of the Word of God. I have seen the power of the Word of God to be the unifying force in building a church. I don't believe you can build a church today on preaching alone. But, I don't believe you build it without that.

I am afraid that we have a generation today that is confusing means and methods and trying to be up-to-date by jettisoning some biblical methods. I think that the end of that process is tragedy. So we want to do the old things in better ways. I can tell you that I've seen this church go from less than 1,300 in Sunday school to last Sunday we had 7,840 in Sunday school. No three ring circus, no "contemporary" music, although we had good music. Nothing except the things that are traditional, but we try to do them with excellence. I don't know why we should change.

Preaching: Any last thoughts you'd want to share with fellow preachers?

Rogers: There's a little formula that I worked out early on for myself in preaching—four little phrases: "Hey, You, Look, Do." This is in my mind to use as a guide in preparing a message. The first word: **Hey**, like you would say to an individual to get their attention. It doesn't matter what you are saying if you don't have their attention. So, I would say, "Hey, open your Bibles today to 1 Corinthians 12. Now look up here. I want to tell you something. You are a gifted child." I am getting their attention. Hey, **You**. "I want to show you how you can discover, develop, deploy your gift and have the best time of your life." Hey, You, **Look**—"Take your Bibles now and let me show you. Here is what I want you to do," and I call them to action: **Do**. That is a very simple little formula that I use just to help me preach—nothing electrifying about it, but it works. Other than that, I've told you more than I know.

If you were to put Johnny Carson, Jay Leno, anybody else, out there and let them speak to the same people three times a week for twenty-seven years, they would be climbing the walls to get out. I don't care who you are. The reason I preach the Bible is first, I'm not smart enough to preach anything else. The Bible is a bottomless well. The other reason is I am smart enough not to preach anything else, because I know that that has the staying power. My people love me today; I don't want to say boastfully, but I know this is true: they love me, they come. This place is packed; we have run out of room. It is not a testimony to the man but to the Bible. If I stop preaching the Bible, these folks will saturate this place with absence. They come for the Word of God. They want it to be warm; they want it to be understandable and applicable. But I have learned that there is power in the preaching of the Word of God.

Preaching without Fear

An Interview with Andy Stanley

In 1995, Andy Stanley, son of Charles Stanley (pastor of Atlanta's First Baptist Church), met with a group of believers to cast a vision for a new church, a safe environment where the unchurched could come and hear the life-changing truth that Jesus Christ cares for them and died for their sins. For three years, the group met in rented facilities every other Sunday night. By 1998, they had moved into their new home on an eighty-three-acre site in suburban Atlanta. Today, North Point Community Church draws more than eleven thousand adults each Sunday. This interview was published in the July-August 2004 issue of *Preaching*.

Preaching: In your book *The Next Generation Leader*, you talk about some of the key characteristics that young leaders need to understand. What led you to write that book?

Stanley: *The Next Generation Leader* was the result of monthly leadership lessons I do with our staff. Once a month, instead of our normal staff meeting, I do training—we do outlines, fill in the blanks, the whole deal. I spend a lot of time developing these talks for our leaders; we have about 180 full-time staff members. That's where this book came from.

I was essentially answering the question, "If there were just a few things I could tell young leaders, what would they be?" These are things I think leaders generally figure out anyway along the way—they're not original—but these are things I wish I'd known earlier. I would have saved so much time and energy if somebody had said up front, "OK, you may not believe this, but just trust me, this is true. Go ahead and apply this stuff and later on you'll look back and be glad you did." So it's basically a few things I wish every young leader—especially in Christian leadership—would embrace because it makes the learning curve so much easier.

The first one is the whole idea of doing less to accomplish more—finding your core competencies and playing to your strengths and delegating your weaknesses. Determine to do that even before you can do that. Of course, when you start up an organization or a church, as you know, you have to do everything. But you know you're not good at everything, and young leaders often make the mistake of trying to shore up their weaknesses and wing it on their strengths. I did that for too many years. I finally figured out that I just needed to do what I was good at and let the other stuff go undone. Then, eventually, somebody else would come along and do it. It was amazing.

We talk about clarity, and how even in the midst of uncertainty, leaders need to learn to be clear. Uncertainty is permanent—it never goes away. I am pastor of this big church with all these wonderful things going on, and there's more uncertainty right now in my ministry than ever before.

This morning, I met with one of our elders, and we talked about the vision for our church. And I'm the guy who wrote a book on vision! Essentially, we are everything we ever envisioned we'd become, so the question is, "Now what? What's next?" And I don't know. I have lots of ideas, but uncertainty is permanent, and learning how to lead and be clear with lots of uncertainty is huge. Young leaders think, "Once I'm a good leader, I won't have any uncertainty," and that's a myth. I say to young leaders, "Learn to navigate through the uncertainty. It's permanent. It doesn't go away. It's not a reflection of poor leadership."

In the book, I talk about courage and the significance of the fact that many times it's an act of courage that establishes us as leaders in the minds of other people. God has gifted us, but nobody knows. God's called us, but nobody knows. How do we become leaders? Often, it's the person who steps out first. Those acts of courage establish people as leaders in the minds of others.

I say to young leaders, "Eventually, there is going to be a defining moment, and everybody will be looking over the cliff, and you'll realize, 'If I jump first, they'll follow me.' And you'll jump, and you'll become the leader. You'd already been called. You'd already been gifted, but suddenly, in that moment, people will say, 'That's somebody worth following.' So be on the lookout for that moment."

Another key is finding leadership coaches. I love to talk about this because it's difficult—it seems on the surface difficult—to enlist people to coach us as leaders. Unlike athletes, leaders think, "I don't need coaching—I'm the leader! If I needed coaching, I wouldn't be the leader."

Nothing could be further from the truth. One of the greatest benefits in my life has been people who have coached me in my leadership—people who, if you met them, you'd be tempted to say, "Andy, they're not even good leaders, so how could they coach you? You seem to be a better leader than they are."

That is the myth about coaching. You know athletes have coaches, and the athletes are far better performers than the coaches who coach them, but they still benefit from coaching. So, leaders at every level—especially young leaders—need people speaking into areas of their lives. I talk about how to find those people and enlist them and not scare them off.

The last thing we talk about in the book is character. Obviously, that's not a new principle, but the thing I say to young leaders all the time is, "You can be successful in leadership and have no integrity." Integrity is not essential to leadership, but it is essential if you want to be a leader worth following. At the end of the day, if you want to be the kind of leader people will say about, "Not only am I thrilled about what we accomplished, I enjoyed the journey. The journey was just great." Not just the goals and accomplishments, but the process. In order to have that kind of experience with the people you lead, you have to be a person of integrity. We just don't enjoy the journey with people we don't trust. There is so much more to say about leadership. I feel like if leaders can begin to embrace those five things—set those up as mile markers and boundaries in their leadership—they're going to go further, faster.

Preaching: One of the topics I particularly appreciated was the discussion of finding your core competencies and focusing there. Lots of us think we have to have our finger in everything. It's a good reminder to work at finding your groove. How did that take place in your ministry, and how has it influenced your leadership?

Stanley: I learned all of this the hard way, and I look back and wonder what took me so long. I am only good at a couple of things in terms of skill set. I'm a good public speaker, and I'm good in a meeting where everybody's in the process of trying to get all the information on the table—I'm good at looking at all the information and moving us forward. I don't always make the right decisions, but I've learned I'm good at recognizing a bad decision quickly. It frustrates my staff, but we've all agreed this is how I am. My temptation is to run down a road, and about the time everybody figures out where I'm going, I'm coming back saying, "That is not where we're going." And they just laugh; they know that's how I make decisions. That's how I make them personally. That's how we sometimes make them corporately. Once I figured that out, I realized the arenas where I need to focus are public communication, vision casting, and decision making at the highest level in the organization.

I'm not a good event planner. I'm not a good organizer. I'm not a good team builder, as far as going out and putting together a team. I'm not an extrovert—I don't even like extroverts a lot of times! I finally figured out there are certain people I don't click with, and that's who they are. Part of this is a maturity thing, but looking at all of it through the grid of, "God, what have you designed me to do?"

I think where it has impacted us in ministry is that very early on I stuck with the few things that I did well. As I say in the book, when you do less you accomplish more, and when you do less you allow other people to accomplish more. I think that if you talk to our leadership team—there are seven of us that are sort of the "they" of the North Point staff—they would tell you, "Andy lets us do what he's hired us to do." I just trust them, and I know that I'm not as good as they are in their areas.

I tell our staff all the time that I'm not the best leader. The reason I get to lead is because I'm the best speaker, and in the church world, if you're the best speaker, they let you lead, whether you're any good or not. I don't claim to be the best leader, but I've created the space for the good leaders around me to lead. I see that with my dad. That's how my dad has always led. And I should have learned this earlier, because he modeled it. He's the guy who just stays in his groove and enables other people to fill in the gaps.

I'm surrounded by the most creative, wonderful, confident people I can imagine. One of them—probably one of my sharpest guys—told me, "If I didn't work for you, I would be a senior pastor, because I don't think I could stand to work for anybody else." It's his way of saying, "You give me so much space to operate, I don't feel the need to go to some other church so I can be the number one guy, because I can't imagine having more opportunity or freedom." And I said, "Yeah, plus you don't have to take up the offerings, so you have it made. I fund all the fun that you're having over there on your side of the aisle!"

I say to young leaders all the time, "Don't look at me and say, 'You've got it made.' You have to look at your own situation and ask, 'How do I apply this principle?' Because the principle is the same whether you're starting alone or with two or three people. Figure out what you're good at, and do the best you can to stay there." When I do this talk publicly, I juggle, and I talk about how I can juggle *three* balls, but I can't juggle *five*. So I juggle my three and I say, "Now if I try to juggle five, guess how many I'll drop?" I'll drop all of them but one. If you watched me juggle five balls, you would conclude that I can't juggle, but that's not true. I *can* juggle. So I'm going to juggle three and let two lie on the floor, and somebody who sees me juggling three says, "You know. I can pick up the one." And somebody else says, "I can pick up the other one," and before long, all five are being held.

That visual says that you just have to do what you are good at because good people love to work for good people. If people can't see what you're good at because you're trying to do everything, they won't join your team. It's just an extremely important principle, and I think there is application at every level in leadership, whether it's a young leader or somebody who's been in leadership for a long time.

Preaching: You talk about the place of courage in leadership and thinking about how that relates, not simply to leadership in general, but specifically to pastors and the challenges they face.

Stanley: It's huge. Speaking from my limited view, I feel like so much of the problem with pastors is they are scared to death. They're scared of their people. They're scared of deacons—they're scared. You know if you're scared of people, you can't lead them; you can hardly even influence them. I tell our business guys all the time, "You'd never go to work for an organization where the customers can hire and fire the president of the company." But that's the church world. The people hire the leader and say, "We'll follow you unless we don't like the way you're leading us. Then we'll get us another leader." In what other organization can the customers hire and fire the leader? So the church is set up upside-down. It's an environment that is not conducive to leadership in some ways. Consequently, to lead a church, you have to have a lot of courage, because the group to which you're saying "follow me" can get together and fire you. Well, that's just the way it is. That's not going to change, but it requires a lot of courage—otherwise, we start bending toward the people that hired us, and we're in trouble.

The irony is that we stand up and talk about Daniel in the lion's den, but then we won't even confront elders. All of these Bible heroes like David and Goliath—we love to preach those sermons and draw those parallels, then we're scared to confront people. I think that dynamic alone is a big part of why the church is where it is. The leadership—or lack of leadership—is just so fearful of people. I don't know where that comes from.

At a defining moment in my life, I saw my dad slugged. When I was in the eighth grade, a man was at the pulpit one Wednesday night. He used profanity, and my dad walked up beside him and said, "We're not going to have that kind of language." The guy said, "You better watch out, or you just might get hit," and my dad stood there. The man hit my dad in the jaw. I can remember where I was standing; I remember the whole thing. That marked me as a preacher's kid and as a pastor. I learned to do the right thing and then deal with the consequences. You don't fear the consequences and do the wrong thing. I think it's been easy for me to embrace that because of what I saw in my father and what I experienced.

When I see pastors who are scared, I want to tell them, "Just lead." If they fire you and you don't think God will take care of you, then you have no message for your people anyway. We get up every Sunday and say, "God's grace is sufficient. He's going to take care of you, he'll meet your every need, and you'll never see the righteous go hungry." It's what we preach, but if our lack of faith in those practical things causes us to not be able to lead, then what's our message anyway?

It's easy for me to say that sitting here, but when I started this church, it was not easy for me to say, because I had to face that whole issue of leaving my dad's church to do something on my own. There were no guarantees; there were no promises. When you walk through that wall of fire a couple of times, you realize it's not so bad. God's grace *is* sufficient. He does show up. Those are the times we look back to and say, "I know there is a God." I just wish pastors would get over their fears. We should be the most fearless leaders. What do we have to fear? We're the ones that say, "If God is for me, who can be against me?" Well, the deacons. Good grief.

Preaching: That connects with one of the other things you talk about: living in the shadow of uncertainty.

Stanley: Exactly. That whole example I used from the book of Joshua, saying we're crossing the Jordan River. We've never been there. I don't know what it's like. I've never led an army, and I don't know what we're going to do, but we're crossing. I want to be certain, be clear—we're crossing. I'm uncertain of what we'll face.

And that's leadership—I've never been there before, but here we go.

Preaching: The coaching issue may sound odd to some pastors. What do you see as the importance of coaching for leaders, and how do pastors use it? How do they find good coaches?

Stanley: I say to pastors, "Every time you preach, your sermon is evaluated by as many people as there are in your congregation. You are being evaluated. You will either learn and take advantage of those evaluations, or you will not. But you're already being evaluated. Your leadership is being evaluated. Every person that sits in your staff meetings, deacons' meetings, Sunday school directors' meetings—every time you lead a meeting, your leadership is being evaluated." So the question isn't, "Should I get evaluations?" The question is, "How can I grow from these evaluations?"

The evaluation is already happening, so engaging somebody to give us input—whether positive or negative or critical or whatever—should be a no-brainer, because all the evaluators are already in place taking mental notes—and sometimes, not just mental. And they are talking to each other about how we're performing. The question is, "Are we secure enough to take advantage of that?" Since the evaluations happen anyway, it's wise to take advantage of them.

The last thing you want to do is ask somebody to be your leadership coach. Everyone will say no. They don't feel competent. What you do is simply ask for people's input. Everybody loves to give input. In our culture, there are some built-in critiques for things that happen every week for every part of our service, including the sermon. There are people that I've asked to tell me after a meeting when I've not been clear, when I've been too dogmatic, when I've been abrasive. I want to know that because I won't know it otherwise. I'm giving them the freedom to give me that feedback.

When you're leading a meeting, you don't know how you are doing. You don't. You think you do, but you're not sitting there watching and listening. So often, it's just giving people permission or asking for their feedback. Get people that you respect—people that you know have done this before in their own realms. There is really no realm of leadership I know of in which you can't get coaching.

A big area for me is in personnel and the few times we've had to let people go. Years ago, I almost let someone go, and it would have been a terrible mistake. There are two guys in our church who are really intuitive about personnel issues. I never make a personnel decision without talking to them first: "Here are all the issues. Here are the details. What do you think?" I've never said to them, "Would you coach me in my leadership?" But what I've said is, "Would you give me input in this area of leadership?" And they are more than happy to. Consequently, they feel the freedom to interject at will. I feel very dependent upon that handful of people that I've brought into that circle.

People say, "You're such a good leader," and I say, "Yeah, but I'm propped up. I'm propped up in every direction." I just can't imagine pastors not finding a way within their own context, according to their own personalities, to figure out how to get that input. They're already being evaluated. They'll either benefit from it or they won't.

Preaching: Years ago, in an interview with Bill Hybels, he told me about using an informal group during the services to provide sermon evaluations. He always tries to have a non-believer in that group . . .

Stanley: To see how they're processing it all. Absolutely. Again, I think it can be for a pastor as easy as asking someone who has brought a first-time visitor, "What did they think?" It gives the person who brought them an opportunity to respond, because I'm not saying, "What did you think?" I'm saying, "What did they think?" You know, we have to have that information. We used to actually do a form—we would ask people in different parts of the building to evaluate everything from lights to sound to sermon to clothing to everything. We haven't done that for a long time, but I think it's a very helpful tool. Again, it's already being evaluated—we might as well benefit from it.

Preaching: Specifically, how has your own interest in leadership impacted both your pastoral work and your preaching?

Stanley: When I hear preachers or teachers, I can tell if they are leaders. There's just a *follow me* thing about every message. Not *follow me* because I've got it together, but follow me because I'm trying to get it together. I see somebody open the Bible and handle a passage, and I think I want to follow that guy. I may think other people are good communicators, but I don't know that I'd want to be on a team with them. I think leaders communicate through their leadership gift, as well as their preaching and teaching gifts.

Preaching: Do you try to lead through your preaching?

Stanley: Definitely. Each January, we do two or three weeks on the vision of the church—what's coming up this year. Here we go. Here's what you need to do to get on board. Then in June, we do a big strategic service Sunday where we sign up all of our new volunteers for the fall. We do it in June and train them through the summer and then start them in ministry in the fall. Those are huge vision casting times for us. It's very much from the standpoint of leading. But those are strategic; that's not every week.

Pastors who aren't gifted in leadership struggle with those sermons. I talk to guys who never cast vision. Well, no wonder no one knows where he's going! But as a leader, it's natural for me—in almost any message—to talk about the vision and mission of the church. I just naturally go there, because it's what I think about a lot.

Preaching: Tell me about your approach to preaching.

Stanley: The guys on our staff that want to become better communicators are constantly asking me to coach them in communication, and when guys fill in for me I do that. I did that earlier today for the guy who's preaching for me Sunday. I meticulously go through the message and outline. I want to help them all become better at communicating.

But people will say, "Andy, can I shadow you one day while you're preparing?" I say no. I can't imagine somebody watching me prepare sermons. You wouldn't understand—most of the time I just walk around the building!

I spent half a day with four of our communicators, a big flannel board with pens and cards, and we outlined my message development process. I just said, "Everybody keeps asking me about this, and I don't know how to talk about it, so ask me questions and dig it out of me, and let's come up with something I can talk about and we can communicate to communicators." It's very different than what I was trained to do in seminary. It's very different than the people I hear preach, but I need to learn how to talk about it and not just do it. Eventually, I think I'll have a tool that will make all that more clear.

On Sunday mornings, I feel like I have to start with the funnel as wide as possible. I have believers, unbelievers, used-to-be-believers, they think. (I say that a lot. It drives the Christians crazy.) I don't think you can be a "used-to-be believer," but there are people who would say that. They would say, "I used to be a Christian." So, that's who I'm talking to. I think you start off as wide as possible. You create tension. You say, "Guess what? The Bible talks about this tension." You look at the Bible, resolve the tension, summarize it and the principle, and then apply it, illustrate it, land the plane, and go home. I don't have multiple points. I usually have one.

I want to come up with a statement that we do throughout a series or a statement that's part of a message. That's the takeaway. My hope and dream is to think that someone could come back to that same passage of Scripture later and say, "I know what that means. I know what that's about. I know the point of that story." That's why I don't like to say, "Paul said" and "John said that again" and "Jesus said that again" and "over in Psalms, David . . ." I hate sermons like that. When I listen to them, I just turn them off. I think just one passage that says it is all we need. Just help me understand the one passage—please don't proof text every point with a verse. I think that's lazy preaching. It would be easy to develop sermons like that.

I feel like preaching is a journey, and I'm responsible to take however many people who show up on the journey. And those are teens, lost people—the ones who say, "I'm here. I'm going to give this one shot." We have all these people, and at the end, I want us all to work our way together to resolve this tension. Whether you accept it or not, here's what the Scripture teaches, and let's all end up together. It's a journey.

Transitions are extremely important. In fact, the only parts of my sermons that I script are my transitions, because transitions are, "We've been here together. Now I'm about to go here, and I don't want to lose you." And if you don't know where we're going related to where we've been, I've lost you. I'm listening to a sermon here thinking, "Why are we talking about this?" We started here, and I'm sure on your outline where we are relates to where we started, but I've lost track—so transitions are huge.

I preach one-point messages. I have a point, and I'm going to make you wonder what it is, take you there, apply the point, and, hopefully, restate it in such a way that you remember it—at least until you get to the car. Maybe forever. Most single sermons I hear are actually sermon series. I think, "Gosh, that would have been a great series. You have four great points. You wasted all that effort. You could have preached that for a month instead of one week!" People aren't going to digest all that information at one time.

And the other thing I do that people say is unique—I don't know if it is or not—is often in a message when I get to a part that I think non-Christians may think is just too strange or unbelievable, I often stop and say, "You know, this next thing is really unusual. In fact, this may be the reason you're not a Christian, or this may make you glad you're not a Christian, or this may give you a reason to never become a Christian." I just feel like if I can state the resistance, they will follow me on the journey to the end, whether they agree with me or not. But if they think I don't know what they're objecting to, in their minds they're arguing with me throughout. I know that I do the same thing when other people speak. But if I get to a place where I think they may check out, I know if I say what they're thinking, they will at least follow me mentally to the end of the message. I've heard that said so many, many times. And when you can say what people are thinking—they know you know that they are aware this is strange: he's aware that this is hard to believe, he's not assuming that just because the Bible says it we should all believe it.

I preached a message not too long ago on the significance of things that are *unexplainable* versus things that are *undeniable*—about how often the unexplainable causes us to doubt God, but there are some things that are undeniable. I talked up front about how much I doubt. Then I listed some of the reasons I doubt Scriptures and, sometimes, I doubt God. I went on and on because it's true. How, at times, I can become the biggest skeptic and cynic. Then I went on and preached the message. The response was overwhelming, because I gave people permission to doubt—we all doubt. But everybody thinks the preacher never doubts.

The next night in my small group a couple of the ladies said, "Andy, you don't know how much it helped me to know that you doubt," because everybody assumes I don't doubt. "But if you can doubt and still believe, that helps me." So I think it helps anytime I can express that—I don't mean make it up, but sincerely say, "Boy, I struggle with this too."

Whenever I mention hell or eternal separation from God, I almost always say, "You know, if God would give me five minutes, and he'd turn his back, I would erase this part out of the Bible." I say, "If we all get to heaven, and we find out that there's a loophole, and everybody got to go to heaven, I'll be so happy. But the reason I believe that everyone doesn't go to heaven is because Jesus taught it. I am as uncomfortable with it as anybody in this room." Well then, they think, "OK, he understands. He's not so dogmatic." And it's true. I'm not making it up. I wish it weren't there. I hope universalism is true. I don't think it is.

I think it's one reason we are able to communicate to the unbeliever *and* the believer. People don't come here and get surface sermons just because it's a seeker church. I've preached on everything. My view on divorce and remarriage is so narrow I might be alone, but one Sunday I preached on it. I told them, "Here's what I believe the Scripture teaches. You know this is the minority view, and I hope I'm wrong, and if you've got something I need to read, send it to me, but here's what Jesus said." I think if we can be authentic, we can let Scripture be the authority, and we're simply the mouthpieces—we'd have all kinds of unbelievers that would come week after week after week and say, "We don't believe it yet, but we'll be back next week." And we have mature believers who flock to this church because they say that the teaching is so rich.

I don't think we have to choose one or the other. I just think that dichotomy does not have to be there. Jesus modeled this—so many people of faith flocked to hear him teach because he spoke with authority. But Matthew and Zaccheus came, too. How did he do that? He took truth and made it clear. The best thing I can do for skeptical unbelievers is to cause them to think, "I didn't know that was in there." The reason they don't believe the Bible is because they think it's irrelevant. If for one moment there is a relevant thought that comes out of this book, it gives us credibility. What I enjoy about preaching, I think, is causing those "ah-ha" moments for people who either have been away for a long time or for whom the Bible has gotten old or stale.

Preaching: Some preachers say they can't preach biblical sermons as they used to because people don't come with an acceptance of the text's authority. A generation ago, people walked in the church and there was a level of knowledge about Scripture that doesn't exist today.

Stanley: Well, they can't preach verse by verse and assume there is interest, and I think that preaching through books of the Bible week after week, verse by verse, is not a good idea anyway. We have a conceptual preaching calendar that we follow every year, and after Christmas I do preach through a book of the Bible. Even when we did James, we picked the key parts of James. We didn't do it verse by verse.

I don't know where that came from. Jesus didn't model it. Nobody modeled it. I don't think it's terrible. I think there is a place for Bible study and learning the themes of Scripture, and I'm so grateful for seminary, but in terms of building people, I don't think it's a good model at all. And I went to Dallas Seminary—that's kind of what we were taught to do! I don't think you leave people with a sense of, "I'm going to take this home and make use of it." It's harder to preach the way we do, but that's just my opinion.

Preaching: Tell me about your sequential preaching calendar.

Stanley: We start with Easter, and Easter in our church is different than a lot of churches. Easter here is not a once-a-year thing, because our church is so young and new. People who only go to church on Easter don't think about coming to North Point. They go to the church that they used to go to—that they go to once a year. Easter for us is when everybody that normally comes all come. So I don't think, "Hey, we've got this one shot because it's Easter, and they're here." I don't feel that at all. Easter is a harvest Sunday for us. Our Easter sermon is, "You know what you've been thinking about, you've been listening to, you've been looking at. Today is your day! Why not put your faith in Christ?" Not because they're only here one time. We're assuming they've been here for six months and they'll remember this day forever. And then we have a big stand-up invitation.

So we come out of Easter with what we call the "big hook." We do a very, very high needs-driven series. Last year, we did a series on parenting, on marriage, and on God and the workplace. It's kind of a secular bent in terms of a big hook coming out of Easter. Then after Easter, we get into Father's Day and Mother's Day, so we do a relationship series. It could be on parenting, or it could be on marriage. I did a series called "Prescription for the Fractured Family"—about healing, forgiveness, and family. That takes us through the May-June period.

In the summer, we come up with a theme, but we don't do sequential messages. They're stand-alone messages under the banner of the theme, because we know people are gone in the summer. This summer, we did a series called "Defining Moments," and it was seven encounters with Jesus, each with a stand-alone message, and the banner was "Ah-ha Moments with Jesus."

In the fall, we always do a spiritual growth series. Last fall, we did a series called "You've Got Style" about drawing near to God through the way he has wired us. Then we did a series on doing the wise thing. It was called "Fool Proof" and was spiritual-growth oriented. So we did two of those, and then it was Christmas. I try to do a Christmas series. We close the church the Sunday after Christmas. The Sunday after Christmas nothing happens here. No services. We put a big Closed sign on the door. It's wonderful. Everyone is off, all staff and volunteers—because during Christmas, everyone's doing double duty anyway, with Christmas Eve, choir programs, etc. So, the Sunday after Christmas . . . nothing happens.

Then the first two or three Sundays in January are all very much church-family oriented sermons: the vision of the church, our mission that year, what are we trying to accomplish financially. Then we do a book of the Bible or a Bible study series. And then we try to do a short series leading up to Easter. Again, our goal is to bring a group of people to a point of commitment to Christ on Easter, so we ramp up. We did an apologetics series last year right before Easter. We did a series on "Why Did Jesus Come? Why Did Jesus Die? Why Did Jesus Rise?"—all leading up to Easter. And then we are back to Easter.

So when we first came up with this idea, my worship service planning team took every series I'd ever done and put them on a big planning board. They put every series in one of the categories I mentioned before. Sometimes they'll come back and say, "We're coming up on the fall. You know four years ago you did this series; I think we need to redo this." Now as a preacher I immediately feel guilty. I can't repreach, because everything has to be new and original! And several times they've said to me, "No, it's been five years, Andy! I hate to burst your bubble, but nobody remembers these messages!" So they'll take an old series and repackage it with a different look, different title, different visual aids, and different sketches. Since it's already categorized, it's already on a place on the calendar, and it's been extremely helpful for me to have a grid system through which to think.

When I come up with a series idea, instead of thinking, "I need to do that next," I think, "That's a relationship series," so I go ahead and file that away for that season of the year. It really helps me stay ahead in my thinking and in my planning, and it allows my team to work with me in finding the right place to put different things as we think sequentially through the year. It's been great.

Preaching: Do you preach for three morning services? And how many weeks out of the year do you preach?

Stanley: Yes. We do six- to eight-week series—usually six, sometimes four—but I'll try to take two Sundays off every eight to nine weeks. It doesn't work out perfectly, but after ten weeks in a row, I'm dying! I can just feel it. I'm dreading Sundays. I'm dreading studying. I'm just dying. So four times a year, I'll take a two-week break. I'll just sit in church and coach the guys who are preaching, if they are staff members. It's not vacation time.

Then, of course, the Sunday after Christmas nothing is going on, so that's nine Sundays. Then in May, I usually take three weeks off, some for vacation. So, I preach about forty Sundays a year. But I'm going to change that. I really want to begin using more communicators, not just to fill in between my messages, but to do their own series.

With our campus expansion, I'm convinced—I've been convinced, but I'm finally going to do something about it—that I need to become less indispensable to this organization. There is no other arena in our organization that is personality dependent anymore. We've grown past that in every arena except in preaching, and as the leader, it's my responsibility to do what I've asked the rest of our staff to do: to replace themselves by apprenticing people into their roles. So last year, at our last elders' meeting, I said, "Guys, I feel it's time to do this. We are healthy enough as an organization that if we take a hit in attendance or finances, we will just grow back out of that, but now's the time." They were 100 percent supportive of that. So I'm not sure how that's going to look yet, but that's the direction we're moving in.

There are all kinds of incredible communicators floating around Atlanta, so it's just a matter of becoming more strategic and exposing our people to them. Even though I know this is the right thing to do, it's really going to be hard for me. I can already tell. Part of me is relieved, and the other part of me feels this, "Oh no! That's my job. That's my responsibility!" It's just something I have to do. It's probably going to be harder than I think.

Preaching: Are there some things you've learned about preaching that you wish you'd known years ago?

Stanley: This is one of the things I love to talk to pastors about. In terms of how I structure messages and memorize them, what I finally figured out is that there are basically three or four, maybe five parts, to every message. What it took a few years to learn is this: if I'll just get those three, four, or five parts in my mind and know my transitions, I can forget the details. I am more free to communicate. I can watch someone preach and tell if he is trying to remember something or trying to communicate—and the audience can, too.

This is just a personal opinion, but I think preaching with notes communicates something. I think it communicates, "What I have to say is really important. I hope that you'll put this in your heart. It's not in mine, you know—I haven't integrated it, but I hope you will." Well, nobody thinks that, but . . . when somebody gets up and is passionate, you absorb it at the heart level.

And so in terms of memorizing sermons, I figured out there are only three or four big chunks, and when I can mentally go through the big pieces, I'm ready. It took me a while to figure that out. It helped my memorization and my communication style tremendously. I became far more conversational. I also discovered it's about a journey, and it's about one thing, not four things.

The other thing I wish that I'd done earlier is involve lots of people in the series planning. Just because I'm a good talker doesn't mean I'm the smartest person on staff. I don't have a corner on the creative ideas. So all of our planning begins with a team of people just throwing things up on a board. At every level of preparation, I bring people into the process and say, "What do you think about this? Does this make sense?"

Now the average person gives me all the credit for that wonderfully delivered message, but it had a lot of hands on it. I think that more and more pastors are doing this . . . involving people in the preparation process. And the earlier on I do that, the better the messages.

I'll never forget talking to my wife, Sandra, one time about a message. I went through this whole message with her in the car as we were driving. I finished it, and she was real quiet. Then she said, "So what do you have for the women?" I said, "What do you mean?" Sandra said, "That was a guy sermon." I said, "Oh, you're right." Because she's a woman, she's listening to it completely different. I benefit from that.

I think the whole team approach to series planning is helpful. My best visual aids haven't been my ideas. When you get a group of people thinking, they all use their gifts. So I wish I'd done that earlier. It takes the creative pressure off. I'll have other people out there thinking about it, while I'm in my study working on the details. So those two things would have speeded things up for me.

Preaching: **When does your planning process take place?**

Stanley: Through the years, it has changed and will continue to change. One of the things I have learned about myself is that I just love change. Even bad change! I get so excited—it's invigorating to me! That's not always a good thing about a leader, but it's true.

Once a year, we sit down and talk about the whole year—sort of the big chunks, filling in some gaps. At the beginning of every series, we sit down and brainstorm through the series. And we work ahead, because with creative elements, you have to be ahead. One thing we do—it's hard to describe—is build sets for a series. We do a lot of sitcoms where the characters stay the same throughout a series. We'll build kitchens or houses that take up the whole stage. So to get all that ready we need to be weeks ahead. I have to give them enough specifics for them to know where to go with the sets. So the series planning big picture is sometimes a couple of months out.

I meet every Tuesday with three other people: our worship church service planning person, our music director, and one of our associate pastors who's just brilliantly creative. The four of us meet to talk through specific sermons coming up. We do an evaluation every Monday afternoon after the service of what went on the previous day.

Every once in a while, I'll have an idea for a series and I will randomly call in staff, men and women at different levels of the organization, to spend two or three hours "just talking about it." Again, I come out of there with a big board full of ideas. I might not do the series for months, but I know when I come to it, I have all that valuable information waiting to draw from. That's pretty much how it works. The schedule changes a good bit, but those components are always part of it.

Preaching: One of the physical innovations you've developed is a back-to-back worship center—which I've heard called the "Siamese sanctuaries." How did you develop that concept?

Stanley: It wasn't my idea, but it's the best thing we ever did. Our original worship center seats twenty-seven hundred people, and we were filling up fast. We filled up two services right away. I was committed to never having three services. (Ha, ha, ha!) We didn't know what to do. Do we build a big worship center? We'd only been in our current worship center for a year and a half. Should we spend thirty million dollars, and how big should we build it? And is this growth going to go on forever? We had no idea what to do. We were doing overflow in our children's theater. Overflow is no new idea.

One of our elders said, "Why don't we just build another worship center this size? It's cheap. It's quick. It's easy. We'll just put screens over there." So we'd just build a big overflow room, and we felt like that was the thing to do. In the meantime, our production people got busy and came up with this incredible technology that has paved the way for our future growth. It was all by accident or providence—it wasn't strategic. We drop down a big center screen with an image from the "live auditorium" that makes me appear life-size in the other worship center. We also do the two image-mag screens up on both sides of the center screen. It worked incredibly.

I came out of the auditorium one day after we had been doing this for about three months, and this guy walked up and said, "You could do that anywhere." And that was true. So sure enough, we leased a grocery store in Buckhead and opened up on Easter Sunday with the same screen setup, on a one-week delay. We use the videotape and play it there. Last Sunday, there were 1,960 adults in worship at a grocery store watching a video a week late. (We are now averaging over thirty-three hundred adults in four worship services.)

It's so realistic that a lady came up after a service in Buckhead and asked to speak to me. I wasn't even there, but because of what they've done with the center screen/side screens it creates a three-dimensional image that causes people to argue, "He was there." "No, he wasn't." "Yes, he was." The two back-to-back worship centers that began as a solution to a problem really became part of the vision of how to grow this church.

Preaching: Do you ever physically go into the other auditorium during the service?

Stanley: Not to preach. I'll go over there and do announcements. I'll go over there and just walk through and talk to people, but I always preach from the same side. We ask people to rotate auditoriums by alphabet, A through M, N through Z. Not everybody does that. Most people probably don't do it, but we ask them to anyway. Some people are faithful, back and forth. But it has worked great. It's saved us so much money because the new worship center seats about twenty-two hundred people and gives us capacity for five thousand people in two rooms, and it didn't cost that much money. It allowed us to grow really quickly without having a giant building campaign and big debt. The music's live in both places. Announcements are live, and then the screen comes down. It's amazing.

The other thing that's been exciting is doing our series on DVD. There are dozens of business guys now that are showing these DVDs at lunch. It's given them a tool to do Bible studies without having to teach. They can drop it in their laptops and put it on their television screens or monitors in their conference rooms. It's been so neat to just give these guys a tool.

Preaching: If you could offer a few words of encouragement to fellow pastors, what would they be?

Stanley: Just don't be afraid. Don't be afraid.

Taking the Word Downtown

An Interview with Jerry Vines

Each Sunday morning, Jerry Vines preaches to a congregation of eighty-five hundred people in the First Baptist Church of Jacksonville, Florida, a thriving downtown church. A popular speaker and author, Vines has also served as president of the Southern Baptist Convention and annually sponsors one of the nation's largest pastors' conferences. Vines recently announced plans to retire as senior pastor. This interview appeared in the January-February 2003 issue of *Preaching*.

Preaching: First Baptist Jacksonville is at the heart of a major urban area. While many city-center churches in recent years have moved or experienced steep declines, your congregation appears to be vibrant and growing. Why are you seeing such success?

Vines: There was a conscious decision made over thirty years ago to stay downtown. The other churches were and have moved out. The conviction was there needs to be a strong witness in the heart of the city. Also, neighborhoods have a way of growing and declining; so to stay in the center of the city, regardless of whatever happens, you still remain central in the city.

Of course, our city has not just moved from neighborhood to neighborhood; it has grown out—the circle has gotten bigger, which means we have to work a lot harder to reach people! But we just believe there's a real testimony to have a strong preaching station and a strong witness for Christ in the middle of the city.

Preaching: Does the downtown location make any impact on your approach to preaching?

Vines: City Hall is just across the street from us here, and because of that I know that what I say here does have an impact on the city's life. And while I don't necessarily just pick topics as they come along—I certainly don't speak on every city issue—what I speak does get a pretty good audience.

Preaching: I would guess that you have a wide range of people—demographically, economically—in this church. How does that affect the way you preach to this congregation?

Vines: What you said is exactly true. Our church is really a people's church. We cross all lines here—we have educated, uneducated. We have all nationalities and cultures. We have people who are poor and living on welfare. On any given Sunday we'll have sitting on the same pew a millionaire and a person living on Social Security.

When I prepare to preach, in my imagination I picture people in the congregation. I picture the businessman struggling with ethical issues. I picture the widow living on a small Social Security check, trying to meet her day-to-day expenses. In my mind's eye I try to picture that high schooler who is facing the pressures of peers. So when I prepare I try to keep in mind all these different groups of people in our church.

Preaching: Among all the well-known Southern Baptist pastors, you are perhaps the most consistently expository in your preaching style. What led you to that approach to preaching?

Vines: I was brought up under a pastor who did exposition, and I knew that was the way you should do it. I had a little church when I was eighteen, and I knew that was the way you were supposed to do it, so I took off in the book of Romans! I had at that point in time, beside my Bible, one other book to my name, George Truett's *Quest for Souls*. Those were the sixteen most miserable weeks of my life! I preached a sermon a week on a chapter in the book of Romans, and at the end of that I definitely knew it was not for me. So for the next ten years of my ministry I basically preached topical sermons. I really didn't know how to do exposition. My training in college or seminary—I won't say they didn't offer it, but somehow I didn't get it. I just didn't pick up the tools to help me do exposition. I guess my unpleasant experience may have colored that.

I was a pastor in the Chattanooga area, and went to a Bible conference to hear a man I'd never heard before, named Warren Wiersbe. Here was a man who opened up his Bible and almost nonchalantly, matter-of-factly, just began to explain the Scriptures. I heard him saying things about the Scripture I'd never heard, and I wondered, "Where is he getting this?" And I looked in the Bible, and he was getting it right out of the text. So it created a real desire on my part.

Taking from him, I determined that I would go back and start trying to preach through books of the Bible. Then along the way I had other influences in addition to Dr. Wiersbe. There was Stephen Olford—I started hearing him on Sunday nights from Calvary Baptist Church in New York. God gave me different teachers like that. Then I started reading books like *Expository Preaching Without Notes*. I just set out to do it, and I'm still learning.

Preaching: Who are some other preachers who have been an influence in your life?

Vines: I love to hear John Philips; he's a very fine expositor. I enjoy hearing Adrian Rogers. I used to love to hear James Montgomery Boice, before his death. W. A. Criswell was one of my early influences; he really stirred my heart.

Preaching: Why would you encourage other pastors to adopt an expository preaching style?

Vines: I would encourage it for several reasons. One reason is what it will do for you personally. I cannot tell you what it has done in my own personal life just to go through books of the Bible—just the study itself. Paul said to young Timothy, "Take heed unto thyself, and unto the doctrine" [KJV]. Just the study of Scripture to preach in an expository fashion is invaluable to your own personal spiritual life and growth.

Then what it will do to the people. It will give the people a well-balanced meal of the Bread of Life. You don't get hung up on one hobbyhorse, you don't neglect areas. It gives a total picture, which I'm a little concerned about today with the trend toward more need-oriented preaching. I think you should do need-oriented preaching, but if you're not very careful, you'll avoid certain things. I'm preparing to preach from Galatians 3—one of the tragedies in today's preaching is we take people straight to Jesus without getting them to Moses, and I think you've got to meet Moses before you're really ready to meet Jesus. You've got to see yourself as a sinner. Because even if you can come to Christ without seeing yourself as a sinner—which I'm not sure about—you won't have that overwhelming appreciation and gratitude for what Christ has delivered you from.

Preaching: Are there some areas in exposition with which you struggle?

Vines: Yes, one thing I struggle with is to work at keeping the method fresh. It can become a very dull and boring enterprise if you don't work to keep it fresh. I mean by that you can get into certain patterns. I have heard some expositors get up and say, "Now, last Sunday we looked at thus-and-so," and then give you a ten-minute recap of last week. That can get pretty dull.

Also—and I need to do a better job on this—the way it is presented, the packaging of your preaching, needs variety. It's not that hard to get the material up. Almost anybody can find enough books to get the material up for an expository sermon. It's how you package it that's the hard part. The manufacturing part is not all that hard; the marketing part is the real challenge! To keep it fresh, to keep it interesting.

Preaching: What are some things you do to keep your preaching fresh?

Vines: I try to approach things in a little different way sometimes. For example, I try to use some facets of drama. To me, good preaching is good use of imagination. Sometimes if you can couch the passage in some form of drama, you can make it more interesting. I'm always looking for something to freshen it up a bit.

I think just the delivery itself—connecting with people where they are. Getting up-to-date, real-life illustrations helps a great deal, especially when you've been at a place for twenty years like I have!

Preaching: How many books of the Bible have you preached through since coming to Jacksonville?

Vines: I have preached through every book of the New Testament one time, and almost half of them two times. I have preached through—not necessarily verse by verse, but a pretty good treatment of all the books of the Old Testament except ten, and I'm down to the real hard ones, like Leviticus! My intention, if God lets me live, is to do something on every book of the Bible, to at least give the people a good sampling.

One of the things I have found is that many of those little-known books—or at least little-preached books—have been the most interesting. Like Ecclesiastes—that was one of the most enjoyable, for me personally, of any of the books I've ever preached. And Job—I preached ten messages in Job. I didn't preach forty-two—that would get them so depressed they'd never get out! I just got done with a series in Ezekiel—that's a challenge. I did about fourteen of those. There's a lot of good stuff there if it's packaged right and put in a form the people can relate to.

Preaching: How long is a typical series for you?

Vines: My series are getting a little smaller. One of the reasons is people are more mobile than they used to be. We have quite a turnover in the city of Jacksonville. The second time I preached through the book of Romans I think I preached eighty-one messages. The last time I preached through Romans I did forty-three. Now I try to make it even shorter than that. Right now I'm doing a series from Proverbs—it's going to be called "Proverbs for Parents"—and there will be twelve messages. I'm doing a series called "A World in a Week" from Genesis 1—I finished preaching through the book of Genesis; now I'm going back to Genesis 1—and there are going to be twelve messages in that series. That's a little more in-depth on a smaller passage.

I'm cutting the length of them down. I have done a lot of verse-by-verse, and I am going back now on some that I have done and packaging it a little tighter. My tendency has been to be very content oriented—that is, give them every "of," "the," "and," and "but." But I have also found along the way—it's been a humbling experience—that they don't get it all. So I'm trying now just to get the real essence of the passage rather than all the details. I think you can get lost, sometimes, in the minutiae and miss the big picture. If it's germane to the understanding of the passage, then I'll deal with that prepositional phrase, but if it's not . . .

If the verse starts with "behold," I don't give an exegesis of "behold," the different words for "behold," how it's used in other contexts, and all that. I used to! My introductions would be my sermons—I wouldn't have time for the sermons because of the introductions! So I'm trying to get a little better. We're in a different day. People have a lot of things to do. I read the old Puritan writers, and I love them, but I think their folks didn't have a lot else to do!

Preaching: How long is a normal sermon for you?

Vines: We're on television, so that restricts me somewhat. I will normally preach about a thirty-seven-minute message on Sunday morning. Our Sunday-evening service is also televised, but it's not live; it's tape-delayed, so I have a little more flexibility. I preach three sermons each week here: Sunday morning, Sunday night, and Wednesday night.

Preaching: Tell me about your planning process.

Vines: I'm doing more planning than I used to. I used to get through with one series and get into the next one, but I am trying to contemplate ahead. I'm working generally three to six months out. What got me into it was the harder books. I found out I couldn't announce a series on Job and start studying it this week for next Sunday. So the harder books got me into doing a rough outline ahead, so when I get ready to start a book, I've already done a rough outline and a lot of the commentary work. So I try to plan three to six months ahead. Then week-to-week, I try to stay two or three weeks ahead, because I've found that you have emergencies come up during the week, and if you lose two or three days there, you can be in real trouble.

I divide my days into three parts. In the morning I stay at home. I have my study at home, and I do my study there in the morning. In the afternoon I come into the office for staff meetings, counseling appointments, anything I'm involved in there. At night, we don't have a lot of night meetings here; I do go visiting on Tuesday night. So I'm able to be home.

My mornings I plan very tightly. I schedule out the entire week, every hour of every day, in terms of study. I don't necessarily follow that every day, but at least I have something I can adjust. For instance, I may get started on my Sunday morning message on Monday morning and it's just really clicking. Where I was going to spend just an hour and a half on the morning message and an hour and a half on the evening message, I may spend the entire time on the morning message because it's just really producing for me. So I go ahead and finish out. I've got a schedule to follow, but I'm not rigid—but the fact that I have a schedule helps me get a lot done.

To have my study at home, I can go in—after my wife and, used to be, my children go to bed—I can go in and study and not take time away from them. I used to be quite a night owl; I quit that these days!

Preaching: How long do you spend in preparation for each message?

Vines: Preparation for Sunday morning, I'll spend about twenty hours. For Sunday evening, about ten. Wednesday night, probably about five. That's a lot of hours, but that includes everything—in the morning, at night.

Preaching: Do you have three consecutive series running simultaneously?

Vines: Right now on Sunday morning I'm in stewardship, but I'll be done with that next week and go back into Proverbs. On Sunday night "A

World in a Week" on Genesis 1, and Wednesday night I'm in Galatians. A lot of things I do on Wednesday night are things I've already done; I've already got outlines, I've already had messages prepared. That doesn't mean I just pick them up and use them; I study again, but a lot of the initial work is right there. I keep all of this in notebooks. It's there for future reference—I've got all my word study, outlines, those kinds of things. A lot of the spade work is done for me.

The big challenge of going back to books you've preached on is illustrations. An illustration you used when you preached ten years ago may not be so hot today! You've got to freshen it up. Or sometimes the outline I used before doesn't seem to work now, so I'll revise it. By the time I'm finished with it it's a new message, though it may have some of the components of the first message.

Preaching: What do you see as the advantage of preaching without notes?

Vines: I do think there are advantages to preaching without notes. You get better eye contact; I think you can be much more extemporaneous without notes. I would recommend it to young preachers.

There is a disadvantage to preaching without notes. As you get a little older, your memory tends to weaken. I think a young preacher would be wise to learn how to do it both ways. I turned sixty-five Sunday, and I'm aware my memory is not quite as keen as it used to be. I used to memorize every poem I used— I still memorize most Scripture I use. I memorized every quote. I don't do that any more: number one, I don't have time. And number two, I don't know that there's a real need to do that. So now on poems or things like that, I have them typed up and printed out in large print; I clip that in the back of my Bible, then when I get ready to use it I just turn there and read. I think I have tormented or afflicted myself enough on that!

There is some advantage to that eye contact, not having to look down.

Preaching: How has your approach to preaching changed over the years?

Vines: I think I have learned that you can make exposition interesting. When I first got into it, I think I labored with it so much, got so caught up in the process, that it may not have been as interesting. I've tried to brighten it up. I've tried to use humor.

If I was starting over, I would study preaching more than I did. I'm still learning. The preacher is facing tremendous obstacles today. Here he is preaching to a group of people who every night watch very polished people deliver newscasts, reading from teleprompters. And here the preacher is, perhaps with limited training, standing before the people—it can be very intimidating. But the preacher who is walking with God has a communicative tool that is unavailable to any other communicator on earth—and that is the power of the Holy Spirit. The Holy Spirit can take a stumbling, stammering preacher's message and use it to bring about miraculous changes.

Purpose-Driven Preaching

An Interview with Rick Warren

Few pastors have become more influential in shaping church life today than Rick Warren, founding pastor of Saddleback Community Church in southern California's Orange County. Under his leadership, the church has grown from the Warren family alone to regular worship attendance of more than twenty thousand each weekend. Warren has taken the insights he learned at Saddleback and shared them in the book *The Purpose-Driven Church*, which has become one of the most popular Christian books of recent years. (The interview preceded publication of *The Purpose-Driven Life*, which has sold more than twenty million copies.) Warren is a member of the board of contributing editors of *Preaching*, and this interview appeared in the September-October 2001 issue.

Preaching: Rick, we were just looking at some examples of *The Purpose-Driven Church* as it has been translated into different languages—twenty-one languages, a million copies; it is just an incredible story. How did the concept of the purpose-driven church come to be a part of your ministry?

Warren: It actually started when I was a short-term missionary in Japan being sent out by the Baptist Student Union years ago in college. While I was there, I began to say, "What is it in our churches that is cultural, and what is really biblical?" As I looked at the Japanese churches I saw that they were adopting a lot of the things that were not working here, so it just got my mind thinking. So I began—while I was in Japan—a lifelong study of what is it that makes a healthy church. Not necessarily a growing church but a healthy church.

I believe health creates growth. I don't have to tell my kids to grow. If they are healthy, they grow automatically. So the focus is often on the wrong thing—on growth. I began several things: first, I read through the New Testament over and over looking for principles, transcultural principles. If it is biblical, I believe it will work anywhere. American principles only work in America, but if it is biblical I believe it is transcultural. So I read through the New Testament over and over and over. I've read every book in print that I could find on the church or church growth or church structure.

Then I also wrote the one hundred largest churches in the United States. I just researched them and personally wrote them a letter and did my own personal research project. I discovered that, of course, it takes all kinds of churches to reach all kinds of people. There is more than one way to grow a church, and I say if you are getting the job done, I like the way you are doing it. The only wrong way is when you think there is one way that everybody should do it—your way.

What I began to see is that God uses all kinds of styles, all kinds of methods, all kinds of formats to reach all kinds of people. But the common denominators were every church that is going to be healthy has to worship, has to evangelize, has to help Christians grow, discipleship, has to do ministry in the world, and has to have fellowship. I began to see these over and over in the New Testament—I really saw them in the Great Commandment and the Great Commission.

The Great Commandment gives us two purposes; the Great Commission gives us three. The Great Commandment—Love God with all of your heart—that is worship. Worship is expressing my love to God. Love your neighbor as yourself—that is ministry. So two of the purposes of the church, worship and ministry, come from the Great Commandment.

Three of the purposes of the church come from the Great Commission. It says to go make disciples—that's evangelism. It says to teach them to do everything I [the Lord] have commanded you—that is discipleship. But right in the middle it says to baptize them in the name of the Father, Son, and the Holy Spirit. Now, why did God put baptism between these two great purposes of worship and evangelism? I think because of what it represents. Baptism does not just represent new life in Christ; it represents incorporation into the body. The Bible says we are baptized into the body of Christ. And so I think that baptism is a symbol for fellowship or incorporation. It says that I am not ashamed to say that I am a believer. I have identified myself as a Christian, and the point there is that we are called not to just be believers but belongers.

I finished Southwestern Seminary in December 1979, moved here with no money, no members, no building. All I have ever had really was a bunch of ideas and knew I was going to build it on the five purposes.

Really nothing more than that. Of course over the years the vision gets clearer and clearer and clearer. I have what you call Polaroid vision. That is, you take a picture and you hold it. The longer you look at it, the clearer it gets. So when I was twenty-five years old, all I knew was I wanted to build these five purposes into the church. But over the years I have learned that you have to have a strategy and structure, and there are certain things that you have to do to make that happen.

If you don't have a strategy or structure to intentionally balance the five purposes, the church tends to overemphasize the purpose that the pastor is most passionate about. So, for instance, if I am gifted in teaching, I tend to produce a classroom church that has Christians growing but maybe nobody is coming to Christ. If I have gifts in evangelism, I tend to produce a soul winning church where lots of people come to Christ but there is no depth. I may have gifts in the area of ministry—we'll have what I call a "family reunion church" with great fellowship, great *koinonia*, but no evangelism, no discipleship. Or you can have gifts in the area of worship and build what I call an "experiencing God" church—God comes down, the Holy Spirit falls, maybe there are signs and wonders. It's great worship, but no ministry or no fellowship or no evangelism. So, I need a strategy and structure to keep me from killing the church!

Preaching: **Where does preaching fit into that whole matrix?**

Warren: The bigger the church gets, the more important the pulpit becomes, because it is the rudder of the ship. Where else do you get an hour of undivided attention with all these people on a weekly basis? Most pastors do not understand the power of preaching. But even more important than that is they don't understand the purpose of preaching.

I probably have the largest library of books on preaching in America. I've read over five hundred books on preaching. Maybe some seminary might come close to that, but I am sure that no pastor comes close to five hundred books on preaching. And as I've read them, the vast majority do not really understand that preaching is about transformation, not information.

So to understand the purpose of preaching, first you have to go back and look at a few things. First, what is the purpose of God for man, and second what is the purpose of God for the Bible? Because once you understand those two things, your purpose for preaching becomes very clear. What is the purpose of God for man? Well, the Bible tells us in Romans 8:29, "For those he foreknew he did predestine to become conformed to the image of his Son." God's purpose from the very beginning of time has been to make us like Jesus. It has been from the very beginning. In fact, in Genesis he says, "Let us make man in our image"

[NIV]. That has always been God's purpose—to make man in his image. Not to make gods but to make us godly. To have the character of his son, to be conformed into the image of Christ. So he wanted to make us like himself. In Genesis there was the fall—Jesus came to restore what was there before. So the goal of all preaching has to be to produce Christ-likeness in an individual. Is that person becoming more and more like Jesus?

Now, what is the purpose of the Bible? Well, it says in 2 Timothy 3:16–17, "All Scripture is given by inspiration of God, and is profitable for doctrine, for reproof, for correction, for instruction in righteousness, that the man of God may be thoroughly furnished unto every good work." People misread that verse most of the time. The purpose of the Bible is not for doctrine, not for reproof, correction, instruction in righteousness. Those are all "for this" in the Greek. For this, for this, for this, in order that. The purpose is "in order that." So doctrine in itself is not the purpose of the Bible. Reproof in itself is not the purpose; correction, training are not the purpose. The bottom line is to change lives. "That the man of God may be thoroughly furnished unto every good work." So every message must be preaching for life change.

I hear people talk about life application as being a genre or type of preaching. If you are not having life application, you are not preaching. It may be a lecture, it may be a study, it may be a commentary, but it is not preaching. To me preaching is for life change. I am not the master of this. Don't make John the Baptist your model. Don't make John Mac-Arthur your model. Don't make Rick Warren, or Spurgeon, or Calvin, or anybody. Make Jesus your model.

In my two day seminar on preaching that we take thousands of pastors through I just keep coming back to, "Now, let's see how Jesus did it. Now, look how Jesus did it." You take the greatest sermon in the world—which is the Sermon on the Mount—and he starts off, "Let me tell you eight ways to be happy." Happy are you if you do this. You are happy if you do this. Then he talks about anger: don't get angry. He talks about divorce: don't divorce. He talks about worry—let me give you four reasons why not to worry: it's unreasonable, it's unnatural. He talks about all of these practical things, and then he goes, "Now, if you put this into practice, you are a wise man. If you don't, you are a fool and build a house on sand." It says the Pharisees were amazed because he preached as one having authority. It is 100 percent application. My model is not anybody but Jesus.

My goal is not to inform; I came to transform. Unless you understand that, your messages tend to be based on the traditional style of teaching. I say interpretation without application is abortion.

Preaching: How do you think through this whole issue of application as you are dealing with the text or the biblical theme? Walk me through that process as you think through how this applies to the lives of people.

Warren: The big thing is building a bridge between then and now. You have interpretation on one side, you have personalization on the other side, and in the middle you have the implication. The key is always finding the implication of the text. The interpretation—commentators tend to live in that world. Personalization—communicators tend to live in this world. It's a fine line, and you can fall off on either side. It is easy to be biblical without being contemporary or relevant. It is easy to be relevant without being biblical. The test is right there in the middle, walking that fine line.

We don't have to make the Bible relevant—it is—but we have to show its relevance. What is irrelevant, in my opinion, is our style of communicating it. We are tending to still use the style from fifty years back that doesn't match who we are trying to reach today.

When I start with an application, I first start with personal application. Nearly twenty years ago, I wrote a book on Bible study methods, on how to apply the Bible. It sold a couple hundred thousand copies. In fact Billy Graham picked it up and gave it to every evangelist in Amsterdam. In it I talk about a dozen different ways to apply Scripture so you start with your own life and you make applications there. A lot of it is just simple stuff like is there a sin to confess, a promise to claim, an attitude to change, a command to obey, an example to follow, a prayer to pray, an error to avoid, the truth to believe? Is there something to praise God for? So I start looking at it like that.

I also go back to the paradigm of 2 Timothy 3:16. Doctrine, reproof, correction, and instruction in righteousness is basically these four things: What do I need to believe as a result of this text? What do I not need to believe as a result of this text? What do I need to do as a result of this text? What do I need to not do as a result of this text? That is doctrine for reproof, for correction and instruction of righteousness. So I use that format. Start with personal application, then you go for the implication—what people need in their lives.

The biggest thing that I would say about application is that every pastor eventually gets to application. I'm just saying he needs to start with it, not end with it. A lot of guys need to start where they end their sermon. They will do about 80 to 90 percent explanation and interpretation in background study, and then at the end there is a little ten-minute application. Now, that is OK if you have a highly motivated group of people who just love Bible knowledge. But the Bible says there are a couple of problems with Bible knowledge. In the first place it says that knowledge puffs up but love builds up, and the Bible says that increased knowledge without application leads to pride. Some of the most cantankerous Christians that I know are veritable storehouses of Bible knowledge, but they have not applied it. They can give you facts and quotes, and they can argue doctrine. But they're angry; they are very ugly people. The Bible says that knowledge without application increases judgment. To him that knows to do good and does it not, it is sin. So, really, to give people knowledge and not get the application is a very dangerous thing.

Here is an interesting thing: look at the Bible and start taking the books of the New Testament and find out how much of the Bible is application. It will really change the way that you preach. For instance, I once preached through the book of Romans for two and a half years, verse by verse. I do both verse-with-verse exposition—which I call topical exposition—and I do verse-by-verse exposition, which is book by book. Two kinds of teaching for two different targets and two different purposes, and they are both needed for a healthy church. To say you only need one, I think is ridiculous. One is far more effective for evangelism, and one is far more effective for edification.

I am teaching through the book of Romans. Romans is the most doctrinal book in the New Testament. Yet how much of Romans is really application? Chapter one, doctrine. Chapter two, doctrine. Three, doctrine. Four, doctrine. Five, doctrine. Six, application. Seven, application. Eight, application. Nine, doctrine. Ten, doctrine. Eleven, doctrine. Twelve, application. Thirteen, application. Fourteen, fifteen, sixteen—application. So you have a book of sixteen chapters, and 50 percent is application. So even the most doctrinal book of the Bible is half life application. Then you go to Ephesians. Half of the book is doctrine, half is application. Colossians, first half of the book is doctrine, the second half is application, 50 percent. You get to a book like James—100 percent application. Proverbs, 100 percent application. Sermon on the Mount, 100 percent application.

So my cry is, "Pastors just do more of it. You already know that you have got to apply in people's lives; you have just got to do more of it." If that means cutting back . . . I think sometimes in our preaching we are far more interested in a lot of the details and backgrounds than people are. A guy who spends three weeks on one verse is missing the point of the verse. Truthfully, it's like looking at the *Mona Lisa* with a microscope. Every single word—God didn't mean for it to be read that way. He is missing the point of it. People who say, "I don't do topical preaching" but they take an entire two weeks for two verses, what are they doing? They are doing topical preaching. They are just using it as a jumping off point.

Preaching: How much of the sermon should be application versus explanation of the text?

Warren: I personally believe 50 percent. I know Bruce Wilkinson once did a study of great preachers. He went back and studied Spurgeon and Moody, Calvin and Finney, both Calvinists and Arminians. Then he studied contemporaries like Charles Stanley and Chuck Swindoll. He discovered that those guys were anywhere from 50 to 60 percent, some at 70 percent application.

What we normally do in a structure of a message is that we do interpretation and then application of a point, then the next interpretation and the next application, the next interpretation and the next application. I am suggesting that if you want to reach pagans, you actually just reverse that procedure. You still get both—it's just the way you do it. So instead of getting up and going through a long background on the Sermon on the Mount passage on worry and explaining, I stand up and say, "Isn't it a fact of life that we all deal with worry? Well, today we are going to look at six reasons why Jesus said that we shouldn't worry." Then you make your application the points of your message.

People don't remember much. If you are motivated, you remember about seven bits of information; if you're not motivated, you remember about two. So if they are only going to remember some things, what do I want them to remember? Well, I want them to remember the application, the lessons. Not a cute outline of the text. The alliterated outline is not going to change their lives. So I say make your applications your points, because the points are all that they are going to remember.

It is more important to be clear than it is to be cute. So I'll say, "Here are the three things that you have learned." Here is the contemporary application, and underneath it you go back and cover the background. Here is the point, and you go back and cover the background. It is the exact same thing—it is just the order—and what that does is it increases retention and it increases interest.

Now, understand that I am pastoring a church in California to a church where maybe 77 percent of the people were saved and baptized at Saddleback. Without question, Saddleback is the most evangelistic church in America. We have baptized 7,800 new believers in the last seven years. No church has ever done that—1,100 baptisms a year. I preached this year at Easter. We set up a 5,000-seat tent. I preached seven services. We had 33,000 for Easter—which is about a typical number—and we had 2,082 adult professions of faith recorded on cards. That is a crusade! To have 2,000 people saved—well, how does that happen? It happens when your focus is preaching for transformation, for changed lives.

Preaching: Tell me about the sermon that you preached on Easter.

Warren: I did a message on "I want to know the power of the resurrection." What is the power of the resurrection, Paul wants to know? It is the power to change your life. I do a little thing called CRAFT, which is a methodology that I developed. C stands for collect and categorize, R is research and reflect, A is apply and arrange, F is fashion and flavor, and T is trim and tie it all together.

As I go through these things, first I sit down and I start praying. I say, "Who is going to be there?" I start to think of one person. When a church gets as large as Saddleback, numbers really are irrelevant. There is no statistical difference between fifteen thousand on a weekend and sixteen thousand on a weekend—it's just a big crowd! So what motivates me is not the number; what motivates me is the individual changed life. I start thinking about people that I know that are going to be there—people that I have invited, like my back doctor who was an atheist Jew who came for Easter. I start thinking, "Now what is going to help this guy know about Christ?" and I will go through that little formula and think about the points, which were actually quite simple.

Point one was "open your mind to God's power." I talked about if your life is going to be changed, it starts with a change in your mind, which by the way, is the purpose of preaching. Open your mind to the power of God. The second point was "open your heart to the grace of God." The third point was "open your life to the love of God." Now, that is extremely simple. But by using metaphors and using Scripture—I use an average of sixteen verses per message.

We write the verses out; we put them on an outline. I do that for several reasons. In the first place, non-believers don't bring their Bibles to church. Second place, even if they did, they wouldn't know how to find it. Third place, it saves time. I once timed a guy, and he took about eight or nine minutes saying, "Now turn to this and turn to this." I don't have that time. I want all of the time for preaching. I preach on an average of fifty to fifty-five minutes. Most people would think, "Well he is preaching sermonettes for Christianettes"—you know, that kind of stuff. I typically preach fifty to fifty-five minutes. You can do that if you can understand features.

I use about fourteen to sixteen different verses. I will use different translations. That is another reason I will use an outline, because I use different translations. Sometimes the New American Standard says it better. Sometimes the New Living Translation says it better. Sometimes the NIV says it better. So I use that. It also allows me to have retention because you can have the people read it aloud together. We actually read Scripture aloud together. We probably read more Scripture aloud than the average church does because I have it on an outline. I say, "Now, let's all read this together." I'll say, "Circle that word, underline that, star that." Then they can take it home with them and put it up on the refrigerator, pass it on to friends, teach a Bible study on it. I'm a firm believer in actually writing out the message, outlined with Scriptures written out. If you are in it for life change, it just makes it a whole lot easier for people to use.

I actually started the message on Easter—I stand up and I say, "You know, if you are not a particularly religious person, if you don't feel particularly close to God, if you feel pretty disconnected, if you rarely attend church, congratulations! This is your holiday!" Rather than making people feel bad, I will say, "I am glad you are here. If you are going to go to church at all, I am glad you came here. And guess what—you don't know what you're in for!" And then I'll say, "What is Easter all about? It is an invitation to a changed life. Would you like a changed life? What does it take?" Just right at the start you roll it out—we are here for establishing a relationship with Jesus Christ. We had over a thousand people saved each of the last four Easters. So it is a great harvest for us every year. Our people bring their friends.

Preaching: Are there some particular insights you've gained over the years that help you preach for life change?

Warren: There are ten things that really form how I figure life can change. The first one is that all behavior is based on belief. If you ask why I do what I do, it's because you believe something behind it. If somebody gets a divorce, it is because they have a belief behind that which is causing them to get a divorce—I think I'll be happier divorced than I will not or whatever. If you have sex outside of marriage, it's because you have a belief behind it.

The second thing—behind every sin is a lie of unbelieving. This has profound implications for preaching. When you sin, at that moment you think you are doing what is best for you. You think you are doing the right thing, but you have been deceived. When your kids do something dumb, at that moment they think what they are doing is smart, but it's dumb. The Bible tells us that Satan deceives us.

The third thing—change always starts in the mind. This principle is taught all the way through the New Testament. Romans 12:2, "Be transformed by the renewing of your mind" [NIV]. The Bible teaches real clearly that the way we think affects the way we feel and the way we feel affects the way we act. Since change starts in the mind, and sin starts with a lie, and behavior starts with belief, number four—to help people change, you have to change their beliefs first. You don't work on their behavior; you work on their beliefs because it always starts in their mind. That is why Jesus says you will know the truth and the truth will set you free.

Number five—trying to change people's behavior without changing their beliefs is a waste of time. The illustration I use is it's like a boat on autopilot. I have got a boat and it is in a lake and it is on autopilot and it is headed north. If I want it to head south—I want to do a 180 degree turn—I want to do a "repentance" on that boat. I have two options: one, I could physically grab the steering wheel of the boat and physically force it to turn around and it would turn around. But the whole time it is turned around, I am under tension because I am forcing it to go against its autopilot. Pretty soon I get tired, and I let go of the wheel—I go back to smoking, I go off of the diet, I stop doing whatever, I go back to my habitual ways of stress relief. So, the better way is to change the autopilot. The way you change autopilot is by changing the way they think. Now, that brings up repentance.

The sixth thing that I believe is that the biblical word for changing your mind is repentance, *metanoia*. Now most people think of the word "repentance" as they think of sandwich signs: turn or burn. Or they think repentance means stopping all my bad actions. That is not what repentance is. There is not a lexicon in the world that will tell you that repentance means stop your bad action. Repentance, *metanoia*, simply means changing your mind. And we are in the mind changing business. Preaching is about mind changing. Society's word for repentance, by the way, is "paradigm shift." Repentance is the ultimate paradigm shift, where I go from darkness to light, from guilt to forgiveness, from no hope to hope, from no purpose to purpose, from living for myself to living for Christ. It's the ultimate paradigm shift. And repentance is changing your mind at the deepest level of beliefs and values.

Number seven is *you* don't change people's minds, God's Word does. So we bring people into contact with God's Word. I can't force people to change their mind. I like 1 Corinthians 2:13; in the New Living version it says, "We speak words given to us by the Spirit, using the Spirit's words to explain spiritual truths." There is both a Word and a Spirit element in preaching, and often we leave out the Spirit element. A lot of preaching today has the Word element but it doesn't have the Spirit element.

We talk about spiritual warfare. I don't think spiritual warfare is like demons. I think the Bible says spiritual warfare is tearing down mental strongholds. Our weapons have power—pulling down every argument, every pretension—that passage in 2 Corinthians 10. By the way, that's why you're exhausted after preaching. If you are trying to pull down strong-holds, you're in a mental and spiritual battle that is going to leave you exhausted. After I do five services every weekend I'm a puddle—there's nothing left!

Number eight—changing the way I act is the result or fruit of repentance. Changing the way I act is the *fruit* of repentance. Technically, repentance is not a behavioral change; it *results* in behavioral change. Repentance is what happens in your mind. So it doesn't mean forsaking your sin. That is why John the Baptist says produce fruit in keeping with repentance. Why would you need to produce fruit? Because the fruit is the action. The fruit is the behavior. Paul says in Act 26:20, "I preached that they should repent and turn to God and prove their repentance by their deeds" [NLT]. OK, so deeds are not repentance. But is that going to change your mind?

I believe, number nine, that the deepest kind of preaching, bar none, is preaching for repentance. The deepest kind of preaching. Life application, on the contrary, instead of being shallow preaching, I believe is the deepest kind of preaching. Shallow preaching, to me, is doctrinal application or interpretation with no application—biblical background with no application. For twenty-one years now, the secret of Saddleback is every week I get up and I try to take the Word and apply it so that it changes the way that they think about life, about God, about the devil, about the future, about the past, about themselves, about their mission in life.

If you go through the New Testament, you will find that repentance is the central theme in the New Testament. When I teach a seminar, I read them all these verses: Matthew 3:2, John the Baptist, "Repent for the kingdom of heaven is near" [NIV]. Jesus, "Jesus began to preach, 'Repent,'" Matthew 4:17 [NIV]. The disciples went out and preached that people should repent. Peter, "Repent and be baptized, every one of you" [NIV]. Paul, "Now he commands all men to repent everywhere." John in Revelation, "Repent." You just go through the New Testament.

To produce lasting emotional life change, you have to enlighten the mind, you have to engage the emotions, and you have to challenge the will. Those three things have to be present in life application preaching. There is a knowing element, there is a feeling element, and there is a doing element. This takes a lot of just being sensitive to the people, because sometimes they have to be comforted and sometimes they've got to be challenged. I can often get that wrong, you know.

This is one of the big weaknesses in our preaching. I think one of the greatest weaknesses is people who are unwilling to humbly stand before people and challenge their will. A lot of guys are great at interpretation. They are pretty good at application, but they are not really willing to stand there and call for repentance. Now I preach on repentance on every single Sunday without using the word because the word is misused today, it is misunderstood. So I talk about changing your mind, and I talk about paradigm shift. But really, every message comes down to two words: "will you?" Will you change from this to this in the way that you are thinking?

Our culture is falling apart. If you are not preaching repentance in your message, you're not preaching. No matter what we cover, it has got to come back to changing your mind, because your mind controls your life.

Preaching: What you are describing is preaching strategically, and a strategic approach requires planning. How do you plan that strategy in terms of what you are going to do in preaching?

Warren: I have a preaching team that I meet with. When you start a church you literally do everything. I set it up, I took it down, I stored all the stuff in my garage. From the beginning of the church it has been my goal to work myself out of a job. And so as the church grew, I began to give the ministry away to more and more different people—to laypeople and to staff and on and on. About ten years ago I realized that I had finally given up everything that I was doing except two things, the feeding and the leading. I was still doing that myself, and so I began to start building a staff of other leaders and other feeders. I now have a preaching team of six pastors who share the pastoral teaching and preaching.

This year, for the first time, I will be preaching twenty-six of the fifty-two weeks at Saddleback. Now, why is that? Well, several reasons. Number one, most people have never done five weekend services, and they don't know what a toll it takes on your body, and I want to live a long time. Since we are doing five we will probably go to six. I will preach in one month what some guys will preach in a year just because of multiple services. So, to protect my own health I did that.

But more than that, I believe you need to hear God's Word from more than just one personality. I think that is healthy. I think a lot of people, you hear a guy for about six or seven years, and he has shot his wad. You've heard what he has got to say, and you either have to start hearing the same stuff over again or move to a different church. Well, I want people to stay at Saddleback for thirty or forty years, so I've built a team of different preachers with different personalities—I do believe preaching is truth through personality, like Brooks said.

It doesn't bother me at all if somebody likes another pastor's preaching better. "Well, I like his style." That's fine. I think that is good. They hear it and they stay here, and as long as they are growing and happy and are being built on the purposes of moving them out into ministry and mission, I am happy about it.

I take that team and we do planning. I am a collector of ideas, collecting future sermon series and ideas. There are some series that I've been collecting on for twenty years that I still haven't preached on. For instance, I did a series through Psalm 23 a couple of years ago. I had collected material for over twenty years. I just knew that one day I was going to preach on Psalm 23. So when I get a quiet time insight, when I hear a good sermon and I hear a quote, I throw it in that file. When I get ready to plan a series, I'm not starting from scratch. I have what I call my bucket file. My bucket file is not real organized. It is just stuff tossed in there. Once you get enough to start making a series—you go, "I want to do this series on the family" or "I want to do this series on 1 Peter" or "I want to do this series on the second coming"—you start the file. Right now I have maybe fifty series in the hopper.

Then as it gets toward the end of the year, I will pick about a dozen of those that I think, "This is where God wants the church to go in the next year," and we prayerfully go away on a retreat. We pray and say, "What direction does God want the church to go? What needs to be done?" I'll tell you one of the ways you know what needs to be done: name the five biggest sins in your church. If divorce is a big sin in your church, guess what you're not preaching on. If materialism is a big sin in your church, guess what you're not preaching on. So looking at just the sins of the people in your church and in your area, you can come up with a lot of pretty good wisdom. I will get a dozen or so messages.

I happen to believe that the audience determines God's will for what you are supposed to preach on. In other words, do I believe in the sovereignty of God? Absolutely. Do I believe in the foreknowledge of God? Absolutely. That means God already knows who is coming next Sunday before I do, and God is already planning on bringing those people next Sunday for you. Why would God the sovereign give me a message totally irrelevant to the person he is planning on bringing? He wouldn't. So I start saying, "God, who is coming?" If I'm dealing with teenagers, that is one kind of message. If I'm dealing with seekers, then that is another kind of message. If I am dealing with mature believers, that is another kind of message. If I am dealing with people who need to be mobilized for ministry . . . We look at that and we pray, and then we will do a tentative outline of the series for the year.

We try to balance it in several ways. I try to give purpose balance. I will always do a series, somehow, dealing with worship, a series on evangelism, a series on discipleship, a series on ministry, and a series on fellowship. I will cover those five things every year because that is the purpose of the church in some way. Now I can do that with a book series, I can do it with a biographical series, I can do it with a topical, thematic approach. It doesn't matter the style, but I will balance the purposes.

I will balance the difference between comfort and challenge—afflict the comfortable and comfort the afflicted—I will balance that. I like to balance Old Testament and New Testament. I like to balance a little biographical, a little didactic, a little doctrinal.

Now what I love to do is to teach theology to non-believers without ever telling them it is theology and without ever using theology terms. For instance, I once did an eight-week series on sanctification and never used the term. I did a four-week series on the incarnation and never used the term. I did a twelve-week series on the attributes of God—the omniscience, omnipresence, omnipotence—and never used the terms. I just called it "Getting to Know God." I love to teach theology to non-believers without them knowing what it is; I find that a challenge. So it's a good balance.

We lay it out, then we never stick to it. If I know that I'm going to cover these ten to twelve themes or books in the year—that is where we are going in the year—I finish a series and then say, "Which one, Lord, do you want to do next?" We will pick it out, we will do it next, then we will go, "Which one, Lord, do you want us to do next?" So there is kind of planning and kind of spontaneity at the same time. It allows for God to move us in the middle of the year. I know some guys, it doesn't matter if it's Christmas, we are going to stay on that book! To me that's silly. If all of a sudden next week America were in war, does God have a word about it? Absolutely! We would stop, and we would talk about "What does the Bible say about war?"

Preaching: How long is a typical series?

Warren: I think the ideal series is four to six weeks. I have often stretched it to ten weeks. Obviously the Ten Commandments are ten weeks. I did a ten-week series on the doctrine of grace. Ten weeks on it. But really, if you go more than four or six weeks on a series, people start wondering, "Does he know anything else?" There is a fatigue factor. One lady said, "My pastor has been in Daniel seventy weeks longer than Daniel!" So I think the best series would be a month-long series of four; twelve a year would be ideal. We almost never do that because you get into it and you want to go another two weeks because there is still more material.

Preaching: The last time I was in a Saddleback worship service you did a "tag team" sermon with one of your preaching team members. That's an example of what you call "features" in preaching. Tell me more about that idea.

Warren: We now live in a society where the attention span is dramatically reduced. Yet I don't think you can really change a life in a twenty-five-minute message. I think it takes a more significant amount of time. If you're moving a person—trying to change the way they think—you have to lead them through a process that takes more than ten or fifteen or twenty-five minutes. But in order to hold their attention, what we do is add in what we call *features*. We have five or six different kind of features.

The most common one is the personal testimony. A lot of churches use drama; we honestly don't use that much drama because most of it isn't that good—it looks more like a camp skit. What I found is why would I use a dramatic fictional story when I have the real-life story of the changed life sitting there in the chair? We have now had hundreds and hundreds of people give their testimonies—we actually fit them into the message. So this week when I'm preaching on "Blessed are the poor in spirit," I'm looking at a series of testimonies right now. One of them is a woman who came out of prostitution, was saved here at Saddleback Church, and she talks about how she learned that, "I was not God, my life was a mess, and I had to give it all up." I'll fit that five- to seven-minute testimony right into the point. Rather than tell an illustration I'll say, "Now I want you to hear this." That's one feature—that breaks it up.

Another feature is what we call "tag team preaching." We developed that simply because we're doing five services, and it's pretty tiring to carry that long of a message five times. Five times fifty-five minutes is a long time! But what we found is that a different voice will often help keep the attention. I will write the message, but then I will assign a point to one of my teaching pastors. That often really adds a dimension of freshness that helps keep the people listening longer.

We have used film clips, we have used some dramas, we have used some object lessons. One of my favorites is called "point and play," which is separate the points by music. We always at Easter and Christmas Eve do a "point and play" message. For example, with my Easter sermon, I took every point and we divided it up into five sections, and we had a song that went with each point. So there is an emotional punch as well as an intellectual punch at the same time. We layer it: tension/release, tension/release.

I learned this when I was a consultant on the DreamWorks movie *The Prince of Egypt* to help keep it biblically correct. One day I was in the hall at DreamWorks, and I noticed something on the wall called an "Emotional Beat Chart." They actually monitor the emotional highs and lows of a movie. I counted up, and there were nine peaks and nine valleys in this ninety-minute movie—about every ten minutes there's tension/release, tension/release. Well, you can do that in a message: you can do it with humor, you can do it with an illustration, or you can do it with a feature, but it allows us to keep people's attention longer in order to give them more material.

Preaching: **You mentioned earlier the distinction between topical exposition and verse-by-verse. How do you see the difference between those models?**

Warren: Let me talk to you about the futility of preaching labels. We often hear modifiers used for preaching. We say there is topical and there is textual and there is life situational and there is expository. Frankly I think that's a big waste of time, and I have kind of given up on trying to label other guys' sermons, much less my own. The reason why I discovered it is because everybody has their own definition. They are meaningless. I have got over five hundred books on preaching in my library, and I have learned that everyone has their own definition. I started a hobby a few years ago of collecting definitions of the term "expository preaching." Right now I have over thirty definitions of the term, many of them contradictory. In fact, at one well-known seminary I got three definitions of expository preaching that were contradictory by three preaching professors in the same seminary!

I read this quote by Clyde Fant in *Twenty Centuries of Great Preaching*; it says it is impossible to define the terms "textual," "topical," and "expository." There is no modifier to explain all that God does through preaching or the way that he uses it. The only question that matters is, "Does the sermon involve itself in the truth of God's Word?" When it does you have genuine preaching and all of the modifiers of the term become superfluous. If you use God's Word to bring light and change people's lives, then preaching has occurred regardless of the message used.

Given that, here is my definition of expository preaching, and I think that it's about as valid as anybody else's of the thirty-some odd that I have already collected: "When the message is centered around explaining and applying the text of the Bible for life change." That definition says nothing about the amount of text used, and it says nothing about the location of the verses, because I think those are man-made issues. I read frequently we need to get back to the New Testament pattern of verse-by-verse preaching. Well, there is one problem there. There is not a single example in the New Testament of it. The fact is Jesus always taught in parables.

What do Finney, Wesley, Calvin, Spurgeon, Moody, Billy Graham, Jesus, Peter, and Paul all have in common? None of them were verse-by-verse, through-the-book teachers. Not one of them. Now the issue becomes how much of the text is a text? That is really the issue. How much text is a text? It depends on who you are talking to. If you talk to

G. Campbell Morgan, he often uses an entire book of the Bible. If you talk to Alexander Maclaren, he would usually preach on a paragraph. If you talk to Calvin, Calvin's general rule was to use two to four verses almost always—two to four verses. Spurgeon usually chose an isolated phrase—not even an entire verse, an isolated phrase. Of course, Martyn Lloyd-Jones would often preach on just one word. He has a famous sermon "But God."

I don't think that God cares at all whether you preach ten verses in a row or ten verses from his Word from different places as long as you adequately expose and exposit those verses once you are there. I don't think God cares whether they are in a row or not as long as you adequately feel that the text wants you there—that you don't use it as a jumping off point. Now the "topical" sermon that just takes a verse and doesn't even deal with it and just goes off—of course that is not preaching.

I believe there are two kinds of exposition. There is verse-with-verse exposition, which is taking verses from different parts of Scripture. That is valid; in fact there are some themes you have to do that. If you are going to preach on abortion, then you need to take verses from several passages of Scripture. If you are going to preach on the second coming, you need to take verses from several passages of Scripture. I believe in verse-by-verse book exposition, too. I do a combination of both. I just finished doing verse-by-verse through James again. Second time in twenty years going through James.

Preaching: Do you vary styles between the weekend and midweek services?

Warren: I will do them in both. I used to do only verse-with-verse in our weekend services, and I would do only verse-by-verse in the midweek service, and we would divide it up that way. We have since taken our midweek service and killed it and taken that teaching and put it on video—we are now putting it into groups. I have just taught through the book of James verse by verse on video, and it is going to the eight thousand people we have in small groups. We never could get eight thousand to show up for midweek, but they are in small groups. So they turn it on and watch it, and they turn it off and discuss it and apply it.

I have done a number of books on Sunday morning. In the last year we have done 1 Peter. We have done Philippians, we have done a Gospel, we've done Proverbs, I've done Ecclesiastes verse by verse. I don't have a hang-up with it. It is just when people start saying it is the only way to preach or the apostolic method. I am saying, "Show me where it is in the Bible. Show me where it is!" I am very opinionated on that!

Preaching: What is the biggest mistake that you have made in preaching?

Warren: We have done more things that didn't work at Saddleback than did. We are just not afraid to fail.

I think the biggest mistake that I made in the first couple of years of my preaching here at Saddleback, I didn't realize the importance of drawing the net. I think drawing the net is an important thing. I didn't know as much as I do now. Forsyth says that what the world needs today is the authoritative Word of God preached through a humble personality. I think that a combination of confidence and humility goes together. I have learned that the secret of spiritual power is integrity and humility.

It is not vision. A lot of people talk about vision being a big thing to grow a church. Vision is a dime a dozen. A lot of people are visionaries who are not growing churches. What God blesses is first integrity, walking with integrity. Walking blameless. That we are exactly what we appear to be. The other is humility. Now, humility is not denying your strengths; it is being honest about your weaknesses. We're all a bundle of strengths and weaknesses. We all have strengths. We all have weaknesses. Paul could be very obvious about his strengths. He would say, "Follow me as I follow Christ." Because he was also very honest about his weaknesses: "I am chief among sinners."

I used to look at Paul and go, "Man, I could never say that." Follow Rick Warren as Rick Warren follows Christ? It seems so arrogant. But then I realized that people learn best by models. At least I am making the effort. I am not perfect, but you know what? I'd rather have people follow me than follow a rock star! I am at least making the effort, and they know what my weaknesses are because I am honest, I am authentic with the people.

I do believe in confessional preaching. I believe that you should confess both your strengths and your weaknesses. You don't dwell on yourself, but in many ways the minister is the message. The Word must become flesh. The best kind of preaching is incarnational preaching. The most effective message is when I am able to get up and say, "This is what God is doing in Rick Warren's life this week. This is what I am learning. This is what I need to believe, what I need not to believe, what I need to do, what to not do." Those four things. There is a ring of authenticity about that.

It is interesting that I have a thorn in the flesh that makes preaching extremely painful for me. I was born with a brain disorder, and I took epilepsy medicine through high school. Although I did not have epilepsy, they gave it to me because they did not know how to deal with it. And I would faint; I would be walking down the street and just fall over and faint. It is a very complex thing, but I am under the care of Mayo Clinic. I have been to the best doctors in the nation. I have a very rare disease that less than two dozen people have—that's what Mayo Clinic told me. What it does is my brain does not assimilate adrenaline correctly. So adrenaline—when it hits my brain—it will tend to blind me, will tend to create headaches, dizziness, and confusion, and all kinds of things.

Any pastor knows that adrenaline is your best friend. If you don't have adrenaline, you are boring. You need adrenaline for passion. Yet the very thing that I need to speak to five thousand people at one time is the very thing that harms my body. So it's quite painful for me to preach, and I just think it is in God's sense of humor that the guy that he chose to speak to Saddleback is a guy who is really quite weak. In my weakness, he is strong.

Sometimes people would think, "Warren, do you ever get full of pride knowing you preached to thirty-two thousand or thirty-three thousand people last week?" I want to say, "If you only knew." When I am up speaking, that is the last thing on my mind—"Oh, how great this is." My thing is, "Oh, God, just get me through this." The reason I do it is because I am addicted to changed lives. That is what motivates me. I love it. People say I love to preach. I don't love to preach—it is painful for me to preach. It is actually painful. But I love the results of preaching. I love the changed lives.

If a guy says, "I love to preach," that never impresses me. They may just be a ham. They may just like the attention. They may just like to be the center of attention. They like the adrenaline rush of being on stage. I don't want to know do you love preaching but do you love the people you preach to? That's the key. If I have not love, I am sounding brass and tinkling cymbal. So when I get up to speak, I do this five times. I have a whole prayer. It is about a thirty-second prayer that I pray every weekend. I pray on Saturday and Sunday at every service. As I get up before the crowd and I look out there, I go, "God, I love these people, and they love me. I love you and you love me, and you love these people and many of these people love you. There is no fear in love. Perfect love casts out all fear. This is not an audience to be feared; this is a family to be loved. So love these people through me." That is the last thing that I think before I get up to speak before every service. It just kind of gives you the pastor's heart.

Preaching: When you get up to preach, what do you carry with you?

Warren: I carry, of course, my Bible, my notes, and my outline.

Preaching: How extensive are your notes?

Warren: A fifty-five-minute message is four half pages one side. I use trigger words. I use transition words. It is very important that I always write out my closing prayer—word for word—because I find that when I get to the end of the message I am starting to get fatigued. And when you do a message five times—you say the same thing with passion five times—your mind just starts shutting down on you on the fourth or fifth sermon, so you need pretty extensive notes. Now, I could memorize the message and not use notes. To me that seems to be an enormous waste of time, because the amount of time used to memorize it I could be in personal ministry, in leadership, in other things. I don't think that people care that much. God uses all styles. We have got a guy on our staff who is a manuscript preacher, but he delivers it with vitality so he is not just reading it. I do walk around a lot, so I can look at something and it will keep me going for two to three minutes, but I do use notes.

Preaching: In your preparation process, do you develop any kind of manuscript yourself?

Warren: No, I don't do a manuscript partly because I don't want it to sound like a manuscript. It's an oral presentation. Having been both a writer of many books and a preacher, those are two different skills—two totally different skills. The guy who thinks he can take his sermon and just put it into a book, forget it. It is not going to be that good of a book. Because the things that make good oral communication—like repetition, redundancy, coming back to the point—just sound goofy in a book. So I don't want to sound like a book.

What I will do is to sit at the computer and talk it out as I type. I am very concerned about how it will sound. This is a big key to a lot of guys who have good content but they don't know how to turn a phrase. They don't know the power of timing. You know, all over America, baseball pitchers stand the same distance from home plate, throw the same ball to the same plate. The difference between pros and amateurs is delivery. No doubt about it.

The difference between a good sermon and an outstanding sermon is delivery. I know this because I preach the same material to five services every week and get different results depending on the delivery. The first message of the weekend is never the best time. You are not as comfortable with the material. You are going to become more and more comfortable. As you say it repeatedly you are going to become passionate about it, and so you learn timing, you learn delays, you learn delivery.

Preaching: If you had just one or two words to encourage or recommend to other pastors, what would they be?

Warren: One of them is never stop learning. All leaders are learners. The moment you stop learning you stop leading. Growing churches require growing pastors. The moment you stop growing, your church stops growing. I don't worry about the growth of the church. I never have. In fact, it probably will surprise most people that in twenty-one years we have only set two growth goals—and they were both the first year of the church! What I focus on is keeping myself growing and motivated, and if I am on fire, other people will catch it. So you keep growing.

And I would encourage people to listen to pastors. Find a style that is similar to what you think you are and learn from it. It is OK to have models. I remember in my early days listening to pastors, particularly in my revival days. I preached over 120 revivals before I was twenty. I was in the typical full-time evangelist, youth evangelist mode. I would listen to guys. You'll develop your own style eventually. You can't help but be you.

I also really am a firm believer in let's share our material. I know some guys say you have got to be original or nothing—Vance Havner said he was both! Plagiarism is borrowing from one person, research is borrowing from five, and borrowing from ten or more is sheer creativity! Creativity is the art of concealing your source! It is forgetting where you forgot it. I would say we are all on the same team. Nobody can be brilliant every week, so we need to share. If you get a good idea, man, send it to me! I'm not proud—I'll use it. I learned a long time ago I didn't have to think everything up for it to change a life. In fact a person who thinks he has to think it all up himself really has a pride problem. The Bible says that God gives grace to the humble but resists the proud. Why? Because the proud are unteachable. "I didn't invent it here, then I can't use it"? That's silly.

So I want to use outlines, illustrations, quotes, ideas from different people. We are all on the same team when we get to heaven. When we get to heaven we'll rejoice for the souls that have been saved. That is why I decided a long time ago to start a tape ministry rather than do radio or TV. First, because I don't want to be a celebrity. Second, because I don't want to raise money. It takes enormous sums of money—it turns you into a fund-raiser.

More than that, it doesn't help the local church, and I am a firm believer in helping the local church. God blesses the local church. If I were to put my messages on radio, I don't help that church, I compete with it. A member listens in the car, and he goes, "How come my pastor doesn't preach like Warren does?" Well, that doesn't help his church at all. So instead of going on the radio or TV, I tape the messages. I don't copyright anything that I do, nothing. I tell pastors, "If God has given me a way to outline, and you want to take that outline and put your meat on it, your bones, go right ahead."

I got a call the other day from a guy in Canada, and he says, "Pastor Rick, I need to apologize. I preached through one of your series." I said, "Buddy, that's the point!"

You know what? If some guys are C preachers and by using my material or somebody else we could make a B, that's a good thing. They may be an A at counseling or an A at administrating, but they're just not good at outlining. So let's help each other.

Preaching to the Unchurched

An Interview with James Emery White

James Emery White is founding pastor of Mecklenburg Community Church in Charlotte, North Carolina—one of the fastest-growing churches in the nation. Using Willow Creek Community Church as a model, White's pastoral initiatives also draw on his experience while serving as preaching-worship consultant for the Southern Baptist Sunday School Board (now LifeWay Christian Resources). This interview was published in the January-February 1999 issue of *Preaching*.

Preaching: Tell me about your church and its background: when you started, the goals you had going in, and some of the methodology you have used.

White: Mecklenburg is a seeker-targeted church that was started in the fall of 1992 for the express purpose of being not simply a new church but a church that would focus on reaching unchurched people. By seeker-targeted I obviously mean that the entry points of the church are designed for unchurched people. In some way, shape, or form we can tap into when they are in a search mode, or we try to help them become active seekers. Because not everyone who is unchurched is a seeker.

After five years, by God's grace, we have about 80 percent of our total church growth having come from an unchurched background. So we have maintained that focus. Obviously, it is a normal church in every other sense of the word, but our entry points have been from day one exclusively designed for seekers, for the unchurched.

We're in Charlotte, a fast-growing area. Obviously, we are in the heart of the Bible Belt, but like cities such as Atlanta, it has become inundated with transfer growth from all over the country. The challenge is huge in terms of the melting pot atmosphere—all different walks of life, all different cultures, all different backgrounds and nationalities. So it has been a fun ride, and it has been a very challenging one to try to speak to that context and try to stay focused on that particular audience in terms of front door issues, while at the same time keeping focused at our midweek service to feed and to care for and to challenge the believer. When you wear both hats as a communicator each and every week, you stay focused or you get very confused very quickly and you start making mistakes all over the place!

Preaching: What is your attendance now?

White: About fifteen hundred after five years. We are at three weekend services now. We meet in a high school. [Since this interview, the church has moved into its own facilities.] We have services Saturday night, and we do two on Sunday. All three are identical and a midweek service—we just have one—is on Wednesday night. Our Saturday night service has been very, very successful. I think the first time we offered it, we had 150 to 200 people; it just really meets a need. They come in at 5:30, and they are out by 6:30 and start to go out and have their night. That's really how it works. Great for young families and those with kids.

Preaching: Can you tell a difference in the personality of the different services?

White: Interesting that you ask that. Yeah, you can; you really can. Saturday night is the smallest of the group. But they are also the most relaxed. They will often laugh the hardest and be into it the most. There is something about it that is even more laid back than on Sunday, even though our services are identical. There is a little more energy perhaps with our Sunday morning services because they are a larger crowd. But I think we all really like our Saturday night folks.

It changes every week. You just have a group of people that likes Saturday night. There is a certain constituency for that, but the truth is that you're just saying, "OK, every weekend here are three opportunities. Choose whichever one is most convenient." And our people have absolutely no loyalty to a particular one. Every weekend, people say, you know, "Brenda, which one is good this week?" "Let's do Saturday because we want to hit the lake Sunday." It is purely a matter of convenience. So if we kill one of them, we would literally lose a lot of attenders because of the lack of convenience.

Preaching: Are you trying to do anything else on the weekend besides the worship experience itself?

White: The seeker experience. And I'm not picking at you; it is just that I fight a lot of fights over that one in terms of understanding the model.

We have a simultaneous children's program that runs with all three of those services, fourth and fifth grade. There is a baptismal service which we will have three or four times a year on Sunday afternoon; we rent out a YMCA. We do nothing on the weekends. Throughout the week is when we have our middle school and high school ministries. We rent facilities. The student ministry meets on Tuesday nights. They have a full band, the whole bit. Our small groups meet throughout the week at all different times and places. So all the other ministries of the church happen other times.

I don't know if that will even change once we have our own facilities. We've got our land, but we don't have our buildings. That will be a few years, but I don't know if that'll change.

Preaching: When you use the term "seeker service," is it fair to say that you are describing an evangelistic tool rather than a worship style?

White: It is an evangelistic methodology. People come and they attend the weekend service, and they just say, "This isn't worship. Well, what a wild thing this is." You're just seeing our evangelistic strategy; you're seeing how we have crafted the front door for a specific purpose. In that service you're not seeing the church. This is a full-blown New Testament, Acts 2 animal. You are just seeing the way we open the front door. That's it.

Some people equate "seeker targeted" and "seeker sensitive." And those are two different models. Saddleback and Willow Creek are two different models. Then people confuse contemporary—just a merely contemporary church—with seeker sensitive. What is even worse is when they start using the term "seeker driven," which is theological heresy. Nobody is seeker driven. You and I and everyone else could sit there and say, "Oh, my goodness." Nobody wants to go there. But that is the phrase that is often attached to this. I'm off of that horse.

Preaching: Would it be fair to say that Willow Creek has really been the model that you have been trying to follow?

White: I think it would be fair to say that before Mecklenburg, when I was back at the Sunday School Board as a leadership consultant for preaching and worship, my plan was to study the most effective communicators, the most effective models around the world. To plan Mecklenburg, I stole from everyone without blushing. I studied every effective model I could. So if somebody says, "I see some Willow Creek at Mecklenburg," well I hope so; it's the most effective church in North America in the last two decades. "I see some Saddleback." Well, I sure hope so; it's the fastest growing Southern Baptist church. If I can't learn from them, then there's something wrong. You'll see a lot of other things, too.

I think that the creativity of Mecklenburg is how we've put it all together. As a result we see a lot of distinctives and things that look fresh and new and different. I would say that I have been most inspired by Willow Creek. And certainly if you visit Mecklenburg, you'll say this looks and feels an awful lot like Willow Creek, and I don't even try to hide that. We have differences in our church structure. We are probably much more like Saddleback in terms of our church structure. We don't have elders. There are many other differences that are probably not important to go into here. But I would say we have probably more affinity with Willow Creek than almost any other church. And there are a lot of close relational ties between us and Willow Creek.

Preaching: You mentioned that when you worked for the Sunday School Board, part of your job was observing and studying the great churches across America. That's a wonderful opportunity! Who are the people who have impressed you as the most effective communicators of the gospel in this culture?

White: Bill Hybels [Willow Creek Community Church] is very good. Bob Russell at Southeast Christian [Louisville, Kentucky] I think is an effective communicator. Rick Warren [Saddleback Community Church] is a very effective communicator to the people he talks to. I confess that the way you have raised your question has me drawing up a very short list because it is one thing to be a good preacher; it is a second thing to be a good communicator. Preaching and communication are two different things. I think the list gets even shorter when you say a good communicator of the gospel to contemporary America.

If you had said, "Who are good communicators of Christian truth to the evangelical world or the Christian culture?" I could come up with a fairly extensive list. When you phrase it "communicating the gospel to our modern culture," I think that list gets very, very short because, quite frankly there are very few communicators where that's even their primary agenda. There are actually very few communicators out there who are specializing in and truly are speaking to unchurched people on a week-in, week-out basis. I do, I know Bill does, I know Rick does.

Then there are some people who I think are just flat-out, drop-dead killer communicators. I think of the Tony Campolos of the world. There are very few people who are actually engaging the culture. Many are critiquing it, many are speaking at it, but not many are truly connecting with it and dialoguing with it.

I wish there were more so that I could steal everything that they do. Every time I even smell someone that seems to be communicating well, I try to get their stuff, and I really find very few communicators who I think that are truly doing that.

Preaching: Are there some preachers who you listen to who encourage and inspire you?

White: Bob Russell I think is good, a pretty good guy for that. I probably should have not put him into the former category, but in this category. There are a lot of resources that I use. The things that I use from an audio perspective, things like John Maxwell's tapes, I enjoy very, very much. I enjoy very gifted communicators that are often in the marketplace. But the people who touch my soul are probably more authors than they are speakers, everybody from Philip Yancey to Larry Crabb. In fact, I want to meet Larry Crabb one day so I can tell him how much he has agitated my soul over the years.

Preaching: You mentioned Maxwell's tapes. What are some of the other resources you turn to for trying to developing the kind of communication you aim for?

White: I love academia and have devoted much of my life to it, but there are very few things within academia that really helped me communicate. And even things that are trying to speak to the interplay between Christ and culture are often almost missing the boat in terms of actually connecting and addressing or dialoguing with the culture. They are very good at critiquing the culture but not necessarily in helping to build bridges of communication. You need to be reading *Time* and *Newsweek*, *People* magazine, as difficult though it may be to wade through sometimes. The newspapers. I insist on seeing the latest films. The latest, the top books, fiction and nonfiction. The latest CDs. For example, in the last six months, my speaking has touched on everything from John Grisham's latest book to the movie *Titanic* to songs of Alanis Morissette to Monica Lewinsky

These things are where people are at, and to me they are bridges into their souls. And so I pull heavily from popular culture. Then I use the more cerebral issues related to Christ and culture, including my theological training to form the foundation upon which I stand in using those tools. Because if you don't have that as your base in bracing and using those tools, then those tools can become the tail that wags the dog, and you can fall into all kinds of trouble.

Preaching: Separating the seeker service from the worship experience—which is your midweek service—as you stand in front of the audience of the seeker service, what are you trying to accomplish?

White: Several things. And certain messages are trying to do different things. But I would say there are probably a half dozen things that I am always trying to do that continually pop up. One is really contend for the truth in Christianity. Now, I can do that through contending for its relevance; its practical help for life, its reasonableness. I can do that in all kinds of ways. One of the biggest things I do is just to explain Christianity. I think that's the best approach; I think it is often the best evangelism. Let me just explain this to you. Let me take a few weeks and just talk about grace, what is that? So, a lot of it is explanation, a lot of it is contending for its truth. A lot of it is trying to show its relevance, its practical help for their lives. Then you can say, "This will work for your marriage because it is true." It is not true because it works; it works because it is true.

The biggest thing I am doing is presenting the Christian faith to a secular mind in a way that they can grasp it and evaluate it and consider it for their lives. Much of that is in removing the barriers. If they can see someone who looks relatively normal on Sundays, if they can hear language that they can relate to, if I can use cultural bridges that help them understand it, and if I can use topics that are relevant to their lives no matter where they are at in their spiritual quest, then I am just continually able to present this for their life. And that is really what I am doing—clearing up misconceptions, all these kinds of things.

To give you an idea of how drastic it can be: we have just come off of twelve weeks going through the Sermon on the Mount, verse by verse—explaining essentially the heart of the teaching of Jesus. Everything from teaching on divorce to money—all kinds of things—and now we are in a series on comparing Christianity to world religions. We've got everybody bringing their Muslim friends and their Hindu friends as we walk through these things, and just explaining the distinctives of Christianity. When we get out of this we are going to spend four weeks on a different issue: guilt. We are going to spend four weeks on just guilt. Good guilt versus bad guilt. Then we are going to come out of that with a real horizontal series, probably something on family or parenting. Then come back at it with something else. So we are just continually coming at people with different ways trying to present this.

Preaching: Do you stay in a series format most of the time?

White: I do. Always in a series. There are several reasons. First, it is very hard to do a topic in one session with integrity, at least to the people I address. They would pick up on a real superficiality if I said, "OK, here is how to have a good marriage" in a one-day talk. You know, they are going to say, "Maybe *your* marriage, buddy!" There is no way you can treat that with integrity. So those are the series that are six or seven weeks. You build credibility that way, and you can really address it with legitimacy. You are going to have a series on marriage. OK, one week: here's how to have a fair fight. Here's how to lay a spiritual foundation. Here's one whole talk on gender differences. Here is the thing on communication. People are sitting there and saying, "Now, this I can use. This I can grab on to."

One criticism of seeker-targeted churches is it is all topical messages. Actually, it is more strategic than that. You have occasional messages on topics like marriage and family and parenting relationships. Then you will also have series that might be nothing but a section of Scripture. We've done a whole series on the Ten Commandments. We've done a whole series on the Sermon on the Mount. Sometimes it is a theological series. We did five whole weeks on the problem of evil and suffering called, "When God doesn't make sense." So you do strike on theological issues and ethical issues. Sometimes you'll do nothing but doctrine studies on the character of God. So, it is more of a variety.

Even when you do these topical studies, it's more of a biblical theology. It may be pulling together a lot of verses instead of walking through one particular chapter of the Bible, although it can be one particular chapter. But it is doing it with great theological and biblical integrity.

The best biblical theologies pull together the wide range of verses and passages and Scriptures. The best way to interpret Scripture is through Scripture itself. Sometimes if you take just one small passage on a subject, you can actually almost do more harm than if you pull together everything that the Bible has to say to get a well-rounded view. So I think if you are a good topical speaker, you are doing good biblical theology.

Preaching: Is there a typical series length for you?

White: For a month. In other words if there are four weeks in the month, I'll do a four week series. If there are five weeks in a month, I'll do a five-week series. That is typical for me. A couple reasons. One, short attention spans. Two, most topics you can get in and out of if you do your homework at that level. Three, it keeps variety going every month. There is a new topic and you can switch gears. There are some topics that could use ten weeks. But, people are dying by the eighth week. You know, "Can we please move on!"

We can be promoting a new series at the beginning of each month in newsletters and things like that. There is a whole list of reasons.

We choose our longer series carefully and always try to say, "Can this really sustain this many weeks?" And often they will prove to become our most poplar series. But we choose them really well. The longest we've done is the Sermon on the Mount; the next to longest was the Ten Commandments, which is probably the most popular series we've ever done.

Preaching: How far out do you plan your series? How do you decide what series to do when?

White: I think there are some things we have tripped onto that I know really serve me well. First, I take an annual study break in the summer, and I actually leave the state and go to a place for about six weeks. It wasn't that in the early days, but when you plant a church you can kind of go into that. But now it is right at six weeks. And I just go and I plow up ground for another year of teaching and leadership. Read books, map out stuff. I come back from a study break with the whole next year mapped out. Now, in reality it is only good for about eight or nine months. Then the focus I have starts getting fuzzy and I almost have to take it month by month for what we are going to do. But I pray about that; I strategize about that. I take everything I know about the church and culture and life and what we've done in the past and come up with these series. It really seems to click.

I take that to a creative development team of about eight or nine people that represent a lot of our programs and ministries. Drama, music, multimedia, people who are just involved in producing our weekend services. I will lay these out, and we will begin to pull together the services. We usually work as much as three months in advance. So it goes through that process, which helps me enormously because when you pull in your creative team they start thinking about video, drama, and music ideas about a topic, and I have not even begun actually to write out the message. I've done some research in reading, books. But it helps me enormously to sit around with seven or eight folks. That's the song you think of, or that's what you think of with guilt.

So there is a study break, and throughout the year I have files on all these series. I'm collecting things as I read books. In my mind I know that I am doing these series. It is like a magnet pulling all of this stuff in. Then as it gets closer it goes through the whole creative team developing process, so every week I'm going through a three-hour meeting talking about these things. I tell you, it is so healthy to go through all those different levels.

When I actually have my writing day, which is the Tuesday before I speak, I pull all the stuff together and I actually write the message, and I am just about to pop. You know it is wonderful—it has been thought out, it has been prayed for, prepared. I've been reflecting on it. I've got all this stuff. The privilege of this is that I'm the kind of person that finds working in advance like that is not difficult. For me, a panic attack would be doing a Saturday night special. I couldn't do that. If I did not know what I was going to be speaking on in three or four weeks, I would have an anxiety attack.

Preaching: How long is a typical sermon for you?

White: About thirty minutes. Short end twenty-five, long end thirty-three or thirty-four, but it is right in that thirty minutes. Very tight. I work from a manuscript. But I work off the manuscript enough until I go up there where it is just an outline. But I don't deviate from that. There's a discipline that I have on what that manuscript length is going to be.

Preaching: You wrote a book entitled *Rethinking the Church*. Tell me in what key ways you have rethought the church.

White: Let me answer first in the context of what we do on the weekends, then we can shift it to the worship context. There are really two different things that we do. If I were to sit down with some pastors and talk about communication, I would say that the most liberating thing I can imagine is the freedom to be authentic and to be yourself. To be able to talk normally to people, to be able to be natural. To not have to be something that is contrived. I think that the most effective thing about what I do at Mecklenburg, by God's grace, is the fact that I'm able to be up there and talk the way I normally am. I'm a fairly passionate person, and that comes out in my speaking. But it is not a contrived thing.

The way I dress, the way I communicate, even the vocabulary I use will alert the listener to just who I am. That resonates with folks. There is a sense where, the people that I communicate to, maybe that's what grabs them the most. They would walk out the door if it wasn't that way. You are going to hear it. You may not like it, and you may not agree with it, but you know you are getting his heart. It also has been a very liberating thing because I know what it is like to be packaged and boxed up and try to talk in other ways.

I just talk to people the way you talk to them every other time. I think that connects. What I would say too about communication is that what happens prior to you getting up to speak is decisive. The first thirty to thirty-five minutes of our service is totally devoted to moving the ball down the field for the message to score. The creative development team uses that first thirty to thirty-five minutes in saying, "How can we introduce this topic and prepare people for the topic? How do we prepare people for what the Bible says about this and move them to a point of receptivity?" When I am speaking at Mecklenburg, it is so fun to be able to get up after what they do.

After thirty to thirty-five minutes, we have done songs that just blow people away. Maybe even the occasional use of a song that we know that is going to be a huge bridge builder. They see a drama, and they are laughing or they are in tears over it; the multimedia just arrests them and sneaks past the defenses of their heart, and all of the sudden by the time I get up there they are saying, "OK, tell me, I'm ready. This is unbelievable!" This is not original with me; I think Bill Hybels has often talked about this.

You know, when you start on the two-yard line, anybody can just kind of fall over and score! That's how I feel, because of what the context does to the communication event. Many times I think we divorce the communication event from its context, and that goes against everything we know about communication. When I speak, I'm part of a context. It's part of an event. What happens before is decisive.

Preaching: Using the metaphor you suggest, it's the concept of a preacher as a fullback driving the ball over the last few feet after the service has carried to that point.

White: You know, it really is an ensemble deal for us. I play a role, and we all have the truth of Scripture on that topic as central. But it is an ensemble performance in which I play the role of communicator. We actually have a couple of other communicators who are a part of the service prior to me, doing announcements or Scripture, communicators of drama, communicators of song. The whole thing is communication. I just have the verbal, spoken part. There is just a power when you are working with a team of communicators to get across what you are trying to say.

Preaching: What is the single greatest obstacle to making that link?

White: The minds of the people. The minds and the hearts of the people that you are speaking to. I think the greatest challenge that I have in talking to religious people as seekers is getting past the barriers they have thrown up to keep Christ at a distance. I need to be conscious of those and make sure that what we say and how we say it—whether it is through music, media, song, drama, spoken word—is doing that effectively and with integrity without watering down the gospel. I have been doing this too long not to know that no matter how, even on your best days, there will be some people that you will not be able to pull that off with.

I think that is the greatest obstacle: knowing how to build that bridge effectively and address those barriers and remove them so that they can consider the gospel. You really have to know their heart and their mind. This goes beyond being a student of the latest pop Christian therapy book on the mind of the unchurched. You've really got to know the unchurched in a relational understanding way. You have to be not of the world, but you really need to be in it. A lot of Christian communicators are uncomfortable around unchurched people. Quite frankly, I sometimes am more comfortable around unchurched people than I am churched!

Preaching: If you could be seminary president for a day, what would you do to address these issues?

White: I would make sure that the courses on preaching were maybe less on homiletics and more on the dynamics of being an effective communicator. The second thing that I would want to add is helping people know how to lead. There's a leadership crisis in the church today. You can go through seminary and never be taught how to lead. And yet that is the number one thing that you're going to do when you get out of there, at least as a senior pastor or any minister in a church—you are going to lead at some point.

I would also help people know how to blend the communication and leadership. Because that's something that is not talked about too much. In fact, I did a little thing in a book you edited [*Handbook of Contemporary Preaching*] on the language of leadership, and it was a little bit difficult for me at that stage. A lot of leadership skills are tied to communication, and the blending of those two is actually decisive. Leadership, how do you lead? That's why everybody is flocking to these church leadership conferences that are put on by churches and major pastors—because they didn't get it in seminary.

The third thing is spiritual formation, which is a hot topic right now at seminaries. When I poke around with people and I say, "What do you mean by spiritual formation?" within ten minutes they are right back to Hebrew and Greek words in terms of even how they understand that. You know, it comes with deepening your theology of God or something like that. No, no, no, you are doing that fairly well. What about actual spiritual formation? Really helping someone enter seminary or exit seminary mentored in being in the Christ-life—to where they are actually mentored in growing and developing and on a course of life where they will be more loving, more joyful, more gentle, more patient, less prideful.

I've had to search for that. I've had to search for mentors, search for experiences. I never was taught about the spiritual disciplines. I know some seminaries are assuming a lot of that is in place. Well, make sure that as part of training to be a pastor of people, that the pastor at least knows how to pastor himself and to engage in a life of spiritual disciplines and spiritual growth. And you just shouldn't assume that is there.

I think the average layperson assumes that if you go off to seminary for three years, you're going off for three years to really reach a higher level of spirituality to be able to come back and to lead us to that level. And I think that many people enter seminary hoping that's going to happen, too. That is not what is happening. Many seminaries are becoming graduate schools, not really preparing people for ministry. Helping people enter the Christ-life and the dynamics of how ministry wages war on your spiritual life—that's never talked about. But there is probably no more spiritually vulnerable role than a pastor because you can confuse doing things for God with a relationship with God. I went that route.

And if I could add a fourth thing, it would be to try to expose people to those who are really doing ministry. The irony is that you have the vast majority of seminary professors preparing people to be pastors, and they have never pastored. You have seminary presidents that have never pastored. I don't mean that you can't count interims or student pastorates. I mean that are really out there doing it. They haven't, but they are heading up the institution to prepare people to do it.

Preaching: What haven't I asked you that you are just dying to talk about?

White: I would like there to be less criticism of the seeker model. There has been a lot of criticism of certain types of churches and certain styles of speaking as if there is somehow a compromise of the gospel, watering down of the truth and an abandonment of the gospel in order to get warm bodies in the door. Seeker-targeted churches are probably taken the most to task for having somehow compromised because of the style. I think that many times because of the style they are critiqued as somehow compromising the truth and watering it down and not being biblical or not even being involved in exposition. Not from firsthand knowledge, not from firsthand visitation, not from anything other than just supposition. And I read a lot of people who just seem to take shots at other communicators or styles—if you don't do biblical exposition a certain way, you are not walking with God or being faithful. If you speak topically, it automatically means you're not being biblical, and on and on it goes. If you are seeker targeted you must not have a theological bone in your body.

I would like to see that stop. I don't fit into that mold. My Ph.D. is in theology. We use a lot of Scripture, and I take biblical exposition very seriously, and at our midweek services we go verse by verse through whole books of the Bible. That is our major style for midweek worship. I just wish we would foster an atmosphere where we welcome a lot of different styles and a lot of different approaches. Obviously let's maintain a biblical base and be biblical and be sound theologically but not try to put every communicator in a particular mode.

Quite frankly there may be people that don't minister to me that are obviously ministering to other people. Well, "Yeah, God!" Leave it at that. I just see a lot of shots being taken. Let's just let all of us communicate in our own ways as God leads and try to remain biblical and theologically sound. And before we say that a particular style or context automatically prevents that, you better make sure you know what you are talking about. I read books on supposedly what the content is like in certain innovative churches, and I say if that's what is going on, I'd be denouncing it, too. But we're not doing that. Bill's not doing that. Rick's not doing that. So, who exactly is doing that?

Preaching: One of the theological critiques that is pressed against this model is the idea that there is none that seek after God—that God is the seeker—and the view that there are people who are seeking God is faulty. How do you respond to that?

White: I am not a Calvinist. I'm not. I don't understand why Calvin wrote the *Institutes* at age twenty-seven to try to figure out why there were some people that responded and some did not. I've studied Calvin. I've studied Jonathan Edwards. I'm not immune or numb to the brilliance of his mind. But he is a man. I like his systematic; I like a lot of his insights. But I'm not convinced of the theological reductionism that leads you to that point. I believe that it is in Christ that we are elect. He is the primary elect one. Predestination is for believers to be saved through Christ.

I don't understand election and predestination in that way. I do believe, as Augustine said, "Our hearts are restless until they find their rest in Thee." I believe as Pascal said, there is a God-shaped void in every human being that they seek desperately to fill. Actually, even if you are a Calvinist, I think that you could still embrace people being a seeker culture. Because even though they may not in and of themselves be able to come to God, dependent on being touched by his Spirit, I still don't know why they couldn't be in a search mode—just filling it wrongly. I don't agree with the critique that people don't seek. I think they are seeking desperately.

Preaching Creatively

An Interview with Ed Young Jr.

Since becoming pastor of Fellowship Church in suburban Dallas in 1990, Ed Young Jr. has led the church from its original 150 members to a weekly attendance of more than 18,000 people. Fellowship Church has been characterized by creativity in worship and preaching, and now the church is sharing its resources with others through its Fellowship Connection network and CreativePastors.com. Young has joined the board of contributing editors of *Preaching* magazine, joining his father (Ed Young Sr., pastor of Houston's Second Baptist Church) in the magazine's first father-son contributing editor team. This interview appeared in the January-February 2005 issue.

Preaching: You have come to be identified as one of the most creative preachers around. What do you see as the place of creativity in preaching and worship?

Young: I feel that all of us are creative geniuses because we're made in the image of God. The question that I challenge pastors and communicators to ask is not, "How do I become creative?" but "What are those things that are keeping me from unleashing the creativity that God has given us?"

We're made in the image of our creative Creator. I always go back to the Trinity—the Father invented creativity, the Son modeled it, the Holy Spirit empowers it, and then on top of that people need it. If you look at Jesus, the master communicator, he was so innovative and so creative in the way he taught. He was consistently inconsistent. The message obviously was the same, but he changed the methodology. Whether he was pointing to someone or sowing seed, whether he preached from a beach or drew in the sand, he was always using the process of identification and then illustration and application, and basically that's what we try to do. We try to model our communicative style after the ultimate communicator, which is Jesus.

If you read the Bible and look at God and God's relationship with man—from an apple to Adam and Eve, salt to Lot, a tree to Zaccheus, a fish to Jonah, a boat to Noah, ultimately a cross to a world—God is sovereign, and he understands that we respond to the message in a multisensory fashion. I think that every communicator, every church, should do that within the context of their particular style. I'm not into trying to force people into different styles. Whether you have throne chairs and a five-hundred-voice choir, whether you have the postmodern vibe or country-western, you get to be yourself. Within that, though, I believe you've got to be creative. God desires it. We need to unleash it. That's why I like creativity so much—that's why I'm challenged by it.

I think the church should be the most creative it can be. Several years ago I went to Las Vegas to see a boxing match—not to gamble!—and there I was looking at all the signage, because no one does signage like Las Vegas. I said to myself, "Vegas has nothing to say but they know how to say it, yet the church has everything to say but so often we don't know how to say it."

I just feel so strongly that the church should be on the crest of creativity—that the most creative things out there should be the local churches. To me the exception should be when the church is *not* creative. But sadly, so often you find churches have somehow taken the Bible—the most exciting book—and made it boring. I tell people, "Don't blame God, because God's not boring. Blame the person speaking."

And I also think that 80 percent of what a senior pastor does should be preparation and the delivery of the message—80 percent. We have a saying around here, and it's pretty graphic. I say, "It's the weekend, stupid." James Carville, when he headed up the Clinton campaign years ago, had that sign that said, "It's the economy, stupid." Everything revolves around the weekend, and I believe in proclamation of the Word, so you can't talk about discipleship or evangelism or worship or children's ministry or student ministry or missions activity unless the weekend is hitting on all cylinders. That's the biggest port of entry in the church. We have to be ourselves, and when we're ourselves we're going to be our most creative. Then when that happens, I think phenomenal things are going to occur.

Creativity is not bouncing off the walls. It's not gimmicky. It has to be biblically driven. We're not above the Bible or on the same level as the Bible. We're under the Bible—we're under Scripture. So it has to be biblically driven. And I believe when it's biblically driven you're going to find that sweet spot of communication.

I think that small tweaks take us to giant peaks in communication. It doesn't have to be these big honkin' things and flying down from the ceiling or painting the walls orange and throwing sand in the foyer. It's within your context, and sometimes it can be as small as changing the time when you speak, or it can be maybe one time giving a message outline or message map and then one time you don't do it. Maybe it's having the choir or your praise team singing in one area in the church one weekend and another area another weekend. Maybe it's using video clips for two straight weeks, and maybe it's not using it for six weeks. Maybe it's being very loud and having all the lights for three or four weeks, and maybe it's totally dialed down, totally simplistic, for four straight weeks.

So the church should be consistently inconsistent, because the higher the predictability, the lower the connectivity. And most of us are so predictable. We all kind of lend ourselves towards predictability, but if we can be consistently inconsistent—consistent in our theology, consistent in rightly dividing the Word, but inconsistent in our approaches to it . . .

I want people at Fellowship Church saying, "What is coming next? I'm not sure what's going to happen next." I don't want them saying, "Wow, I know what they're going to do."

Preaching: Obviously now you are in a large facility where you're drawing eighteen thousand people on a weekend. But you started fourteen years ago with thirty people. Obviously you can do things now that you couldn't do then. What are some ways that you introduced the whole idea of creativity in the smaller setting that enabled you to move to where you are today?

Young: I would say this—I would say that the smaller church has the creative advantage over the bigger church, because a smaller church has the advantage—you can make decisions about creativity quicker, and you can also use more stuff and smaller stuff, and you can read people and feed off people more. The bigger the venue—now we have to think in advance; I have missed this about Fellowship—I mean let's face it, the only people who like huge churches are pastors!

One time we did this talk called "Life Savers," and it was on evangelism. So what we said was that too many Christians are on the spiritual yacht and we're just worrying about ourselves; we're working on our spiritual tan, we're playing around on the deck, yet our friends and the people in our community are drowning and they're facing a Christless eternity. Its time to get up off our lounge chairs and throw life savers—throw the life preserver. I said, "Who has God placed in your path in your life that does not know Christ, and what are you doing about that? Are you throwing a life line?" So then we handed out thousands of Life Savers to everybody in little individual packages, and we said, "Hold that in your hand, apply a name to it, and don't eat that Life Saver until that person steps across the line and becomes a Christ follower." Very creative idea but the execution of that with thousands of people is tough.

When our church was smaller I did a message on the soils, and you could show the seeds, and I remember bringing plants up there. I think the smaller church sometimes has the creative advantage.

Now the bigger church deals on a bigger scale. For example, I did a series on spiritual warfare, and a friend of mine has a tank—a real tank, a British scorpion tank—and we drove the tank on the stage. To do that we had engineers to measure how much weight our stage could take—just being able to pull that off and the turret and how to do that and how I can get in the tank and climb up on the tank. It's a great visual—it's just more difficult to pull off. I just like the advantage of a smaller venue. Does that make sense? You can just do things quicker—faster. Like the night before or two days before you can just get an idea and carry it out. Here it's more difficult.

Preaching: How far out do you plan your worship services?

Young: We have our series planned out, generally speaking, within a year—I kind of know where I'm going. At least every six months it changes! Like the series I just ended called "Who's Kidding Who? Parenting Is No Joke." We had that planned like three or four months out—that topic. The one I just finished—I just finished a two-week series on questions—asking the right people the right question to get the right answers; that just came up out of the blue.

This one I'm doing next called "The Table" is a series on vision. This series on "The Table" is going to be about communication. In John 6 Jesus said, "I am the bread of life," and that's the ultimate complex carbohydrate. We're talking about who is around your table—who are you inviting to the table—and then we're talking about bringing a high chair out, talking about sometimes Christians cry and throw food and how do you deal with that, and we're talking about evangelism and putting a leaf in the table and expanding the table when we grow and all that. Those are just some things we're brainstorming.

Preaching: Will you have a table out on the platform?

Young: A table and we'll have chairs.

Preaching: **What are some other series you've done that you think made a real impact?**

Young: We did a series recently that was very controversial. The topic was phenomenal. The topic was on forgiveness, and I did a bunch of research on it—looked at some old messages, read some stuff, listened to a tape series of a friend of mine. Then I had something kind of wild happen to me. I was filling my car up with gas, and I saw a jogger with a Doberman on a leash run past me, and I saw the guy tie the Doberman up to the park bench outside the convenience store; then the guy went in to get something to drink. The Doberman got scared and ran towards the freeway, jerked the park bench out of its supports, dragged it across the lot—sparks flying—and he was headed towards the freeway. I thought, "Man, we're going to have a horrible accident!" He ran into the freeway dragging the bench, and cars came to a screeching halt, and he had such torque on the bench that the bench slammed into an SUV and a Volkswagen and messed it up. Then the owner chased him down and untied him and led him to safety.

When I saw that I just knew it was a story that God wanted me to tell. I was thinking about forgiveness, and I thought, "You know, I'm like that Doberman because I'm leashed up to unforgiveness. I'm dragging around a park bench that's causing all of this collateral damage here and there." I started thinking about unleashing unforgiveness and starting thinking about who's sitting on your park bench—maybe a parent, coach, an ex-spouse, whatever—and I framed that series around that story. I said, "Unleashing unforgiveness is unnatural." I said I don't like to do it. I talked about someone that I held a grudge against for years and years and years. Then the next week I talked about "unleashing unforgiveness is unending." It should be something that we do as believers regularly. And then I talked about "unleashing unforgiveness is unbelievable"—the benefits.

God just gave me that story, but I try to always ask myself this question: "Ed, what can you create? When you're talking to someone—whoever it is—and when you're observing life, what idea, what illustration, what slant do you want me to use to bring form for that into the pulpit?"

That was one of those series we've done, and we gave it a very controversial title. We called it "Forgiveness—the real 'F' word." Before we did that title, I probably emailed over a hundred pastors and talked to them, plus people here, and over 90 percent said go for it. A few said maybe not but we had forgiveness with it. So sometimes in creativity I think there's a line that you need to be very, very careful with. For example, I would not use an R-rated movie in a clip or even refer to one. You have to be very careful.

When we talk about creativity it's not compromise. I think when you talk to someone or when you hear an idea, you have to put it through your creative filter. Every time I hear someone speak or I'm talking to someone, I'm saying, "What can I create, or what can I copy from them?" I don't mean plagiarize—I mean copy. How can I put that through my creative filter, and how can I use that?

The biggest thing I would tell preachers about creativity and about message preparation is something that I just fell into over the years. We call it now Team Creativity. For years and years I was doing the lion's share of all the creative thought behind the message preparation, and I found myself being kind of the creative bottleneck to it. I love to ask people questions, and early on I asked several people questions about the content of my message and "what do you think about it, what other angles do you see?" But as our church grew I became like the bottleneck of creativity, and it's just due to the stress and the load of preaching.

I thought, "I've got all these creative geniuses around me. Why don't I leverage their innovation and have them help me craft a message?" So we developed this thing called Team Creativity, and it's changed the course of my communication. I think my communication over the last two or three years is a zillion times better than it was even five years ago. I'm a totally different communicator, and it's not because of me at all. It's because of leveraging creativity with others.

Here's how I do it: I have to be the one that knows the direction and content before we have these creative team meetings. They know that the buck stops with me—that I have veto power. So normally we will meet two or three times a week, two or three hours each time, and we'll craft the message. I'll walk in and give them the direction, talk about some research I've been doing, what God's doing in my life, and I'll put it on a dry erase board—introduction, different points, thoughts I've had—kind of do a mind dump. You know, here's where I'm going. And then when I meet with them they'll begin to give me ideas; they'll begin to critique what I talked about Monday or Tuesday concerning what I'm thinking about.

For example, today right before you walked in we were talking about "The Table" series. I had some ideas I've been writing down in my journal, and our creative team is just listening; then they begin: "Have you thought about this, have you thought about that, have you thought about whatever?" So I'll begin to write those concepts down, and then usually by Tuesday I'll take a Dictaphone out, and I'll just kind of go through it. I'll just talk it through, like kind of an introduction, some major points, application, different Scripture verses. Then my assistant puts it in the computer and we all get a hard copy, and we come back for another meeting and we go through it and just start changing it around. Then I'll spend some time by myself—I'll just go through and add stuff, take away stuff. Then usually on Wednesday we'll go through the whole thing again. People might say, "Well, Ed, you used that illustration, or an illustration like that, a couple weeks ago," or "The message kind of has the same slant as one you did." So they help me to be consistently inconsistent, and they critique the message while I'm preparing it.

I've got people in this creative team from different seasons of life and different backgrounds. Men and women. So when I'm speaking I'm thinking about different groups. That has taught me so much. Then when I deliver the message on the weekend, after our first service we usually have a critique meeting—we'll go through and critique it again. Let me tell you what else it does. I am training people to speak who are in the creative team meeting, and they don't even know it, so when I'm not here they speak and they know how to do it. Now, they know again that I have the veto power. I don't walk in and say, "Let's go over the sermon." No, no, no. You've still got to do the work, but it takes a huge amount of stress off, your creativity goes way, way up, and it keeps you fresh. It keeps the introductions and the points and the flow and everything fresh. To me, since we've really been doing it, it has taken the sermons to the next level.

On Monday we'll probably spend two hours doing it. Tuesday is when, after we spend two or three hours again talking about it, I'll actually dictate it. Wednesday we'll get the hard copy and we'll go through it, and then it's usually done Wednesday afternoon or sometimes Thursday morning. I take Friday off. Saturday I come in at about 1:00 or 2:00, go over it.

The team is constantly changing. We have some people who are in here always, but it's constantly changing. When I did a series on parenting I had some people who are grandparents in here. I had some people who are single. You do a series on parenting, and singles are going, "Wait a minute, Ed. Is there any application for me?" Had a single person not been in there, I would have not talked about single persons. Ninety percent of all singles will get married and most will have kids. So I said, "Singles, you better show up for this series because this is like pre-marriage, pre-family training." I would have never thought about that. Or I'll say something in the parenting series, and someone will go, "How about the blended family?" It has added a depth, a richness that I would not have had.

If you listen to a lot of preachers, we all have our topics we like to talk about in our kind of style. I would challenge the speakers to broaden your horizons, talk to people about it when you're formulating messages, and you'll not believe the ideas you get. Some of the most creative ideas will come along. I did a series one time called "Everything you need to know about life is in your fishbowl," and I compared different fish to Bible characters and the struggle that Bible characters have with different relationships in their life. I didn't have the idea—someone gave me that. It was an incredible idea. We did a series on the Trinity for five weeks. The title was incredible. I did not come up with the title. The title was "Try God." Brilliant. And that was from our creative team. I wish I could take credit for these ideas. I did have the dog illustration though!

But going back to the dog illustration: several years ago I found out it's important that if you're using a visual, if you can use the visual throughout the series it's great. If the visual does not stand alone, then throw it out. If you have to explain the visual too much, it's a sorry visual. Some people force visuals. I see some people becoming the movie clip or television series preacher. Everything is after a reality television show, or everything is named after a movie, or everything's after sports, or you can turn into the prop guy or the video girl. Change is the key. All those things now and then are great, but to do that almost all the time is almost a whip. Some people I talk to, it is always about the show or movie—predictable. Predictable! I would say even the most cutting edge church out there—postmodern or whatever it is—can become predictable, and many of them are as predictable as the most traditional church you can think of. So again, it's not the model. You can become predictable no matter where you are.

I'm all into the postmodern scene. I love the fluidity, the arts, all that. I love it, and I agree that there's no way you can answer every question in a message, but here's what we have to be careful of—we can become so into the experience, we can become so into the feelings, that we lose the authority of the Bible. Another danger of postmodernism is this: if the churches aren't careful—the postmodern churches, whatever that means—relativism can infiltrate their theology, and then they just leave everything open. There are no answers. You've got to answer some questions. Truth is truth.

My friend Lee Strobel told me this. Lee said, "You know, Ed, that's the reason I became an atheist—because everything in the church I grew up in was open ended." So again, that's the danger. We have to be very careful to rightly divide the Word. I'm all for the arts, I'm all for experience, I'm all for the surprise, and I understand that preaching is a journey and all that stuff. But when you take a journey, you don't just drive and drive and drive and drive; you don't just fly and fly and fly and fly—you've got to make pit stops. You've got to stay somewhere. You have a map, and when you're flying somewhere you've got to refuel. My word to the whole emergent church is you'd better be giving people answers and you better be bringing people to the point of decision. We have to lead them to a point of "Am I going to step over the line or not?" I am sometimes concerned about some of the things I see out there.

Preaching: How much time do you personally invest in preparation for preaching?

Young: I spend at least twenty-five to thirty hours a week on a weekend message. The Team Creativity helps me because some of that time now is with people and we have a great relationship—we have fun, we laugh, we storyboard, we dream, and this [a conference area adjacent to Ed's office] is like a family room. We designed it like this because this is where we do all our planning. It's not like my office. My office is around there. I spend 10 percent of my time in there and 90 percent in here with people talking through things. Now after I talk through things—we're writing things down and all that—nothing is as demanding as thinking in an innovative, creative way. Nothing is. We always say you have to ask the right people the right questions to get the right answers, and the questions we have to ask ourselves about preaching are, "What do I need to know, what does my audience need to know, what do they need to do?" If you can answer those three questions, then you've got a great message, but the work is tough.

Pastors and speakers often take breaks, and it's important to do that. I think that too many of us don't take enough time off. When we're in a relaxed state that's when we have the most creative ideas. We have these great ideas in the shower or maybe driving in our car listening—it can be a country-western song or whatever—or maybe we're playing golf or fishing and we have these incredible ideas. Those are fadeaways, and we need to make time for that. And then, also, when we take breaks regularly it gives us a chance to really think in a creative way. My best, my most innovative stuff always comes after breaks. Maybe it's for a week, or maybe it's for three weeks.

You have to learn to take breaks during the week as well. What energizes you? What gets your creative juices flowing? You need to find out what that is. And it's important to take a day off where you totally unplug from church. You've got to do that. Also, pastors need to miss the natural days—like Memorial Day weekend. Miss that weekend. Let someone else speak. Like Thanksgiving weekend, Christmas weekend, and the first week of the New Year. Labor Day—miss that. That's five weekends a year you can miss. And on top of that I would have you miss at least four others. I would challenge people reading this article to miss at least three weeks to a month straight every summer. And they're going, "Whoa! I don't have anyone to speak." Yes, you do, because when you plan in a creative way and use a creative team, you've trained two or three people.

I learned that from my father. I learned from him about the importance of taking breaks, because if you don't take breaks, your schedule will break you. That's true because preaching is brutal! I mean, it drains me. On Monday I say I have a holy hangover. It's kind of funny, but it's true. You're wasted. That's why you need that day off or that date night with your spouse. We're running a marathon, not a sprint. I'm challenging a lot of my friends to do that. Andy Stanley used to never take time off. This year he's taking three three-week breaks. He's never done that. He's telling me he loves it. It's awesome.

But no matter who you are—even in the smaller church—people will never tell you to take breaks. Never. If they do tell you to take breaks, they'll invite you to their beach home or mountain home, and then they'll want to come with you and it's not a vacation. You need a vacation after that.

Preaching: When you're preparing your message, do you at any point write a manuscript? Then when you preach, what do you have with you?

Young: Yes. When I am meeting with the creative team we are writing it out word for word. We go through sentence by sentence; we don't just talk in concepts. We talk in concepts first, but then on Tuesday afternoon and Wednesday we're doing exact transcription. Exact stuff.

For example, I started off with the story of the Doberman being tethered to the bench and smashing the cars and—this was four or five months ago. Then I stopped and made my transition: "Every person hearing my voice is more like that Doberman than you care to admit. We're all leashed up to unforgiveness, and it's causing all this collateral damage in our lives. Who is holding the leash?" Do you know why I know that? Because I memorized it. We crafted that transition. Messages are all about transitions.

We go through it word for word. It'll end up being eight to ten pages. I don't memorize it. Then after I've gone through it once again and corrected everything, I put it into a mind map, a message map. A mind map is on one legal page. Your big idea is in the middle. You start with the introduction, and you move through counter clockwise. I color different key words. Then I read the mind map—I read it on Saturday and read it and read it and write a couple of notes, and then I put the mind map down and I'll walk on stage and do it. Now, I will have with me in my Bible the Scripture verses typed out—I don't flip back and forth in the Bible. It takes too much time. There are too many translations out there. And we always view a verse, usually on PowerPoint.

Do I have anything written down up there? I'll have an outline. My main points are in the Bible. Sometimes I look at them, sometimes I don't. But that's all I have to say. Because the creative team worked on it, because I've told it and spoken into the Dictaphone, and we've gone over and over and over it, and because we've corrected it all and we've read the mind map—it's just in me. But I do that discipline of writing it down. Every word. Creativity emerges from order. Order is not emerged from creativity. That's again a postmodern view. You've got to do the work, the hard work, and then as the Holy Spirit leads—because I know the message so well as the Holy Spirit leads—I can chase a quick rabbit and come back as he leads.

If I didn't know it well, I would be wheels off. Everything I've done in the last fourteen years is on manuscript. Every word written down prior to walking on stage. I have gone through a period where I write it out, handwrite it. But now I'm dictating it and my assistant is typing it, but then I correct and go through everything. I use the group, and then by myself again on Saturday I'll go through it.

Preaching: Some critics might believe that with all the emphasis on creativity it would be possible to give less priority to the Bible in preaching. Tell me about your use of Scripture in your messages.

Young: If you're thinking about topics or an expositional series or a character study, it all comes from the Bible. For example, one of the most popular series we've done is a series called "Just Lust." It's a topical series, but everything from that comes from the authority of the Bible. You know what I'm saying? On the other hand I did a series like the "X-files." This was an expositional series through the book of James. Taking James and just exegeting Scripture. Another series was called "Ignite." I traced fire through the Old Testament. That was cool. It was a kind of expositional preaching.

Everything we do comes from a biblical worldview and according to the Bible, like a series I just did called "RPMs—Recognizing Potential Mates." Those are biblical, scriptural principles. So even if it's a topical series, I'm always in the Bible.

When I look at the balanced menu of messages that we try to do during a year, we'll have exposition series, and then we'll do topical stuff—maybe some about felt needs, some about family, marriages—and we kind of try to keep a balance. We're a biblically driven church. Also, I try to tell people that we're application-driven. You don't need a Bible study; you need a Bible-doing class. It's great to study, but do it. We try to say things to people—I want them talking about what I'm talking about during the weekend.

Preaching: You've done some very creative things over the years—the tank, and I think you drove a Mercedes up on the platform one time. Have you ever done one of those kinds of things and you look back and say, "Boy, did that bomb. It just didn't work."

Young: I've felt good about almost all of them recently because of the creative team. If you don't have a creative team, you're going to mess up a lot on that. Some things will bomb; some things won't work. Too many people try to force visuals or creative elements. If you have to force it . . .

One thing that I did that I didn't like it: I was talking about John 10:9–10. Jesus said, "I've come so that you would have life and have it abundantly; the thief comes to steal, kill, and destroy" [paraphrase]. And the word "abundant"—the picture behind the Greek word is if you pour water into the glass, it overflows. And I said something like, "God wants us to live a life of overflowing, an abundant life." I said, "But if we allow Satan to rob it . . . ," and then I poured the water over my head—it was pitiful. It didn't work right. Isn't that terrible? I don't know why I did that. I probably had too much caffeine before the message. That did not work.

But most of the time, I will say it works because we just painstakingly go over the visual before we do it. We try to go through all sorts of elements. Like I did an illustration a while back, a visual where I talked about marital drift. We had a guy dressed up in a tuxedo and a woman dressed up in a wedding dress, and we went round and round about "do we use pictures or do we use live people?" And then not only how do we use them but how do we get them off the stage, because the point was once you have kids and a career you have marital drift, and we showed that continuum on the stage. It worked really well because of the work a bunch of us put in prior to that event. The best stuff is the stuff you're going to have worked out. Like the leash and the bench—we spent a long time practicing unleashing and how to tie it up and how to keep the eye contact while I'm doing it so I knew it so well it was just natural. Where do we place the bench on the stage? We'll actually go out there and sit in the audience—we said, "We can't use that visual, you can't even see it, it doesn't look right."

One time I used a chainsaw to talk about worship. The fact that too many of us have the compartmentalized view where we think that worship is something that we do just Sunday morning and it should transcend everything we do and say. We have this compartment, and I took a chainsaw, and I chainsawed through all the compartments, and I opened it up to show everything. The chainsaw got stuck. You know what though? Sometimes when you do those things, those are the best things. The funniest things.

One time I was talking about popcorn, and here's the illustration I used: my wife and I went to a hockey game, and we were getting something to eat during the game. Going to the concession stand, she was walking just a few steps in front of me; I was walking behind her. I slipped and knocked her feet out from under her. She fell on top of me, and we rolled down the steps during the seventh game of the Stanley Cup playoffs. People thought we were drunks, messed up. I had slipped. Security had come over. It's so embarrassing when you fall in front of people like that. You try to act like everything's cool. You look back at the steps like the steps caused the problem, and we kept going, "Why'd you fall on me?" You know what it was? A piece of popcorn on the bottom of my shoe. Greasy popcorn. And here's the illustration. I said, "You know what happens in life? We slip and fall in our number one position—that being husband and wife—and we're tumbling down the steps. We're chasing career. We're chasing money. We're chasing the kids. We're chasing extracurricular activities. I've seen too many popcorn parents."

And we talked about some of us are cheesy popcorn parents. Some of us are caramel popcorn parents. Some of us are buttered popcorn parents. There are so many incredible illustrations about parenting in the Bible. Eli, his sons are totally wheels off. So I talked about caramel popcorn. Caramel popcorn parents are parents that are overprotective and cover their kids—won't let them do anything. They never give them any responsibility. Always with them 24/7, like caramel covers popcorn. And I took a kernel of popcorn, and I kind of just put it on my face to show how we stick to our kids. Well, this popcorn stuck to my head the whole message. I didn't know it was on there. It was funny to see it on video.

We don't use a visual every week. I'll go for a long time without using anything—many times I don't use a visual at all. Many times we dial it down to very, very simple. Sometimes the most basic thing you do is the most creative. Sometimes, though, we have gotten to the point where creativity can also cloud what you're trying to say. Just say it. That's the balance. And again the creative team helps you with all that. We've had lights and drama and different interviews and videos and all this, and then the next week we'll just dial it totally, totally down. Acoustic only. I'll walk up and sit in a chair. Consistently inconsistent.

Preaching: Who have been the most significant influences in your ministry?

Young: In my life obviously my father growing up. As far as preaching, Dad's a great influence there. Number one, he's my father. There are several people in addition to my father. One would definitely be Bill

Hybels. The reason I gained so much from Bill, I think, are his incredible angles of Scriptures. Also, his passion for evangelism. The first six or eight years at Fellowship Church I probably listened to Bill Hybels preach more than he heard himself preach. Also Rick Warren. Rick is a systems genius. Making something simple, not simplistic. Those three—it'd be Dad, Bill, and Rick.

But you know what's so funny is that I'm such a different speaker. I feel I'm not at all like him, but I just learn a lot from them. I've learned you never want to stop learning. The best thing that I have—God's shown me over the years—is to be yourself. The more you are yourself, the better speaker you are.